Every Day, Just Write

Persons interested in the subject matter of this book are invited to correspond with our secretary, c/o GN Press, Inc., P.O. Box 445, La Crosse, FL 32658.

Rādhā-Govinda, We Hardly Knew Ya

Library of Congress Control Number: 2002111799

The Lord Reigneth

Library of Congress Control Number: 2002111801

ISBN: 0–911233–03–2

GN Press gratefully acknowledges the BBT for the use of verses and purports from Śrīla Prabhupāda's books. All such verses and purports are © Bhaktivedanta Book Trust International, Inc.

Cover and inside art by Satsvarūpa dāsa Goswami.
Cover design by Guru-sevā-devī dāsī.

Contents

Authors Note . . . . *i*

Rādhā-Govinda, We Hardly Knew Ya
Every Day, Just Write, Volume 16

November 15, 1997 . . . 1
November 16 15
November 17 28
November 18 40
November 19 55
November 20 61
November 21 65
November 22 72
November 23 85
November 24 95
November 25 106
November 26 117
November 27 127
November 28 138
November 29 149
November 30 165
December 1 177
December 2 188

The Lord Reigneth
Every Day, Just Write, Volume 17

December 3, 1997 . . 195
December 4 208
December 5 220
December 6 230
December 7 237
December 8 245
December 9 251
December 10 263
December 11 270
December 12 284
December 13 294
December 14 302
December 15 306
December 16 315
December 17 325
December 18 337
December 19 349
December 20 360
December 21 368
December 22 380

Glossary 387
Acknowledgments . . 397

Author's Note

WHY THE VOLUMES OF *EVERY DAY, JUST WRITE* ARE NOT PUBLISHED THE YEAR THEY ARE WRITTEN

Devotees who like to read *Every Day, Just Write* sometimes ask why the diary is lagging so far behind in time. They want to know what I'm thinking now, but find themselves reading things I wrote three years ago. This note is to answer that question.

I am a bibliophile; I love books. I love the feel, weight, and texture of a book in my hand, and the comfort of sitting and reading one. Therefore, when I write, I don't imagine publishing an online journal or a quick, photocopied piece of pass-around literature. I want to publish a book. I don't think the pleasure of reading an actual book can be matched by the experience of peering into a computer screen.

The fact is, however, that books cannot be published so quickly, at least not at GN Press, which is short on help and money. That means I cannot get my recent writings out immediately. Books take time to edit, lay out, and produce, and of course, it takes time to collect the money to pay the printer.

But aside from this practical reality, there is a more important reason for the publishing delay. I want my books to be as candid as possible. When I write, I want to be full of as much passion and truth as I can hold without being afraid of censorship. It's likely that all writers fear revealing their innermost secrets. I work hard to overcome this because "no holds barred" writing is what we want to read in a book; we are not as attracted to canned philosophy or fictional personas. I try to write as nakedly as possible. I'm able to do that because I know that what I say will not be published immediately. This both provides me with a sense of privacy while I write—I don't have to worry about what the audience will think, because they won't think it for a least a couple of years—and it also gives me time for deeper reflection on any particular topic. As the months go by and issues clarify, the truth of what I want to say also becomes clearer. I then have time to adjust or even intensify what I might have uttered on the spur of the moment. My editor helps me in this process, protecting me from printing something that is not worthy of print. This system therefore allows me to write with more courage, which in turn allows me to give the readers my best.

So I ask the readers of *Every Day, Just Write* to please be patient if the events and thoughts described in these books seem behind the times. *Every Day, Just Write* is not a newspaper or even monthly newsletter; it is meant to be enduring literature.

Rādhā-Govinda, We Hardly Knew Ya

Every Day, Just Write

Volume 16

November 15–December 2, 1997

Satsvarūpa dāsa Goswami

GN Press, Inc.

November 15, 1997

12:12 A.M.

Kūrma Brāhmaṇa says to Lord Caitanya, "Let me go with You. I can no longer tolerate the waves of misery caused by materialistic life." Yet he appears to be well-born, and has both good family and wealth. Śrīla Prabhupāda states that even in a so-called happy materialistic life, we have to extend ourselves to people and feel anxious to save them. "Thus one must become freed from the materialistic way of life. One has to merge himself in the ocean of transcendental bliss." (Cc. *Madhya* 7.126, purport)

If you wonder why you cannot taste the bliss even though you chant and read *śāstra*, and even though you are free of family encumbrances, it's because your anchor is still stuck in sense gratification.

We're surprised that Lord Caitanya says so strongly, "Don't speak like that again." His words are comforting, yet they break the stereotype we might have of what a renunciant says. "Better to remain at home and chant the holy name of Kṛṣṇa always." (Cc. *Madhya* 7.127)

Don't run away from home, but chant always (*kṛṣṇa-nāma nirantara*). Lord Caitanya must think that it's possible to become a chanter even within one's home, or why would He recommend it? But it will require a change of consciousness.

It's clearer now in ISKCON that we don't need to tell people to leave their homes and families and come live in a temple. How rashly we advised them, "Come live with us," as if that would solve all their problems. It seemed possible, and so many were doing it—either giving up their young families or raising a family in the temple. Śrīla Prabhupāda supported it. He bought up half a block on Watseka Avenue. Now what? Now we call it *nāma-haṭṭa*.

Maybe we were wrong. Or perhaps what worked in the '60s and '70s doesn't work any more. We have Śrīla Prabhupāda's purport that the devotee can live anywhere and practice Kṛṣṇa consciousness. "It does not matter whether one lives in a holy place like Vṛndāvana, Navadvīpa, Jagannātha Purī or in the midst of European cities . . . If a devotee follows the instructions of Śrī Caitanya Mahāprabhu, he lives in the company of the Lord." (Cc. *Madhya* 7.129, purport)

SWING WITH IT

𝄞 Can you swing with someone when you don't
feel like it—initially?
That's the whole point of life.
Someone or some
thing wants us to swing
in a certain way and we
resist.
"But I can't stay at home and be happy," said Kūrma.

I'm no rubber band or ping-pong ball.
I want it *my* way. Let the world swing with *me*.
O fellow, you're no God.

Where's that other mood where you and I can make it, carrying
a tune one to the other. We must get deeper. What we have been given
may seem trivial, the
inspiration gone. But get deeper
find
the heart
then
help someone from your own discovered reservoirs
of Kṛṣṇa conscious knowledge, whatever you have
now.
A Kṛṣṇa conscious tune
to feel a mood and to let go
in piano and guitar, although not too much electric.
O preacher-devotee, are you happy?
Then you're ready to meet death
as an act of faith.

5:10 A.M., POST-PAINTING IMPRESSIONS

On a 24"x28" Bristol board came a childish parade led by a curvy-spined yet erect human (man or woman?) wearing orange *yogī* pants. Right behind him/ her is a red monster, facing backward, with its mouth open. It has a long tail ending in a hairy protuberance. Behind the monster is a bent-over horse (green) with the words "Hare Kṛṣṇa" written over it. At the end of the parade is a human with a bear-claw hand and bluish hair blowing across the front of his face. Behind his head it says, "Pay your dues. Branch out."

Then I did two small paintings, one of a bug with a purple thorax and yellow head, and another with tonal mixtures—not clearly representative of anything in particular. Ambiguous expressions.

5:20 A.M.

The *pradhāna* is the stage before matter becomes differentiated. The next stage is the *mahat-tattva*, the total material ingredients. All this comes from *sa-īkṣita*, the glance of Viṣṇu.

It's inconceivable to me how
my denture looks so pink and sturdy—
it's as valuable as a good wristwatch.
Pulmonary.
Auricular-ventricle-coronary
Hives from too many strawberries,
serious people
gathered around after the accident or to buy tickets for a basketball game, a concert.

A stalwart person asks them to chant Hare Kṛṣṇa or to buy a book. It's natural that preachers develop lines when speaking to people in such situations. Whatever works. But the sensitive might be offended. Preachers take that chance and distribute books.

DON'T BE AFRAID

𝄞 Watch out, this one might get wild.
I'm not afraid of
jungle madness.
My Mama told me, "Don't
be afraid, it's only a movie.
It's not real,"

but it was, or it was close enough,
a real fight brewing.
I held her arm. Until I saw
Snake Pit and realized the people
were crazy.

She said, "I told you so," and
encouraged me to blank out,
pretend it isn't happening,
that thing that wasn't real.
A strategy for life.
We can blank out
bullets and big-dog attacks—it's just a film.

So I'm here
with tears pouring from
my eyes—tears of fatigue
although I know
I'll be okay after a little rest
and a vision of sunshine rising
on the day after Kārttika.

The bazaar
        is empty
onion skins on the ground
to be eaten instantly by dogs
        while two spiders watch
in their poverty.

They're not interested
in Kṛṣṇa's dayglows.
Swami, I know you understand.

Swami, you said they were ruined
by their bad habits, those
who were born in God's land, who hope
        only for money enough
to buy Goodyear tires.

8:45 A.M.

Yāre dekha, tāre kaha 'kṛṣṇa'-upadeśa. Lord Caitanya tells the *brāhmaṇa* Kūrma to tell everyone to follow Lord Kṛṣṇa's orders. "In this way become a spiritual master."

You have to receive Lord Caitanya's order before you can become a spiritual master. You have to be empowered or trained in Kṛṣṇa consciousness so you will teach the right thing. If you follow this instruction, Lord Caitanya says, "You will never lose My company." (Cc. *Madhya* 7.129)

In his purports to these two verses, Śrīla Prabhupāda does not describe the qualifications for becoming a spiritual master. Rather, that information is implicit. He does mention it in the purport to verse 130. "It is better not to accept any disciples." Stay at home as a householder—that's the context here.

Am I looking for ammunition in my fight to establish myself as a bona fide spiritual master? What about *nikuñja-yuno* and all that? What about the NOI purport that we must select a *mahā-bhāgavata* as guru?

Mahā-bhāgavata? He chants sixteen rounds and is always engaged in spreading Kṛṣṇa consciousness. You'd better . . .

Lord Caitanya followed the same pattern wherever He went in South India: He stayed no more than a few days in each place, instructed and inspired people to surrender to Kṛṣṇa, then left those people to carry out their surrender in their practical lives.

The leper Vāsudeva was enlightened. Lord Caitanya cured Vāsudeva's leprosy and asked in return that Vāsudeva "preach about Kṛṣṇa and thus liberate living entities. As a result Kṛṣṇa would very soon accept him as His devotee." (Cc. *Madhya* 7.148) Śrīla Prabhupāda writes, "That is the process of the International Society For Krishna Consciousness. Each and every member of this Society was rescued from a very abominable condition, but now they are engaged in preaching the cult of Kṛṣṇa consciousness." In other words, Śrīla Prabhupāda asks that we preach as *guru-dakṣiṇā*. Preach and Lord Kṛṣṇa will recognize us as devotees.

Let me go out now and take a walk. It will be good for me.

9:25 A.M.

Didn't want to meet anyone. Turned back short of the cow gate in case the owner was there. In fact, I jumped a little because when I saw the cows, I thought I saw their owner among them. When I came to the most private part of the walk, the "tunnel" into the woods path, I saw a man, probably Bhakta Andy, and his dog, at the end of it. I backed out and walked again on the main road. A little later I tried reentering the woods because it seemed empty, but the dog was in there and began to bark at me.

I thought of devotees with whom I correspond—thought of what I might say to them when we meet. Decided I would like to tell each of them what I like about them best. Then noticed how my walk was cut off and how much I desire my privacy. Interesting how we are setting up a place in Wicklow. Should we have a telephone? I am aware my mood is rather empty right now. We all have days like this. I knew if I came back to the house to write I would be forced to write in the moment, despite the emptiness.

Part of the emptiness is my ineligibility to be deeply touched by the reading I did before going out. Read about Lord Caitanya, Kūrma Brāhmaṇa, and the leper Vāsudeva. At least I read it.

Tonight there's a Hare Kṛṣṇa festival and Madhu will sing his songs. I should use my time well. Yesterday a package arrived with two books I had written. My custom is to read them again in their published form. I will, when I'm done looking at the muddy puddles. Ireland is not so cold at this time of year except in the early mornings. The dog is out in the weather; I see him seeking shelter under an eaves.

People ring the brass bell to get over to the island. We each find ways to express ourselves. I also seek ways to make myself comfortable between headaches. If one comes today, I can't take a pill—already used up my quota. Tomorrow I am scheduled to give a slide show of our trip to Europe, and I plan to improvise. In the beginning I may say, "One might wonder how with so many troubles in the world and so many urgent pressures on ISKCON devotees, why I am holding a homey show with pictures of my trip."

No, we all need refuge from the pressures, even if the respite is only temporary. I don't have to answer that one more than that.

If people could just live simply without trying to *solve* so many problems . . .

No, I know I can't say that.

Anyway, here will be my show. I hope they like it. No apologies necessary.

Oh, man, this
is the way to go,
he said, and he walked on,
a chill creeping into his boots.
Hare Kṛṣṇa—a delicious round.

O Prabhupāda, today I thought of a disciple of mine who wants to please me but who doesn't always do the most surrendered thing. It occurred to me that I am asking of you what that disciple asks of me—that you please accept me and see the good in what I am doing. I also take solace in the fact that many of your leaders have fallen.

Solace?

I mean, Śrīla Prabhupāda, I may not be doing as much as you wanted of me, but at least I haven't fallen down. At least that.

A weak argument for winning his love.

A weak strategy for going back to Godhead.

One of Prabhupāda's disciples once wrote an homage centering on the line, "I'm still here."

I'm still here. I didn't bloop. It seemed to me at the time a weak argument for expecting Prabhupāda's favor, but it's our truth.

KC BLUES

𝄞 We are blue, and
I don't mean
in Missouri

where there is a preaching center now,
Kṛṣṇa-sneha dāsa cooking
halavā for guests.

KC blues—state of ISKCON
women's issue, the full moon waning,
accusations that
we poisoned our *ācārya*.

KC blue no
more master to
sit on the *vyāsāsana*.
Now two hundred little guys
with five hundred other
little guys
attacking them on forty-two
schisms, the
near gurus
underground
and no fun allowed.

Blues you have to get it out
get it out
        get it out
                to feel good again
unhappiness chased like a
whistle in a round sound.
They say, "He's okay. I *know*
It." Too bad they went off
into fusion.

Monk under eye of master
didn't explore too far
from home. He *can* grow
on his own—I mean, not just
be a mimic a
parrot
lost in the old times when
he was more of a
prototype. ‖

8:57 A.M.

Forms, music, drawing, and ideograms could come closer to each other. Express the art and deliver Kṛṣṇa in surprising new ways. 1976 New Māyāpur—questions and answers: "Can we see Kṛṣṇa?"

Yes, what is the difficulty? See Him in the Deity in the temple. The devotees laughed. See Him in the sun and in the taste of water. Thus *man-manā bhava mad-bhakto*. Think of Kṛṣṇa as God. Don't forget Him. *Rāsa* dance. Our mixtures forbid us from reaching such heights. But you know, we will all conclude in purity.

12:28 P.M.

Lunch will arrive at any moment. Please redeem eating lust by offering to the Lord, the kind Lord. Remember Him and be saved.

2:40 P.M.

Small, pale tan spider on my page. I blew him off to wander elsewhere. Paintbrushes lined up. Other bugs, flies, and gnats remain on the windowpane. The sky is solid gray; it's not so cold out. M. phoned and said he'd be home by nine tonight.

"But those who always worship Me with exclusive devotion, meditating on My transcendental form—to them I carry what they lack, and I preserve what they have." (Bg. 9.22) Good, profound statements, and they deserve to be recited again and again. I intend to take my pocket-sized English-verses-only *Bhagavad-gītā As It Is* on the plane to New York and the Caribbean, and I plan to center on the meaning of Kṛṣṇa's words. My mind and intelligence are weak, my piety poor, my interests splayed. A pure devotee is engaged mentally and physically twenty-four hours a day in one or another variety of service to Kṛṣṇa, "so that his only desire is to achieve the association of the Supreme Personality of Godhead. Such a devotee undoubtedly approaches the Lord without difficulty." (Bg. 9.22, purport) Kṛṣṇa gives him special help.

We can't expect to receive Kṛṣṇa's help if we don't go to Him to show our desire to serve Him and our clear detachment from the material world. It's not just words or theory, but where our hearts are at.

Even if we have material desires, we should pray to the Supreme Lord to fulfill them (although that is not an expression of pure devotion), rather than go elsewhere to have them fulfilled. By constantly approaching the Lord with who we are, we can one day hope to burn with a pure flame.

If a Godbrother has left his duties, that doesn't mean I am more virtuous to stay. Mediocrity is not virtue.

It's quite dark in here, and I don't have enough light to read or write comfortably. I can get by as long as it doesn't get darker. When death approaches, some artists become depressed. Others turn up the heat of their creativity. The main thing is to get beyond worldly life and to focus on eternal Kṛṣṇa and our own relationship with Him. Anything else is temporary and therefore not worthy of prolonged contemplation. " . . . simply by chanting the Hare Kṛṣṇa mantra one can become perfect in this life and go back to home, back to Godhead." (Bg. 9.25, purport)

Bhakti is all we need. It's everything. Pure devotees, pure love. How to get it? *Desire* it. Concentrate on it. We all have read of those who have dedicated themselves to their own art or business. Well, we must do the same thing in God consciousness. The inspiration to do so comes from Kṛṣṇa.

PLEADING HIS OFFERING

𝄞 "There is no way except 'The Way'"—
a Shambala catalogue hits
the trash, although it contained books
on the virtues
of the quiet life.

Dark, dark sky—you're in no city where
they play their own way
each trying to learn the vocabulary of a
collective past then speak it in their own tongue—
that improvising art
of squeaks and belches,
caresses and croons,
the truth of a life lived
heart and soft
from New York pushcarts—
New York City, that city
I have never forgotten
although now I'm alone with no
more adventures.
Nothing hot and twisted.
Kṛṣṇa is always on my side trying
for the best
for me
in all
circumstances

and I'm hearing
chanting
remembering Him.

I repeat, I'm in the official camp now
but seeking the authentic
title. I live alone
this last of November, a
clever artist musing over what I can't do
and the paintings I have never painted, but
I won't give up—not
this year.
My voice is tired but
I'll still make songs.

NO MOONLIGHT DRUNKS

𝄞 It is really just okay we
are okay—
they are friendly bears
        and say what they have
to say

I asked if he would
like to be the man in
the moon—
no
Li Po down on earth
drunk in moon
reflection.

No, he said, I'm a
Vaiṣṇava wannabe
We don't get drunk
        except on *kīrtana*
and moon drops—Govinda
in the moonlight
        no wine
        no Tao
and we'll never go home
again.

Or if we do then
sādhana—pradhāna
to *mahat-tattva*
and clear notes of anguish
bugle calls from the hill
from carrying danger home
on our heads.

(They went out and sold as
many books as they could.) ‖

4:30 P.M., OUTSIDE SHED

There are many clouds low on the ground, fluffed like layers of blankets. Behind them I see a little of the sky's light blue. It's already getting dark, although it's only 4:30. The wind feels unusually warm. Strange, it's almost like a late March masquerading in November. The long unkempt grass out here always seems to be wet.

6:05 P.M.

If you hear the pastimes of Śrī Caitanya Mahāprabhu with great faith you'll "surely very soon attain the lotus feet of Lord Śrī Caitanya Mahāprabhu." (Cc. *Madhya* 7.152)

Wow, Śrīla Prabhupāda is relentless about how his followers should preach. The verse says to hear the pastimes, but Śrīla Prabhupāda brings it to preaching. " . . . everyone should engage in preaching, following in the footsteps of Śrī Caitanya Mahāprabhu." It's a fact that Lord Caitanya was a preacher. He told everyone He met to chant; He induced them by His own ecstatic dancing and chanting. Almost no one could resist Him. "Actually a devotee of Śrī Caitanya Mahāprabhu must engage in preaching in order to increase the followers of the Lord." So few people in this world have even heard of Lord Caitanya. They don't accept Him as the Supreme Lord. Those who do love Lord Caitanya must therefore spread His glories.

Lord Caitanya's teachings are the essence of Vedic knowledge and can benefit everyone.

Now we have come to the holy river, Cc. *Madhya*, Chapter 8, talks between the Lord and Rāmānanda Rāya. These talks were originally recorded by Svarūpa Dāmodara Gosvāmī. Let's go through the copper and proceed to the touchstone.

6:32 P.M.

Good first day. One year at this trade. Don't puff yourself up.
Up, up goes the soul—long hippie *śikhā* flying he
passes the U.S. space satellite beyond,
enters Kṛṣṇaloka where
Kṛṣṇa
and Rādhā live.
He does it by chanting his *japa*—all of it—
the artist's simplified rendition, 1969. Easy
journey
so easy
for Bharadvāja
he sang and painted, Jadurāṇī too
and I still flinch to recall it—the
raw innocence of those days—
Parīkṣit and Rukmiṇī
and all those
boys and girls, Advaita,
Uddhava, their olive drab uniforms.
So easy, but
not. Still we're joyful, innocent, following Prabhupāda, staving off *māyā*. Still confident, still sheltered
in ways in which we could never dream
in those early days.

Who'd have thought I'd suffer so much, get so many headaches? Who imagined I could live delicious alone like a Vedic sage? And yet I preach
like Prabhupāda wanted.

Yes, I know. I read his books.
I know too now
we're no Peter Pan
flying out of this world into outer space
or Nārada with *tamboura*
on no outer space missions
not pure
not yet.

November 16

12:05 A.M.

"Śrīla Prabhupāda, should we remember that Kṛṣṇa is God?"

"After reading the *Rāmāyaṇa*, someone asks, 'Whose father is Sītā's?' Your question is like that."

"No. I'm asking because you said in a lecture in Māyāpur that we should remember that Kṛṣṇa is God."

"Yes. Then why you have forgotten?" Kṛṣṇa is God.

When I awoke this morning I remembered that I have to be "on" at 8:00 A.M. for the slide show. Then I thought of my little bodily mechanics—to pass urine, wash my face, put on my warm clothes. I also remembered to give Śrīla Prabhupāda his Dictaphone and to sit down and open *Caitanya-caritāmṛta*. Here the author says, "Śrī Caitanya Mahāprabhu, who is known as Gaurāṅga, is the ocean of all conclusive knowledge in devotional service." (Cc. *Madhya* 8.1) See it with your mind.

The temple at Siṁhācala is mentioned in the purport. I hear the wind outside this house and I think of the temple opening at Bangalore. I wasn't there. The Hare Kṛṣṇa festival in Ireland last night—I can't attend these things. This hour is quiet. Stay with the book. It's like bathing in the Yamunā. Lord Caitanya, Siṁhācala, Jiyaḍa-Nṛsiṁha. Lord Caitanya recited prayers and danced and chanted in ecstatic love (*prema-veśe*) before the Deity of Lord Nṛsiṁha.

Śrī Caitanya Mahāprabhu was always ecstatic. When He walked, it mentions, He moved without knowing if He was walking in the right or wrong direction. I can't imitate that, but I can be constant in returning to Śrīla Prabhupāda's books and lectures and chanting on my beads. My love for writing is the closest I own to "*bhāva*." It's a scratching down, you could say, a physical reflex, a vain practice of art, but for better or worse, it's my preaching and I love it wholeheartedly.

Śrī Caitanya Mahāprabhu bathed in the Godāvarī, remembering the river Yamunā. Then He sat and chanted the holy name of Kṛṣṇa. A few minutes later, Rāmānanda Rāya and his entourage arrived. "Rāmānanda Rāya, seeing the wonderful *sannyāsī* [*apūrva sannyāsī*] then came to see Him." (Cc. *Madhya* 8.17)

YOU DON'T KNOW WHAT LOVE IS

𝄞 It's a sad thing your not knowing
you don't know unless you know
the meaning of the blues, sleepless
nights, tears,
        soulfulness—not
worldly 'cause
the *gopīs*' love is something else.
But it's that grief
so many sing of
in reflection perverted.

Be true to your way—sing it
the sadness
of this world and
ISKCON's failure to fix it
to be
the boat on which all can travel.

Still there's comfort, O wise man,
foolish man.
Feel it in whatever way you can.

O Kṛṣṇa,
please give us
      devotional service in a variety of ways
and let me be cheerful and grateful
for what
we've been given.
Please excuse me my pious
utterances and actions
      I tell them, but we are
a community and
tolerant.
      We know the truth don't we?
We walk the earth, part of it
although   strangers
oh man/ how good it is
He is/ this
God/ He gives the
rain/ the pain
reminds us to get out.
We dally, though, and possess,
work, do something else,
try to pass it on.

Kṛṣṇa, love is
    tears love
is
separation
    from Kṛṣṇa, beloved
Rādhā, Viśākhā—I know
it not. ‖

SAY IT (OVER AND OVER AGAIN)

𝄞 Some things should be repeated:
I love it—love you

It's true: I love you, say it
good man
go high and low to tell

I love You/ I love You
it can be said

people who don't talk say it's
foolish but
I say it to myself, to the wind the
air
    I want to be a devotee
    I'm no good one
    but want to say something good
    something that won't
    hurt others the
earth

say it I love I
write
    I Kṛṣṇa's devotee
want to be

my saying is weak
    doesn't make the love thing happen
but it's still truth
    to say it

Hare Kṛṣṇa Hare Kṛṣṇa, Kṛṣṇa Kṛṣṇa Hare Hare
Hare Rāma Hare Rāma, Rāma Rāma Hare Hare

over and over on beads
finger wearing down with saying it

"Distribute books, distribute books"
here comes death
in walked Bud
be careful
mind the preacher
Swami's boss
Lord is nigh

say it—I'm afraid
    get headaches
    repeat and repeat
    be quiet
proved by actions, O *Gītā*
forgive me
—the same old thing—an
iron rod in the fire. ‖

Dreamt I was cooking, but no one would eat. They were waiting for evening. The dog jumped up on the table, and Baladeva said that it was because they had spoiled him with special treats delivered on the table after *maṅgala-ārati*. When people finally came to eat, they were so offended by the dog and wanted to kill him, but I didn't allow it.

Then I dreamt that I was running to work in St. Paul, Minnesota. I was with a woman and her two children. I suddenly dropped three pennies on the ground and the children rushed to gather them. The woman's son suddenly sat on the ground, holding his stomach. He said he felt hot and cold. Even though I was sure he was pretending to be ill, I indulged him. Finally he asked, "Would you visit our home one more time before Christmas?"

"Sure." The boy recovered instantly and I went off to my job.

In the mood of dream theorists who assess each personality in the dream as part of oneself, perhaps the little boy is a side of me who wants me to promise something before he won't fall sick anymore.

5:20 A.M.

I'm resting in bed, listening to the wind, so I'll be up for my 8:00 A.M. meeting. O Hare Kṛṣṇa mantra, I seem to need to keep an easy pace. It has become one of my mottoes.

Kṛṣṇa conscious mottoes:

1. Take on headaches.
2. Tax your brain.
3. Work now, *samādhi* later.
4. Don't expect smooth sailing.
5. Fight for Kṛṣṇa.
6. Don't go to a secluded place to chant Hare Kṛṣṇa for cheap fame.

I could list other mottoes too about looking within, chanting Hare Kṛṣṇa, how our legal formulas won't save us, we must be mad after Kṛṣṇa, read Prabhupāda's books or how will we preach, etc.

When words fail, draw squiggly fill. When the spiritual battery seems to run out of power, turn to crips, licks, tricks, and fill that space.

No *mauna;* talk of Kṛṣṇa. Lord Caitanya beheld the governor of Madras' pomp and fanfare as Rāmānanda arrived on a palanquin surrounded by a military contingent of *brāhmaṇas,* workers, servants, and a musical band. Lord Caitanya wasn't fooled; He knew Rāmānanda Rāya was a pure devotee and not a sense enjoyer. The Lord's mind ran to join Rāmānanda Rāya, but He sat patiently, waiting. The governor came to Him.

I am hearing Śrīla Prabhupāda's lectures on the second chapter of *Bhagavad-gītā*, given in L.A. in 1969. The devotees read aloud from the abridged Macmillan edition and Prabhupāda comments. Kṛṣṇa smiled when Arjuna looked so serious. Kṛṣṇa became guru. When we accept guru, we don't argue with him as we might with a friend. We have to find a person to whom we can surrender. Do whatever the guru says. Such a relationship is uncommon in the West, even unheard of. People think it's slave mentality to accept someone as absolute in their lives. It's not easy to surrender. Since the bona fide guru represents Kṛṣṇa, however, he is as good as God. He doesn't give his own opinion but provides a transparent medium to God. The guru is realized in Kṛṣṇa consciousness, and he controls his mind and senses, absorbing them always in Kṛṣṇa consciousness.

11:05 A.M.

Even before the first slide went on the screen, the audience began to laugh. They were in a jolly mood, looking for a good time. There was nothing I could do to alter the tide. Uddhava kept up a steady line of quips. Of course, I had my own jokes to make, but I didn't really want the crosscurrent. In fact, I felt sober and wanted to make some quieter points. Almost anything I said brought a laugh though, and I couldn't control the situation because the visual images provoked laughter no matter what I said. Each picture as it came on was a challenge to the group to think of something funny to say. As the show rolled along, I thought the exchange remained external.

I felt lucky to get back to my room without having had to mix more with the devotees, but I am sorry I couldn't give them something "soulful." Some of them traveled for hours to get here. There were even devotees here whom I haven't seen in a long time—Bhakta-rūpa and Vidura. They came to see their guru, but they didn't receive any heavy spirituality. I accept the blame for that. I should have foreseen that this format was too light, even frivolous.

12:10 P.M.

Am I going to continue to feel sorry about that too-light slide show? Guru is heavy. I should prepare next time, and stick to *śāstra*. Forgive me.

Am I going to get into being alone, thinking that no one can understand me? It underlines how important this is—the relationship with disciples.

But if I say, "No pretense," then take this too—you can't win 'em all. I was not heavy. They traveled here, saw the show, giggled, got a cookie, headed back to wherever they came from, and maybe later felt it wasn't deep. If they fault me for it completely, that wouldn't be honest.

Now dig out of this mood. Pray to Kṛṣṇa that you don't want to fail in this service. The best service for me is the inward. I want to share it, but not like that. A new book is out: *Radio Shows*, Volume 2.

2:40 P.M.

Out to the shed. What is good and what is not good? Is there anyone who can help me? Can I think of how to ask Kṛṣṇa and Śrīla Prabhupāda for help?

In Bg. 9.26 Lord Kṛṣṇa says He accepts a simple offering of food if it is made with love. We have a method of offering food—put it on a plate before His *mūrti*, bow down, utter set prayers, ring a bell—but how to discover the method of loving? We follow the pure devotee's direction, but we cannot imitate. We feel only what we feel. At least we can always act on that.

We should always examine our personal faith: do we believe in Kṛṣṇa? Do we believe that Kṛṣṇa is the Supreme Personality of Godhead? Do we concentrate our thought on Him? Is He too great for us to know?

"I don't know Kṛṣṇa. I only know my Guru Mahārāja."

But he knows Kṛṣṇa.

Hare Kṛṣṇa.

If we don't offer our food in sacrifice to the Supreme, then we are eating only sin. Each mouthful entangles us in karma as thieves and/or murderers.

So many lessons. O Kṛṣṇa.

Kṛṣṇa-nāma, Kṛṣṇa

truth. Hear from the pure devotee. Most people in this world don't know Kṛṣṇa despite the many religions. We each pronounce the word "God", but the word means different things to different people. O Kṛṣṇa.

If all I have is blind faith in Śrīla Prabhupāda coupled with a long-term commitment, then all right, I'll go with it. I pray to you, dear Lord, dear guru, to please help me. Let me be fixed and aware. I have the duty to live in Kṛṣṇa consciousness and then to give it to others. Please don't let me fail in that.

SOLO DANCER REGRETS

1

𝄞 On the road
like an army
        following
the Leader

but one wants to go solo
to dance
alone. He
asks his Boss
who wants nothing maudlin—they're
sick of it.

"You want to leave the pack?
They're arguin' and moanin'?
If you go alone won't
you do the same?"

"I think I found a Kṛṣṇaite to
talk to. When I gave her the beads
and she chanted for her first time
it was great, wonderful."

Yes, yes, I sit back and read it,
home, I endorsed it
with a simple remedy: don't eat too much
or drink too little
and don't go out or over
with regret.

2

O Kṛṣṇa, I don't want to feel empty
when I read Your words in *Gītā*
don't want to finger empty beads and
utter *nāma* vacantly
solo or not
        Please *help* me.

But I know Kṛṣṇa's comin'
through the rye
    the fog or uplifted dust
and I have only to laugh at
myself to feel His presence.
Never alone. ‖

4:10 P.M.

Outside the shed. Dusty pink in the clouds. One cloud is jutting out like a long peninsula or a swan flying, heading toward the island—yes, a giant swan. Pink stuff down by the horizon too, along the low hills.

And the watery chill. Last gnats flying. Clumpy abandoned meadow here down by the water.

Well, I'll leave this place behind soon.

On my way out, I met a devotee who says he has lost his faith in me. We both made little Chinese bows, then he made a deeper one. Just as I was passing by, he kneeled on the ground to offer his obeisances. It's unfortunate the way we are entangled in rituals when our faith is gone. It becomes unnatural and awkward. I wish it could be simpler and we could act as we are, act out our truth but without offense.

November 17

12:11 A.M.

I woke when the alarm went off at midnight. I was dreaming of a big machine that moved forward and cleaned as it went. The machine was cleaning a tall building, and workers had stationed themselves on different parts of the machine. I too moved from place to place on the machine, supervising. Was I trying to impress someone, or was I being effective in my attempt to supervise the entire machine?

Anyway, back to Lord Caitanya and Rāmānanda Rāya. The door is closed on the *līlā*. I'm cold and want to enter. Remember? Lord Caitanya and Rāmānanda Rāya embraced as master and servant. The *brāhmaṇas* accompanying Rāmānanda Rāya were outsiders. Rāmānanda Rāya was an intimate associate, what I hope one day to be. I have always wanted to be in the inner circle surrounding Śrīla Prabhupāda too, and by his grace I was permitted. Now people criticize me and other insiders for being inside. In my dream I also wanted to be an insider. I don't want to admit that I'm not. I especially don't want to admit what holds me back.

Rāmānanda Rāya said to Lord Caitanya, "You don't fear the injunction that says do not associate with a *śūdra*?" In his purport Śrīla Prabhupāda writes that a devotee should not associate with a materialist, but elsewhere he also writes that a devotee may constantly meet with nondevotees to help raise them to Kṛṣṇa consciousness. A devotee isn't contaminated if he's actually preaching.

This world is filled with difficulties and controversy. I try to remove myself from such things to some extent, but it really is impossible.

Rāmānanda Rāya praised Lord Caitanya as Patita-pāvana; He helps the fallen. His devotees are all sweepers. We sweep our hearts with *hari-nāma*. That big, forward-moving machine in my dream could be compared to the Kṛṣṇa consciousness movement (or process). It's so important to have approval, and it starts within one's self.

4:20 A.M.

Now hold on, sir, don't fall asleep. Just speak in gentle tones. I know you are worried that people have called you a killer of your own guru and a puffed-up usurper, and you are always concerned about whether you are doing the right thing. I know you'd also like to write an interesting book. But I tell you . . .

Here's the latest news: we published our first issue of "Discovering Our Voices," a literary periodical by devotees and friends of Kṛṣṇa consciousness. Nice to be a part of that. Wrote letters this morning. M. came in last night after midnight from playing music in a pub in Ballygowen. I thought about Coltrane, his way of urging through his music, and how I once thought I knew something about the message and the person. He was not as light and happy as Gillespie. Ah, but you were wonderfully intense, John, as you searched for God and expressed feelings we hardly ever felt.

Now you've got the news, our minister will give a blessing:

I bless this day, November 17, to go on without pain. But if there is pain, please accept it and the diminished writing output. I bless you to feed and rest and read and type and walk and sojourn and pray and pray and pray to Kṛṣṇa and Prabhupāda. May you make this day a bridge to the next. Help others by being assured of Him yourself.

The letters I wrote—were they sincere? When I told that devotee that Kṛṣṇa would protect her, or when I told that fellow about the holy name, did I speak from experience?

Śrīla Prabhupāda says ISKCON is not as popular as Lord Caitanya's movement was when He was in charge as a young teenager in Navadvīpa, but we shouldn't let that bother us. We have to push on. O Kṛṣṇa, the needle, the nipple, the cakes of butter and rum, the ice frozen in Lake Walden and carted off to Boston and put into ships and carried to Europe—they used to do that. And me with this opportunity to hear and read about Kṛṣṇa, yet saying I can't take very much. O Kṛṣṇa.

O Rādhā.

Madhu will get up around five, shower, and make breakfast. Then we will have our business meeting. Hare Kṛṣṇa. I asked my disciples in Wicklow, some of whom are quarreling, to please communicate with each other and give peace a chance. Who has to pay for the llamas? Whose children get educated?

I must convey to you, sir, our regret that your magazine subscription has run out. This means that you miss out on the world of fascinating financial advantages. You lose your membership in the most prestigious club of alligators, and the free 1942 pinstripe suit will not be yours. You cannot use the travelers' lounge for elites but must ride with the herd. All this for only twenty-five dollars. Last chance.

Kṛṣṇa makes offers too: chant Hare Kṛṣṇa and make a quick connection with Me. You doubt it? Try it for just one week.

A man bought his wife a parrot—because he didn't want children? I don't know. I don't inquire into those things. I chant Hare Kṛṣṇa instead.

The wrench and grind. You
listen to mundane weather sounds.

No, they're not. What I hear is divine because it reminds me of Kṛṣṇa. A melody from an introverted machine? I'm working at it. Unless I practice relentlessly, how can I expect to be there to receive the inspiration? Or when my well has dried up, I'll have to practice so that I will be there the moment the moon appears on the lake so I can scoop it up in a pitcher and take it in. O Kṛṣṇa, Hare Kṛṣṇa.

O heavens. "The yellow and white decor of the temple looked like a Betty Crocker kitchen," said the news reporter, and he noted that we wore Hush Puppy slippers and that our *tilaka* was messed up. He noticed that we talked about money for Spiritual Sky incense and that we said George Harrison chants Hare Kṛṣṇa. All true.

A strange dream in which a young man stopped me to explain something he had learned from my books. I couldn't understand what he meant, but I thought I should be patient and listen to him because he was a reader. Then I thought, either in the dream or out, about old age. There are many advantages to being old: you become more mellow, understand life better, and begin to be wise. The problem is that you can't take advantage of it because you have lost the enthusiasm and energy of youth. If I had that same enthusiasm, would I really be so much better? Perhaps not. I would misuse it as I already have. It's bewildering.

8:03 A.M.

Just by seeing His bodily features and the effect of His chanting to the one thousand members of His small party, Rāmānanda Rāya concluded that Lord Caitanya was the Supreme

Personality of Godhead. They agreed to meet and speak in the evening in a *rahaḥ-sthāne,* "secluded place." Don't discuss Kṛṣṇa's pastimes with the *gopīs* in public.

Śrī Caitanya Mahāprabhu ordered Rāmānanda Rāya to "recite a verse from the revealed scriptures concerning the ultimate goal of life." Rāmānanda Rāya replied that perfection is to awaken Kṛṣṇa consciousness while performing one's prescribed duty according to *varṇāśrama.* Do your work and make devotional service the center of your life.

Lord Caitanya said this is external. Rāmānanda Rāya then said, "Give up the results of work to Kṛṣṇa."

10:30 A.M.

Black-stained fingers and sheets of rain. I walked in the rain without my glasses and I felt a strange, dislocated pain in the back of my hip. Big and little I seem to be. The world was far away and foggy. I'm Mr. Magoo, or determined to see myself like that—not a hero.

I fear they'll get me one way or another. Imagine such a loyal fellow as me accused of betraying my master in every conceivable way, accused even of killing him. Do other religions have such craziness and failure? Yeah, we're small and genteel compared to the Mafia or Hitler—just little guys—but a brother told me if the ISKCON politicians had the chance, they'd be just as totalitarian.

Why am I saying this? Because I fear the outside world. What, the e-mail dragons?!

P. writes me regarding a quarrel of my disciples in Peace Village, "You better get involved, but if you don't want to touch it, I can understand."

So he says, and the rain comes down. Lunch ahead, but first, Prabhupāda *pūjā.* Then I'll have a chance to be just with him—him and me as we actually are—for those few minutes.

11:58 A.M.

The wind blows different pitches and ebbs and flows. It drives hard and high, wide and low. It can shape matter, and just as a flute player blows into a hole and stops another hole, the wind travels and echoes and sounds through valleys and against mountains. I have heard the wind move along the telephone wires and beat up against this stone house like a surf on land.

Did you know that Śrīla Prabhupāda said the babies attending his lecture (in 1969) had "immense duration" of life ahead of them and therefore hope, whereas someone like him, what hope could he have? He wouldn't be living more than another five or ten years.

I'm still hoping.

Maybe a change in my mentality? Something radical, but I'm no mystic.

What *is* a mystic, anyway? In the West it refers to a person who is aware of God, although usually that awareness is tinged with impersonalism. He or she is aware of the inconceivable. In Kṛṣṇa consciousness we say a pure devotee may see Kṛṣṇa; Kṛṣṇa may talk to him. Viśvanātha Cakravartī Ṭhākura has described how the devotee becomes mad when he sees Kṛṣṇa, then loses sight of Him. That happened to Nārada and Dhruva both. *That's* mysticism, to see God face to face. "I regret that during this lifetime you will not be able to see Me anymore. Those who are incomplete in service and who are not completely free from all material taints can hardly see Me." (*Bhāg*. 1.6.21)

I'm not eligible for any of that, so I'm no mystic. But still I hope.

2:45 P.M.

The wind has driven rain through the shed's closed windows and soaked the outer cover of my *Bhagavad-gītā As It Is*. I hesitated to come out because of the rain (finally decided to put on my blue rain pants) and slightly less than clear head (decided to ignore it), but here I am. M. went to Dublin for about twenty-four hours—"My usual passionate nature," he said. My usual keeping to myself and getting something done in a day, I thought. "Thus, it is the duty of everyone to mold his life in such a way that he will not forget Kṛṣṇa in any circumstance." (Bg. 9.27, purport)

Steer to Kṛṣṇa. Use the compass point to head for the North. What does it mean, North? It's an abstract concept, especially ultimate north, the North Pole. For the hiker, however, north is an immediate and practical direction, distinguishable from northeast and north-northeast. For a devotee too: we point ourselves to pure Kṛṣṇa consciousness, to Kṛṣṇa in Goloka Vṛndāvana.

Because our path swings to the left and right as we try to focus our compass needle on the correct direction, Kṛṣṇa gives us some directions in *Bhagavad-gītā.* He starts with verses like *yat karoṣi*—do what you are already doing as duty or inclination and offer it to Him. He works up from there.

It's barely protected out here from the slashing rain, but it's not so cold. I can take about an hour and a half out in the shed, and then I've had it. I feel like I'm seated in a cockpit facing the weather as it rolls over the strait. The sheets of water are moving horizontally, and no rowboats cross except in an emergency. Devotees know it's better to stay where they are for the time being. I can't call the wind and rain music exactly, but I see the pattern.

Kṛṣṇa is clever in giving us a method for easy and active transference back to His lotus feet. We are already in motion, us *karmīs* and mixed devotees, so don't slow down. Do what you are doing and offer it. Here's how: if we are inclined toward meditation (which is fashionable nowadays), chant the Hare Kṛṣṇa mantra.

We all want to know Kṛṣṇa, especially the devotees. Someone wrote a poem to make this point. She asked how she could give Kṛṣṇa her life if she didn't know Him in truth. She was trying to understand the Deity, the holy names, but she wanted the process to be tangible and realized. As I read her poem it occurred to me that we cannot demand realization. She knows that, I'm sure, but we become impetuous. If only we could follow up our impetuosity a hundred percent. If only we could mean it when we say that we must say His names and hear of Him, that we can't live without Him, even if we can't know him directly right now. Prabhupāda told us to be patient. Know that " . . . the devotee who has always lived his lifetime here under the direction of the Supreme Lord, as stated, has evolved to the point where he can, after quitting this body, go back to Godhead and engage directly in the association of the Supreme Lord." (Bg. 9.28, purport)

NO LARK

𝄞 A slow meditation a
killer pace

chords showing what we know—
no lark, sad as can be,
the stark
    no lark
a piano cortege—rain sweeps
in here seeps
in. Savage thrusting
wind and
a lonely ache.

When you have Kṛṣṇa it's
not so bad but
where is your Kṛṣṇa?
Better not . . . yes,
preach what's in me
even a little.

Face a stark-dark day the
light in your breast a hope
always
would like to give it to others but
I sometimes fear they may take
it from me—those savage
demon atheists attacking
my *bhakti* creeper. ‖

MOOD INDIGO

1

𝄞 You can just feel
okay
it's "blue"   You Irishmen
don't know blue?

You Bengalis?
You pure spirit
          it's when rain sprinkles
in through shut windows

and you think of no home
you can't reach—the transcendental—

you can't reach up
there to care enough

the *āśrama* is cold—so are
hearts it seems

a virtuoso stands by a
professional blue
a passing mood
        be *niṣṭhā*

I wanted to see a *sādhu* but
nothing seemed to go right
and I left wondering
why Kṛṣṇa left me
in material straits

2

now as for transcendental blue
        it's totally different—what
I heard they
are fixed in spiritual meditation
on a blue boy
the indigo mood means
Śyāma on the mind pure
bliss for
pure souls

no intox left of this world
I hope my friend won't die
but we all will and
grief goes black

but blue blue
that world reaching up—
        we know we'll make
it somehow

when we love to chant
and won't give up.

5:38 P.M.

Lord Caitanya pronounced *varṇāśrāma* external. "Śrī Caitanya Mahāprabhu belongs to the spiritual world, and His methods for propagating the *saṅkīrtana* movement are also imported from the spiritual world." (Cc. *Madhya* 18.60, purport) Rāmānanda Rāya listed three actvities: (1) *varṇāśrāma;* (2) the offering of the results of work; (3) renunciation. Lord Caitanya rejected all three as activities on the material platform. Then Rāmānanda Rāya offered his fourth suggestion, *jñāna-miśra-bhakti*, devotional service mixed with empiric (non-Vedic, speculative) knowledge. Lord Caitanya rejected that proposal also.

Please never think that your spiritual master is less intelligent than you. Don't kill your devotion in that way. Bow down. Ask him to give you faith. Pray to Lord Balarāma, the original spiritual master. Go before your spiritual master as Lord Caitanya went before Īśvara Purī. Consider that you don't know anything about the science of Kṛṣṇa. You need to be instructed and enlightened. It's not ordinary knowledge but *divya-jñāna*. The spiritual master is not an ordinary person. *Arcye viṣṇau śilā-dhīr guruṣu nara-matir* . . . and *ācāryaṁ māṁ vijānīyān* . . . *sarva-deva-mayo guruḥ*. Don't think of the guru in material terms, as if he is merely a philosopher or a teacher. He *is* a teacher, but in *paramparā*, carrying Kṛṣṇa's message—he doesn't invent his own. If we criticize him, we criticize Kṛṣṇa (*sakṣad-hari*), because the Supreme Personality of Godhead is the origin of the *paramparā*. Śrīla Prabhupāda established Kṛṣṇa consciousness all over the world simply by his faithful teaching and chanting. He established worship of Rādhā-Kṛṣṇa and book distribution. He translated and gave Bhaktivedanta purports for the most essential Vaiṣṇava books, which can now function as law books for the next ten thousand years. And during Prabhupāda's lifetime he worked tirelessly to manage the Hare Kṛṣṇa movement with its more than one hundred centers and many, many problems.

6:15 P.M.

Soak your foot
ease your head—you never had
this fog. It's not like you.
You were a lover?
You . . . I don't remember. You
were a lost soul. You wanted to become a famous writer, get enough money, maybe marry a beautiful woman who

understood you . . . and listen to Eric Dolphy on the phonograph and in nightclubs. But Eric died young. There are always other musicians, and some of them live until older. I could have surrounded myself with such people for as long as I lived, and they would have accompanied me through life. But they would have cheated me, too, in a way. The bona fide spiritual master will not do that.

November 18

12:05 A.M.

Rāmānanda Rāya quoted the Tenth Canto verse, *jñāne-prayāsam*, and Lord Caitanya replied, "*Eho haya*—that is all right, but you can speak more on the subject."

To read in the *smṛti* of the ascension of states through karma and *jñāna* to pure *bhakti* is assuring intellectually, but simply to hear it again and again doesn't bring us to pure devotion. It becomes "study." We pride ourselves that we belong to the best religion, and that's fine, but such pride could become a source of complacency. To be always thinking of Kṛṣṇa, to be moved to render Him constant service, and to tell others about Him is the desired state. I don't mean to say reading of the ascension of states is unimportant. I'm confessing, however, that this study isn't moving me right now. I will look up this conversation with Rāmānanda Rāya in Śrīla Prabhupāda's other two books, *Teachings of Lord Caitanya* and *Search for the Ultimate Goal*. Perhaps that will help.

I have been so long without tasting *prema-bhakti* that I'm quite aware my kind of reading doesn't change me. I read of a distant subject, like reading of the stars and galaxies. I read that I too can go there, live there, but I don't go. I read that if I die in an incomplete state of spiritual progress, I'll have to be reborn in the material world. That strikes me as true, but I can't seem to "do the needful" to go back to Godhead after this life. Rāmānanda Rāya composed a verse addressing my predicament: "As long as there is hunger and thirst within the stomach, varieties of food and drink make one feel very happy." (Cc. *Madhya* 8.69)

I lack this intense hunger and thirst. Physically my power of digestion has reduced; I can't eat as much as I did when I was a young man. I've tried Āyurvedic medicines and naturopathic treatments to increase my digestion, but nothing has worked. Now I take aids such as Lavan Bhaskar, Trifalla, and Hajmola every day. Spiritually, I also don't have strong digestion for *kṛṣṇa-kathā*. I say I can read only one hour a day and chant only sixteen or nineteen rounds at most. I also hear only one taped lecture a day. Then there is my writing, to whatever degree that helps me become Kṛṣṇa consciousness.

Perhaps all my activities are connected to Kṛṣṇa. Lord, You see all. I desire to increase but lack strength, it seems. I lack the love that makes hearing and serving so relishable that one can't have enough of it. "Similarly, when the Lord is worshiped with pure love, the various activities performed in the course of that worship awaken transcendental bliss in the heart of the devotee."

Rāmānanda Rāya stated further, "*Kṛṣṇa-bhakti-rasa-bhāvitā matiḥ:* Pure devotional service in Kṛṣṇa consciousness cannot be had even by pious activity in hundreds and thousands of lives. It can be attained only by paying one price—that is, intense greed to obtain it. If it is available somewhere, one must purchase it without delay." (Cc. *Madhya* 8.70)

PUT YOUR LITTLE FOOT

𝄞 I'm here for you, Lord Kṛṣṇa
twenty-four hours a day trying to become Your
devotee

self-conscious though I am.

Rāmānanda Rāya says you need love and
devotees write of their shortcomings.

Put your little foot right in
put your little foot—
well
I tried, he says so sour-
sounding

I want to be Your devotee, that's
a sweet state I know
young men dancing in *kīrtana*
men and women going out on marathons
of devotional energy.

I don't put down my life
here or in the shed—
the wet quay is fine with me and
I like to chant the holy name

Lord, You are kind to me
give me what I asked—
peace in this place
with rain down

Lord, in here I can seek
You always while
    in my heart the
familiar I go over

afraid to ask more if
    I have to wrench, take
out things I'm so attached to
although I can't even see them

afraid
    to give up what?

I need love
and don't complain
except to rouse myself

desirable: alone
    beads,
true friends,
work I can do
ease of body and mind
    —but more
the confirmation
of inner flame
and You the great one
dear one.

"Mystics" in Kṛṣṇa consciousness are not vague
    abyss-falling
They are with You face to face
forgetting even Greatness
for love
Put your little foot in
that ocean
    prema-bhakti-sindhu

or stay on the edge sorrowful
you can't drown
or swim stronger. ‖

5:04 A.M.

Cleaned the bathroom. Many clots of dirt on the floor, hair and gray stuff. Blackened the sponge again and again, then rinsed it out—filthy water down the drain. It's a pleasure to see a place become clean. In a dream did a Christian Santa Claus curse me? Was that connected to the infamy I called down upon myself later? The Hare Kṛṣṇa mantra will save me. I am like the sorcerer's apprentice who doesn't know how to handle the magic.

I'll have to chant Hare Kṛṣṇa with better quality if I want to be saved. And don't rush through *gāyatrīs*. Will it take a cyclone of infamy to bring me to my senses? What I thought I had is torn away and I am left with . . .

Cling to the Hare Kṛṣṇa mantras and stay alive. Float on a log in the wreck. Survive.

Lord Caitanya is the ocean of all conclusions. He rained down on the hill of Rāmānanda Rāya, or—how does it go? Rāmānanda got some of that rain and poured it on Lord Caitanya, meaning it went back into the ocean.

Creation by the Viṣṇus. What is my little creation of paintings or word sketches compared to *that*? I am such a tiny, inconsequential creator. What creative force can flow through me? How many volts?

Not so many. I shiver and blister easily.
I can't take stress or
else I have to
lie down.
Similarly I can't take on spiritual rigors. I'm peaceful
nowadays and
maybe that's Kṛṣṇa's response to the service I offered Śrīla Prabhupāda.

Don't live on laurels, please.

It's a fact I don't ask for rigors. I can't handle more pressure.

Then are you not ready to face the purification necessary to become a pure devotee? It requires *total* surrender. Want cheap redemption?

Kṛṣṇa-bhāvitā . . . how much am I willing to pay? How much *laulyam* do I have?

I think I will go put paint on a Bristol board. Think of making it an offering. I do it as devotional immersion, not to produce anything particularly valuable. Kṛṣṇa is *bhāva-grāhī janārdana*, He can accept the good in *any* offering, fortunately. At least I can stamp it with "Kṛṣṇa" and add *tilaka*.

The truth is in Fort Knox in the gold. I will not take my gold pen west but keep it safe here for when I return.

Then I'll have to write with this Sheaffer recessed pen. It deposits ink on my forefinger and could poison me.

Well then . . . I could die before my allotted time, poisoned by ink.

No, that won't happen—or
it could.

Hare Kṛṣṇa. This is ridiculous, I know.

The truth is in the minister's snuff box.

No imagination please, and no heroics. The fat man ate ten full loaves and said to the waitress (in the Carver story), "We don't usually eat this much. This is delicious. Thank you."

That night the waitress, who usually had to bear the weight of her so-called lover, whom she didn't love and who was not tender—the waitress imagined that she was making love to the fat man. That's a story of a forbidden sort. We want to meet the Supreme Spirit who will love us and save us from having sex with unloving persons.

Form and essence, pretense and design. He went to college and learned a few things. He wanted to find good in his mother culture and offer it to Kṛṣṇa, so he told stories and wrote poems. I remember Jean Shepherd and Alfred Hitchcock. No, I am actually completely Vedic. I forget the past and remember only my purpose.

8:05 A.M.

Windy and cloudy dark at 8:00 A.M. It's hard to whip myself to read this morning because I feel the need for ease. Will I take a walk later? Whitecaps. Sounds in the house. White BBT van parked down by the boathouse. Don't let the mind get carried away.

"Please quote some scriptures about the ultimate goal of life," Lord Caitanya asked Rāmānanda at the beginning of their discussion. A faithful preacher is enthusiastic to discuss Kṛṣṇa consciousness even though he's heard and spoken on the same topics many times. Similarly, I am not tired of seeing the sky and water at Inis Rath. *If* I can touch that freshness, aliveness, and not fall into a rut.

Repetition is for emphasizing an important point or to assure that the student retains the information. Or it occurs emotionally to someone experiencing ecstasy. All life is cycling, repeating, but changing, changing.

Out for a walk. It's windy but not cold. It seems like days since we've seen a clear sky. I'm like the Irish weather in that I have frequent cloudy days. As I have become used to the Irish weather, I wonder if a day will come when I won't mind the clouds of a headache. Could I even welcome one? Bill Evans played a tune, "Here's That Rainy Day." His mood was not sad but reflective, poetic. It might be perverse to enjoy a headache, but I could resign myself more to the experience without becoming glum or upset.

The problem for me is the strong desire I have to be productive each day. To be satisfied on a headache day I have to see the stepping back from my activities as a path to more intense Kṛṣṇa consciousness. That would be all right, but the headache so much robs me of energy that I don't have the vigor to focus. When I learn how to intensify my Kṛṣṇa consciousness despite pain, that will be the success of living with this chronic disease.

WE'RE AHEAD

1

𝄞 The theme is blues—more
repetition, big sound
dwelling on
stars, mind, the same old thing

of Kṛṣṇa in the heart
in mine, *is* mine
and the reverence
and love
I feel—that same old thing
and can someone
teach me to pray?

I limp along—same old
thing—
        To feel to
feel
        the need
to make art
to express
that thing
in a way
that is not the same old
thing.

That takes practice.

2

O Kṛṣṇa. I
walk down the same old
        spattered-leafed path
        wet mud but
me alone
a little dry

while the door bangs closed
behind me and I think it's someone
the Raven quoting
nevermore?

Nevermore—no more youth
I laugh
no more young ISKCON
hear the bugle?
We're lost but found
and have something to say.

3

We each
take a turn
speak from soul
as close as we can to a
self of selves
we know
so much more but
can't get it out—no
jñāna.
We go to India to feel it

and make pit stops for marriage
and other endeavors—
all for Kṛṣṇa—rowing boats
cooking lunch
and eating.

"Govinda comes naturally
to me,"
she said, "You, Govinda, can fool
Mother Yaśodā, but not me! I've been on Vraja-
maṇḍala *parikramā* and
heard all the secrets."

I prefer a simpler act
liking putting Him to bed—
nothing to imagine in *that* realm.

4

Lord, here's another with strong
hands, doesn't want to use them to hurt,
    but to make music,
to help, to work
    and mine grips the Pilot.

Lord, You are in all things
    we know nothing more no
    science
    but work
    and to read and chant and
preach.

This is the confidential
    circle of my world, what
    Kṛṣṇa says. ‖

2:32 P.M.

I took a pill at noon so I could be active. I pay for it. I can't always be pain-free and active because the price is sometimes too high and I can only take so many of those pills. Anyway, since I paid for this afternoon with an afternoon later in the week, I should use it well.

Other voices, drop by drop. Someone went by in a car. Another works in a glass studio. She says she'll return to Belfast to live with her parents—there's no heat in the *āśrama* and people don't take care of her. The comings and goings of other people. He wrote a book and sold it. Whose got it now?

I love to woodshed. I come out to the shed and blow out scales and melodies and chords of prose and poems. I look into my face like a fortuneteller gazes into a crystal ball.

I don't want to accept a superficial, merely official Kṛṣṇa consciousness. I must have real experience. But I don't want to drift away from Śrīla Prabhupāda's teachings. It was comforting today hearing him speak in a fatherly, kind way to devotees in L.A., 1969. Inviting them to control the tongue: "Śyāmā dāsī will make you nice *prasādam*." Fill up with those lectures and nearness to Śrīla Prabhupāda.

It's astounding how ninety-nine percent of people in the world are ignorant about the soul, the Personality of Godhead, and the laws of transmigration. They live for only this life.

Carl Sagan has another bestseller answering questions on life and death and speculating on the next life. He's a first-class atheist. People will hear from him but not from a devotee of Kṛṣṇa, whom they think is dogmatic.

The Supreme Lord feels special consideration for His devotees, although He is generally impartial to all. He's wonderful. He has given us sufficient access to Him.

"I live by your inspiration," a devotee wrote me. I feel like tempering that and reminding him of discipline and patience. What is his daily *sādhana*? Why not more of it? Pure devotees don't demand of Kṛṣṇa. It seems hard to imagine. We excuse ourselves, justify ourselves, balk at the idea of surrendering private interests. How can we be so empty and selfless and just do what He wants, we wonder. Yet that is the point. Those in the spiritual world have attained it. Here, we practice compassion toward others and also ourselves. We hope Kṛṣṇa will save us quickly.

TWELVE-TONE SONG FOR MY FATHER

1

𝄞 He composed a twelve-tone song for
his father.
I can't remember mine—my father
spawned me and spermed me—so physical
a small yellowish

emerging from my mother
flesh and spots and moldings and
a strange funny head to boot.

But a soul. Somehow. My father now
my spiritual master. I've
been adopted.
I entered the storefront on an off-day
from work
my strange head full of the new jazz
and the daily marijuana high.
I was heading downhill but had enough
sense to stop and
listen.
Śrīla Prabhupāda signed me up
to serve Lord Caitanya for lifetimes
but even then, I had to
reenlist
daily
and now again
amid the institutional doldrums and
personal insanities.

No, I know no twelve-tone scales
have no horn, although I like them—
their crazy sad sorry music about
people squirming here and squirming
there and
coming together in some
important, internal way.

My head hurts. He says
his father hit him. Imagine
an average, square father
hearing his son's twelve-tone song,
knowing he was always crazy,

because he didn't train for business
or make money
or at least give him grandchildren. ‖

"NO STORY" PAINTINGS

𝄞 I write in a shed
poorly recording those days
when we knew how
to play dirty

I mean how harsh and quick we
were we
knew
not what we
did.

Now my church pink
and red
a *cakra* on top
no story
other than this one.

Paint heads—one blue
one Rādhā's
(why not?)
added squiggles, someone
eating a banana
shrinking, no
leaning, back

then a woman a quickly
entered holy word
        signature of
Kṛṣṇa's feet.

Painted a monster and
a yellow horse
came, more words: "I love You,
Kṛṣṇa"—something like that.
I dared
to add Kṛṣṇa everywhere
like legato-staccato
conspirators and me
no shakedown melancholy baby. ‖

4:15 P.M.

Outside the shed. Dusty pink again in the lower sky where the clouds are. Overhead (lo and behold), see the first pale blue in days. While I was in the shed two bands of rainbows appeared suddenly after the rain shower. At the time I was so busy writing I barely noticed. Handsome island from here, home of Rādhā-Govinda's secret. Those who work there know it.

I feel satisfied. I paid for the afternoon by taking the pill, but it was worth it—a good way to spend a Tuesday. See those birds flying as if their wings were stone? I can't comment on them. The grass is too wet.

"When one's dormant Kṛṣṇa consciousness is awakened, it spontaneously flows to the lotus feet of Kṛṣṇa without impediment." (Cc. *Madhya* 8.70, purport) Whatever Rāmānanda Rāya says now based on spontaneous love will be agreeable to Śrī Caitanya Mahāprabhu, and He'll ask him to say more and more.

The Lord is my Master. I want to serve Kṛṣṇa. That's part of *mamatā*.

Śrīla Prabhupāda chose my name. There were no Sanskrit secretaries in those days. He called me Satyasvarūpa, Satsvarūpa, and sometimes Steve. Go back to Śrīla Prabhupāda, to that time, and recall. I cherish the link. Read his books.

6:30 P.M.

We will review the steps from *dāsya* to *mādhurya* and on. There is nothing like this in other religions, although others also try for authenticity, faith, and experience. I don't judge *myself* better than other religionists just because I read of *mādhurya-rasa*, but I do believe we have more. All of us, regardless of our religion, must work for sincerity and faith. It's available through prayer and pure following.

Faith: do we believe? Accept authority? We have been trained to do so for many years now. "If you want to know your father, you ask your mother."

"But that's for children," the reporter said to Kīrtanānanda.

"Spiritually, you are a child."

We presume.

I accept authority; I don't disrespect it. I'm not a devotee—still aspiring. Vaiṣṇava humility helps. If I had love of God, how could I live in separation from Him? I'm lower than a worm in stool. One who actually has love of God is symptomized by feeling that he has no love of God. These are comforting sayings, because they show that our *sampradāya* is not arrogant. We don't claim we are better or even that we have been saved just because we joined or we belong. Hare Kṛṣṇa.

November 19

3:10 A.M.

Woke wondering if I should (or want to) take time off from EJW to do more directed free-writing on a topic. Where am I going anyway? What am I doing for ISKCON? I seem to be boxed in. I appear to have no genuine interest in the nitty-gritties of social development in the Inis Rath-Geaglum community, the question of education, the problems of temple maintenance, etc. I want to leave those topics behind, or at least aside for the time being. I have a different service. I have faith in that. And then there's the disease, which is a full-time occupation in itself.

Maybe there is nothing I urgently need to know about myself that I don't know already. I am compromised. So what?

I'm doing what I can in a less than perfect body. So what? ISKCON doesn't inspire me. So what? I'm almost sixty. Where else can I go? For my disciples' sake I need to maintain a live connection to ISKCON, yet I negotiate the nature of that connection. No more jockeying for position in this lifetime for me.

8:32 A.M.

I'm not going to feel obliged to read *Soul Making*. Rather, I'm going to take it easy—because of my headaches, you know. I'll write down what I feel and hang loose (hang tough). Thus I'll remain simple with no rigorous reading program forcing me to ask myself too many difficult questions: Am I suffering interiorly enough? Am I "looking, weeping, and living joyfully" according to the motto of Desert Spirituality? I like what he says, but I just don't want to come under that man's spiritual funk or angst or program for heart work. Maybe later. Give me these last two weeks in Ireland to read *Bhagavad-gītā As It Is*. Keep everything else simple. Hare Kṛṣṇa, because actually, I live in the shade of both followers and enemies, and that creates too much mental anxiety.

2:30 P.M.

In the shed with a head (can't be headless). Happy is the man who prays to the form of the Supreme Personality of Godhead. Rare is the soul who knows and believes—and is attracted to—the name, form, and pastimes of the Lord.

Questions people ask nowadays: Do I need another mentor from another camp? Can I teach myself? Can the Lord teach me?

Of course, Kṛṣṇa can teach anyone He finds eligible. When we give Him our affection, He reciprocates by giving us more of Himself. O Kṛṣṇa.

In the meantime and as part of my attempt to become eligible, I look out the wonderful wide TV screen of a shed window

Vande Guru Sri
Caranaravindum
head-
ache

Now where does this begin?
Two guys
Preach to Them
GO HOME, B. ack To Goahead
OH

Sada
Krsna

PURDAIVAN
Got
No
taste

KRISHNA

I'll teach
OH? Yeah?

Hare
Krsna

Krsna devotees

NITAI
Radha
Nay
Sudhha
habe
Hey
please

Deenatarine
Bhajatam

top
Krsna

Bhaktivinoda
I am sorry
he said
Hare Krsna is best medicine
for a
Cough
theres no
better cure than
chanting
Gods Names
Hare Krsna

at the moving picture of Nature herself. The wind blows across the lake and roughs the surface. Nature is only a fragment of the transcendental.

Should we believe it because we are supposed to? Because the authority (*śāstra*) says we should? Or because of its innate truth. Because it moves us? What do we *know* of the ideas and opinions of those who sought the Absolute Truth? "O Kṛṣṇa, O Lord," he said, aware of mockery and self-mockery and disbelief, of emptiness and death.

Clinging hope. Please let a little of the faith-giving potency stick to *me* from guru's words, from *śāstra's* power. Since my mind is prone to be overcome by the modes, and since it's also its nature to serve, please let my mind serve Kṛṣṇa and my spiritual master.

Look at the verse, read the familiar purport. Consider it. Even if a devotee of Kṛṣṇa accidentally falls down, he is still a devotee. Don't deride him. He will quickly attain lasting peace. Chanting Hare Kṛṣṇa mantras "should be continued without stoppage. This will protect a devotee from all accidental falldowns." (Bg. 9.31, purport) We should praise the holy name's power and sweetness. Why don't I write another book about chanting?

Because I'm too poor, I have no good experience to report.

Better I continue writing "Hare Kṛṣṇa" on my drawings and in my writing.

Tell us what that feels like.

Well, I feel an urge to canonize my whimsical writings and drawings, so I add the holy name.

I count those moments as chanting, but otherwise, I chant my sixteen rounds in one stretch from 1:15–3:15 A.M.

And what is your experience at *that* time?

I gloss. I utter. I stay awake. I get the mantras out.

MEMORIES OF YOU

We are alone
improvising is
not like playing at home
by yourself
a tough-guy provocateur—
no, but giving the heart
making a tune
of aloneness
or company
and memories
of you.

O Prabhupāda, you reminded me how bad
I wanted Kṛṣṇa, how much
I needed Him
how happy I could be.
Kṛṣṇa, the most
relishable of all forms of
Godhead. Yes, you said,
approving.

Prabhupāda, you knew God in
a special way, and you gave us His
loveliness and His power His
eternal reality

and we lived in faith
no one else could teach us
faith abounded with
capātīs and *dāl*—as real
as that.
O immediate friend, mentor
I accept your rule—my master
I want to live with you.

I recall the rough times when my mind
        couldn't surrender—I wanted
my space and needed it
and got it
and I thank you

but please enter this space
because I can't live without you—
foreign voices invade and I
begin to forget.

O Prabhupāda,
will you come to me at death?
Death will simplify me, I know,
and I will be reduced only
to the hopes I have placed
in you. ‖

REVIVAL

𝄞 Shout blues blind—
faith, I grab for you and
Śrīla Prabhupāda:
I will get it from my God/ in
his pants
        the little boy dances
tap
(he didn't, but I do)

and incline myself
to the *śāstras*

to prayer and
obeisances—keeping away evils
staying in tune
with the good a man can
do/ although no one seems to like
it much.
        "I don't understand."

3:50 P.M.

Outside the shed. Again I opted for my little life. It may not be so dramatic, but it's not static either. Different things happen. Right now birds are flying over the island. I never saw that before, at least not in the present. They say there is no past or future; the present moment is all we have. We Kṛṣṇa conscious people hope for much more than that, for eternal life beyond the moment. We preach it too.

5:50 P.M.

The Fuehrer fumed. I said, "Wait, I was in East Germany before the wall came down. We stopped our car-van to West Germany from Berlin in an area where you're not supposed to stop. We couldn't read the German sign. The green-uniformed East German policeman came and told us to move. I'm glad he didn't arrest us."

Sir, I'm a naturalized citizen. I used to live in the spiritual world, or so the *śāstras* tell me. You can't expect me to . . .

Śrīla Prabhupāda says to put faith in his books. Be humble. The *ācāryas* accepted the *śāstras*. I should too. It's a method. Give up mental speculation on topics beyond your purview. My puny brain can't figure God out. That's our method. The book Bhūrijana Prabhu recommended has a somewhat different view. Kierkegaard seems to have faith in *śāstra*, but he says faith is rarely attained. Alan Jones is thoroughly aware of psychoanalysis.

We avoided much of Western education when we came to Kṛṣṇa consciousness. We still don't consider it essential. We read only *śāstra* and the śāstric viewpoint. That makes us oddballs in our home cultures. We are accepted more in India, I suppose, but we don't really belong in either world.

Sunday is coming around again. I'm thinking to not prepare so much for my talk. They are famous verses—of Lord Caitanya speaking to the Kūrma Brāhmaṇa. I can probably improvise, and I should trust my training more.

Putting the pen down for the night. See you at midnight, if I'm lucky.

November 20

2:15 A.M.

"Generally, a devotee who is engaged in the nine kinds of devotional activities is engaged in the process of cleansing all material contamination from the heart." (Bg. 9.31, purport) A devotee places the Supreme Personality of Godhead in his heart, and thus sinful contamination is washed away. Therefore Kṛṣṇa says, "He quickly becomes righteous and attains lasting peace." That doesn't mean he continues sinning. We're not talking about unredeemed persons. One has to become sinless to become a pure devotee—or an active devotee becomes sinless. Regular, constant chanting of Hare Kṛṣṇa mantra will protect us from accidental falldowns.

Dear self, please take heart in this *Bhagavad-gītā* message. It's addressed to me. Continue the journey. I'm on the best path in this dangerous material world.

The world is not a happy place for anyone. "It is clearly stated here, *anityam asukhaṁ lokam:* this world is temporary and full of miseries, not habitable for any sane gentleman." (Bg. 9.33, purport) There is another world, eternal and blissful.

"Everyone should attach himself to the bosom of the Supreme Personality of Godhead so that he can be eternally happy." (Bg. 9.33, purport)

4:12 A.M.

I heard Śrīla Prabhupāda say we can't stay here. We may tell Death, "I can't go. I have permanent residency in America. I have too much left to do there."

"Damn your business! Come on!"

I played the tape excerpt for Madhu, and we enjoyed Śrīla Prabhupāda's powerful speech. To some degree the message sunk in. Then I thought that we as devotees have our devotional business. We're not ready to die either.

I have sent messages ahead to America to be sure my compact CD player and new CDs are waiting for me during our stopover in New York City, along with a fresh supply of Esgic. Yes, we will continue sailing, despite the obstacles and despite the dangers. Material life, Śrīla Prabhupāda said, means for every advantage there is an increased danger. The point of it is to see that this world is undesirable and transfer our thinking to Kṛṣṇa in the spiritual world. We can go to Him and not return for repeated material suffering.

When Prabhupāda was seventy-three, he said he couldn't live much more than another, say, five years. He said it calmly, philosophically, providing himself as a living example. We were young—in our late twenties and early thirties—when we heard it. We thought we would live a long time and see the Kṛṣṇa consciousness movement grow strong and more joyful. At least we are mostly still around, still operating new temples in Gujarat and Bangalore, and another just now coming in New Delhi. Yes, this was a wonderfully expanding movement.

While drinking his mint tea, the reporter wrote up his report to send to headquarters. This was no *Photo Preaching*, just mint tea and thoughts to while away the time.

You know, I used to sit on the floor and type for the Swami at my First Street apartment. I had a manual typewriter and made carbon copies. I used an eraser for mistakes. It was real labor—no one likes to work like that nowadays. I learned to type in the Navy. Later I move to Allston, but I continued to type with the machine on the floor. How much longer would I be able to do it without eyeglasses, without giving into my senses?

Looking back at those days: Would we be able to withstand *māyā*? Would we remain faithful in the Kṛṣṇa consciousness movement? Would the movement itself remain? Would we progress? Would we be able to keep faith in that narrow way, looking neither to the left nor the right? Or would the world's various influences gradually filter in, especially after the spiritual master left the planet?

Oh, he never left, I know.

They are waiting still for Rādhā and Kṛṣṇa to appear. They still don't drink tea (except mint) or coffee, and quell their hunger at breakfast. A routine life.

The moon is shrinking and the waters are choppier. Arjuna dāsa is becoming stouter as he looks at the lake and rows mightily back and forth with his passengers. I told him he's not like Charon of Greek mythology, carrying people across the river Styx. Rather, he is carrying them to eternal life, to the *darśana* of Rādhā-Govinda. He liked to hear that. O Kṛṣṇa. At the beginning of a Shakespeare play, you're supposed to try to understand what's going on through the thick, ornate poetry. A lot of it starts with "O."

5:40 A.M., POST-PAINTING IMPRESSIONS

I spent quite a bit of time on two paintings and now I'm exhausted. I am not so pleased with the results. Did I waste my time? I don't want to have blind faith in the creative process, but still, I seem to need to feel creative energy and to link it in a tangible way to my attempts to attain pure Kṛṣṇa consciousness.

Guy standing beside a horse, redeemed by the presence of the holy names. The other painting consists of four figures in various postures. Ask me what it means—what they are doing—and I can only imagine. The man on the far right is on his knees, naked, in a mood of supplication, his hands upraised. The Hare Kṛṣṇa mantra appears over his head. Next to him is a womanly shape, posturing like a department store mannequin. I drew her hips down as a heart shape, then gave her Vaiṣṇava *tilaka*. Next to her is the biggest of the four figures, with a Humpty Dumpty head and a sad look. He has violet arms and a brown torso, again like a store dummy. To his left stands the vaguest figure, an orange man with his hand uplifted and the word "Rāma" written over him.

9:00 A.M., MORNING WALK

I felt a twinge of pain, but decided to take my walk. Just before going out, Madhu and I discussed how young musicians tend to be naive. It takes time for them to realize the commitment it takes to become skilled with their instrument. We related it to devotional service and said that unless we work under a master and take one step at a time, we will not attain success. There is no cheap way to achieve perfection.

I am still young, even naive, in devotional service. I'm like a naive musician trying to learn how to copy the master, but I know now that first I will have to pay my dues.

On the trail of this small patch of land leading into the woods, just me and the leaves and the closeting of the little forest: Hare Kṛṣṇa, Hare Kṛṣṇa, Kṛṣṇa Kṛṣṇa, Hare Hare/ Hare Rāma, Hare Rāma, Rāma Rāma, Hare Hare.

November 21

1:00 A.M.

"Pain is hideous," said the materialistic doctor to the abbess of Lisieux. She replied, "Not here. Here pain is glorious because we suffer for Christ, who suffered for us." The nuns believed that if one of them was in pain, it was God's will for that soul. It should be used for devotional service.

I agree, but it's hard to accept pain at the price of my ability to read, write, and chant with vigor. Actually, I don't want to suffer. But if I knew the pain was my ordained devotional service, shouldn't I be willing to experience it as love? Shouldn't I be able to see pain as purification, or at least as something which I could do meekly rather than miserably?

Anyway, I took the second Esgic of the week around 6:00 P.M. last night. The pain gradually subsided. The noise from M.'s room also began to subside. Today I face lunch with a Godbrother without the cushion of a pain pill. If a headache comes, I'll have to cancel. I won't have the solace that he will understand or even believe my plight.

4:28 A.M.

"To him [Arjuna] also the Lord says, 'Take to My devotional service and come quickly back to Godhead, back home.' No one should remain in this temporary world, full as it is with miseries." (Bg. 9.33, purport)

Then the Lord tells us how to go back to Godhead: "Engage your mind always in thinking of Me, become My devotee, offer obeisances to Me and worship Me. Being completely absorbed in Me, surely you will come to Me." (Bg. 9.34)

LOVE SONG

(Love is a romantic story, especially when a guy loves his girl, because he can see her inner beauty, even despite his own less than handsome features—when they find the heart. It's an allegory for Kṛṣṇa consciousness, in a way—how we transpose it, feel the sadness of lost love or our wanting to be loved despite our lack of personal beauty, our hope to please the most beautiful God of love. But this, a love song . . .)

1

𝄞 Love knows itself immediately
and keeps a quiet tone
as quiet and breathless as a hushed choir.
Life's sad but
he's together with his love
      the sweetness and the light
the touch of tears of yearning
well-earned—no

old-guy cynic living ironic
left alone and
dry.

Love is earned through suffering
by becoming the sacrifice
by growing old with the love.
"My mind boggles at the
relationship between Kṛṣṇa and Arjuna—
  it's so dramatic!"

2

Realization—a funny Valentine
  offered to Kṛṣṇa, constructed from
a Brijbasi print
  an awkward *mūrti's* eyes—awkward
dress—he holds it to his heart.

O Kṛṣṇa, my
words are false but
I love You
and I try to be kind to others
for You.

My days run down
and Death (as Emily described it)
  will come
in its impersonal way. I mean,
it will take me no matter
how much we want to stay.

  O Kṛṣṇa, may I live the truth
going to a temple in the dark,
maṅgala-ārati, hearing
the scripture once again
in earnest.

O Kṛṣṇa, I
love You in this private
song. ‖

Dreamt I saw the full moon rising. I was walking on an island, similar to Inis Rath. Suddenly I heard someone sobbing. It felt like something magical, as if the moon itself were crying. I was afraid it was a curse upon me to have heard that sound. When I pronounced something to protect myself, the moon eclipsed.

9:05 A.M.

Śrīla Prabhupāda says that it is easy to know Kṛṣṇa, the Supreme Personality of Godhead, if we follow the process: hearing about Kṛṣṇa in the association of devotees. We repeat this statement with faith, and apply ourselves to the process. As the decades pass and we find we still don't know Kṛṣṇa, we must take it humbly, patiently, that we are not yet qualified. We simply go on practicing.

Or, we may pretend (fake) we know Kṛṣṇa more than we do. Prabhupāda said, "I don't know Kṛṣṇa, I only know my Guru Mahārāja."

We might choose to blame our lack of advancement on the Kṛṣṇa conscious process itself. Or some may find it easier to pursue a tangent, since the goal seems so hard to attain.

Or, seeing some defect in ourselves, we might resort to self-work—depth psychology or other forms of therapy—thinking our inability to receive Kṛṣṇa's full mercy is some blockage within ourselves of which we are yet unaware.

There are other alternatives too, such as giving more emphasis to active service than to internal development, or giving more emphasis to *japa* than preaching, thus possibly avoiding the surrender set us by the spiritual master, or traveling around the movement and especially to the holy *dhāmas*, spending endless time with friends rather than within our own hearts, etc.

But you know, it's up to Kṛṣṇa to reveal Himself to us or not, as He likes.

12:05 P.M.

What will I say to my Godbrother, who will visit in a few hours? I will, of course, be kind to him as I expect him to be toward me. We are not better than others, so we should always offer respect. It's usually our own insecurity that causes us to become defensive or to criticize others.

Why don't I ask him what he's reading in Prabhupāda's books? I'm concentrating on isolated "prayer" verses in *Bhagavad-gītā* right now.

3:10 P.M.

The meeting with my Godbrother went all right. He was gentle, and I was able to speak too. He's not to blame for anything.

I read the purport to Bg. 10.2 describing how Kṛṣṇa is inconceivable even to the demigods, yet He does exist. He is the Supreme Personality of Godhead: "We can actually understand Kṛṣṇa, who is eternal, full of bliss and knowledge, simply by studying His words in *Bhagavad-gītā* and *Śrīmad-Bhāgavatam*." He is far away even as I say this. While talking with my Godbrother, I thought this wasn't a likely topic to discuss. I couldn't say, "You know, we talk of Kṛṣṇa and assume we are Kṛṣṇa conscious, but I feel He's so distant it's alarming. I function in our movement because I have been here for so many years but not because of my direct experience of Kṛṣṇa's *darśana*." Of course, I *could* have said it, but I didn't think it would help me attain the intense state of *kṛṣṇa-smaraṇam* that I desire. Can someone speak to me who knows what I'm talking about and who is able to touch me?

Ah, Henry,
Hermes . . .
and other words.

I don't think I will paint today. Kṛṣṇa is the Supreme Personality of Godhead, and He can't be known by my endeavors. Devotees are going to India. Would that help? I told my Godbrother I would be going to the Caribbean soon. Will that help? What *is* it I need to do?

You say read more, and that sounds right, but I have already read quite a bit.

He told me how devotees leave ISKCON because they don't feel loved. He's doing his bit by serving as a counselor. I didn't presume to have the answers, so I said . . . O Kṛṣṇa, Kṛṣṇa, Kṛṣṇa.

B. Leo looked at me as if expecting something. He prostrated himself before me, as is the custom. What does it mean?

3:50 P.M.

When he said that he's too busy helping devotees to write, I thought, "Writing doesn't help the devotees?" He said, "I haven't eaten sweets in four months." I greedily devoured two pieces of delicious apple pie. I said my headaches have triggers—the arteries are spastic. He listened. He said in counseling you are taught to lean slightly forward while the person talks and occasionally say, "Uh huh," to show that you are listening. It's called empathic listening, he said.

Oh. You do it from life experience; they solve their own problems.

Shed is getting cold, but I won't turn on the heat. I'll go back soon and try Alan Jones.

Satsfer is a mysterious entity. I couldn't see his face, only his reflection. His *tilaka* was clean in the middle. Needs a haircut and a shave and to be fed at regular times.

Don't.

Don't.

They had a meeting and said, "Hare Kṛṣṇas have to be more relevant, not always claiming to be absolute."

The sun is going down. Fires on an island.

Premi. Sleep and rise.

5:10 P.M.

No more being disloyal to Śrīla Prabhupāda, thinking I need another *śikṣā-guru* and all that. Prabhupāda can teach me how to grow up. Alan Jones speaks of how many people can act as angels in our lives, even when only briefly met, when they give us a revelation of ourselves and of our falsities.

Look, be attentive and be patient. Admit what you lack. We simply don't love enough, and we prefer to deceive ourselves about that. How to go forward? It doesn't seem "enough" to read the scripture a little, chant a little, and keep together or apart from others.

November 22

12:10 A.M.

Getting back into scripture. How will we know Kṛṣṇa unless we read His word? Woken at midnight by the alarm. Didn't know whether it was night or day at first because the earplugs were in tightly. I was deep in a dream that I was with another devotee, a swami, who was telling me that it might be necessary to murder someone on *saṅkīrtana*. Incomprehensible fragments. Everything was so dark and the meanings so unclear. I never dream of Kṛṣṇa or the spiritual world or something to convince me deeply, but I have learned not to complain.

My Godbrother asked about my headaches. He said it's been great for me to have headaches because it has allowed me to avoid ISKCON management.

"Yes, perhaps I am unconsciously willing the headaches upon myself for that reason, but why should I *have* to do that to myself?"

He said he has a big head, and when devotees used to wear wigs on *saṅkīrtana*, his wig always hurt. He thought it was because he was not enthusiastic. Rather, it was simply because his wig was too small.

"Why did you tell me that?"

"Because it wasn't that I was actually unenthusiastic or to blame for my discomfort. Similarly, your headaches don't indicate your lack of . . . whatever. It's your suffering, that's all."

I didn't always have the pain, but yes, I like the life I have now. I have also made a major personal discovery because of the headaches: I like my freedom from ISKCON management. Some people are forced to accept a life not to their liking, and they become depressed, unable to see how Kṛṣṇa is blessing them.

I WANT TO TALK ABOUT YOU (ACCEPT, ALONE)

𝄞 I want to talk of You, Kṛṣṇa.
I know it's possible.
I must start alone—no one should
hear. Prayer
is never public, well
rehearsed
but heart to heart.

Kṛṣṇa, I want to be with those persons
who can induce me
to hear Your voice.
I surrender to You, Bhagavān,
Lord of all, as I hear You speak to Arjuna.
Junior ones remind me, the one
bowing down, the
one who loves *Bhagavad-gītā*,

the one praying to be number two
in the all-England book distribution
party.

I want to pray to You alone
    in my desert my
room. I want my prayer
to become an oasis
    of plenty
a flowing of faith and
realization.

O Kṛṣṇa, I want to talk *about* You
in Trinidad.
I'm not the center of the universe I know,
but it is not selfish to have faith to
admit I'm part and parcel.

O Kṛṣṇa, I want to find You
in the lines and between them.

O Kṛṣṇa, when I go alone to talk to You,
I won't feel pain, but
    if I do, I'll accept it
    if You give me the strength.

Only alone can I know You
and not be a mere small
suffering deceived person. ‖

4:11 A.M.

The persona is a nice guy who doesn't particularly like mint tea, but that's what he has been given, so he sips away. Too much tea fills up his belly and steals his appetite for breakfast. He has time to work on his appetite; he doesn't have to rush off to work like a *karmī.* Neither is he a *jñānī* meditating with the material mind. Ah, he is above those two, a *bhakta* in transcendence, serving and loving Lord Kṛṣṇa, daring and active, living in Him. Or perhaps he is something less than that.

I have written notes to Bhūrijana Prabhu on my reading of the book he recommended. When I finish the book, I'll arrange my notes and write him a letter—how it affected me. No big changes expected. By practicing spirituality, we come to the *bhakti-mārga* and the specifics Śrīla Prabhupāda gave us: chanting Hare Kṛṣṇa, reading *Śrīmad-Bhāgavatam.* A book never seems to make a profound change in our actual, routine lives. It may be interesting to read, and in rare cases it touches on profound subjects. We may admit it has exposed us as deceivers. Then what practical result comes from reading? We return to our way. We are not about to go off and follow someone else.

Come back to ISKCON, devotees. So you experienced Scott Peck's therapy group—tasted what you have not tasted since your first *kīrtana.* Or you learned about Reiki or some other process. We tell the devotees to return to ISKCON; it's vastly different than those earlier days. We acknowledge more the interior way, we have good times, less big shots manipulating, and we won't send you out to collect money. Neither will we demean you if you are incapable.

He said they complain that the leaders don't mix with the juniors and . . .

Yes, yes, but it's all different now. We all stay together as one happy family and love the morning program. Come back and enjoy the evening milk and *Kṛṣṇa* book reading.

And Swamiji has never left. He is sitting in a cabin in the mountains. At least one devotee dreamt that. He said that the GBC had been hiding Śrīla Prabhupāda all these years. He was angry at the GBC for doing this, but surprised and relieved to see that Prabhupāda was actually there in a room in the house. Hare Kṛṣṇa.

Live with death. Clear day yesterday. Who knows what to expect today?

The *Bhagavad-gītā*, Śrīla Prabhupāda says, is only the ABCs; it's preliminary knowledge. No one understands it even so.

Madhu stayed up last night looking at his chord book and memorizing new chords. I don't understand the process because I can't read music. I was asleep, deep in a dream filled with obscure, disturbed nonentities. Repetitious—I use my last days here in one way and my nights seeing dreams. It was cold as the night wore on. Finally had to get up and put on a sweater.

"Please see that the cat doesn't kill the pheasant," I said. I saw them both yesterday. The cat was looking at the pheasant from a distance. When the cat saw me, however, it ran away. It ran so fast I thought it was a fox. Then I realized that the cat wasn't running from me, but from the collie, who was coming up from behind me. Confrontations. I'm a powerful human being, right? I could kick off all attacks because I'm a tall caveman. What a waste we make of our time. O Kṛṣṇa, may I use this caveman body not to feel my power but to think of You.

5:24 A.M.

If we know some of Kṛṣṇa's opulences, our faith in Kṛṣṇa will increase because we will better understand how He is the Supreme Personality of Godhead. "I am the source of all spiritual and material worlds." Later the question is answered how Kṛṣṇa can make such a claim. Arjuna's acceptance is cited, along with the acceptance of Vedic sages such as Vyāsa and Nārada.

A contemporary Westerner can remain unconvinced. He can say that the Universal Form is simply a myth and that there were either no real Vedic sages or that they were ancient, sectarian persons who might not have known everything there was to know about the nature of God, especially as He manifested Himself in various world cultures.

We have our standard answers to these.

Mahā-mantra dāsī will be back Monday or Tuesday from India, hopefully carrying a *mūrti* of Rādhārāṇī for me. Kṛṣṇa is the source of all. "The wise who perfectly know this engage in My devotional service and worship Me with all their hearts." (Bg. 10.8)

Had a dream of being away from my disciples. It occurs to me now as I read *Soul Making* that we need a "stop the world" experience. That means getting a shock when a person is forced to abandon his or her provincial views. (I thought of how we used to think of LSD, but that was just another hallucination, wasn't it?) Such experiences come in times of catastrophe. My dream showed me that I may have to live without my usual support system. A devotee wrote a similar fear in her letter: "Life at my temple is peaceful and meditative. I feel I've been through a subtle change. I'm more at peace inside. The children are really happy here, and I have been appreciating Kṛṣṇa through His beautiful, ever-changing works of nature . . . I feel this is right for me at the moment. I do pray to Kṛṣṇa to be gentle with me when it comes to purification. When I see the hardship other devotees go through, I think, 'O my God, what lies ahead for *me*?' for it seems the more difficulty one is in, the more Kṛṣṇa conscious one becomes. I'm afraid of these difficult times."

Religionists often talk about "dying to the self," but I tend to resist that phrase. It sounds too much like ultimate voidism. Still, we say we must abandon false ego. I seem to resist that too. I'm afraid my writing will be taken away—and my Esgic, my bed, my servant, my disciples, the money coming in, the gentle people who live with me in this insular world of devotees. Leaving all this—is it akin to dying to the self?

Śrīla Prabhupāda never told us to renounce everything. Rather, he wanted us to use whatever we had and to risk our lives to bring other people to Kṛṣṇa consciousness. He told us to remain simple, and to live devotional lives with other devotees. He told us to prepare ourselves for going back to Godhead. He told us that we would be changed by the happy, easy practice of chanting and hearing about Kṛṣṇa.

But did we do these things? ISKCON seems burdened with worldly or ecclesiastical preoccupations, schisms, and heresies.

There's no need to weaken our faith.

8:00 A.M., MORNING WALK

The tallest tree on "Geaglum Road," which leads off the property, is leaning at a sharp angle. It seems to be dead, although green vines have wrapped around the trunk and all the way to the top. If someone pushed against it, it might come crashing to earth.

On the inner woods' path I noticed that two trees had been chopped down. Andy probably cut them for firewood. I'm not involved in the management of this project, but they should agree not to chop down their own forest.

While walking, I thought of the Jones book and the discussion on how we should become awake to reality in order to understand that we are not the center of the universe. This happens when our self-centered world is torn apart by calamity.

In *Soul Making*, Jones discusses how mystics live with death as a friend. St. Francis referred to death as "Sister Death." In that way, they don't meet Death only at the end, when they are terrified, but befriend it during their lifetimes. As a friend, Death can help shape our activities.

A disciple wrote saying how she feels she's been talking too much to her Godsisters and house visitors. She said her tendency is to share with them her innermost secrets and aspirations for spiritual life, and she suspects she does it so she'll be seen as a good devotee. When she talks out her secrets, however, she feels empty. She describes how she felt after spending an afternoon with a friend, talking too much, and then returned to her more usual solitude: "The loss I expressed in my poem about this is real—real enough to cause tears in my eyes and a tightness in my chest as I turn to my dear friends on my desk, *Bhagavad-gītā*, *Śrīmad-Bhāgavatam*, *A Poor Man Reads The Bhāgavatam*, *Japa Walks*, *Japa Talks*—my daily companions seemed somehow closed to me this evening—like I had been unfaithful to them. Please let me enter again into their real yet incredibly subtle spiritual reality . . . "

10:17 A.M.

I can't be clear of pain every day. I had no pain yesterday, yet today I live with it. Lordy lord, if I can't read and write, I can sit on a chair or lie down on a bed (and I don't mean like a vegetable) and manage to see calmly, without unnecessary guilt or disappointment, that Kṛṣṇa is in control. I can chant a few mantras in my mind and wait. I have so many gifts in this life, including the letters I receive and the ones I must write in return.

For example, I just wrote a letter to a devotee who recently changed from saffron to white cloth. The *brahmacārī saṅkīrtana* leader told him that he was no longer welcome on their team. I wrote a letter to encourage him, ending with, "Be humble, be friendly, and feed your preaching spirit." To be able to write a few lines like that and to hope to give another devotee encouragement is a gift. I quoted *kibā vipra, kibā nyāsī* to prove he could still preach. I also quoted *asat-saṅga-tyāga,—ei vaiṣṇava-ācāra* to show that he should always be careful about associating with sense enjoyers and nondevotees.

We each look out from our world and try to see into the heart where we can focus on Kṛṣṇa's names and presence: Hare Kṛṣṇa, Hare Kṛṣṇa, Kṛṣṇa Kṛṣṇa—it is often a tepid, piddling, leaking *bhajana*, but at least we keep it going—Hare Rāma Hare Rāma, Rāma Rāma Hare Hare. This tired donkey with the eye twinge wants to chant and wishes his *japa* weren't offensive. Kṛṣṇa Kṛṣṇa, Hare Hare. I'm sorry, Lord, that I misjudged, underestimated, and remained ignorant of the power and sweetness of Your name. Thank You for maintaining me while I make my attempt to improve myself. I don't want to be governed merely by Your material energy; I wish to serve You in spiritual life, beginning with hearing and chanting: *śṛṇvatāṁ sva-kathāḥ kṛṣṇaḥ*. May I touch the lotus feet of submissive hearing, as I did today for a moment.

ALL OF YOU

𝄞 I want the soft lotus feet of You
the east, west and north of You the
unlimited One
the glories of You
as I have heard them in *Bhagavad-gītā*.

I want to hear You
softly in my reverberating
        heart and mind
and heart and
I've heard

I will be with
You
even when my head is
cracking with pain

living smooth and sublime
in what You have said but

I want *all* of You
and I want all
of me
to surrender to You—
my talent (given by You)

my ability
my fun
my anger and fear
given
to You.

Looking out at Your changing
nature, lake and sky and island trees
glory I say it too—
got a right—
the soft and smooth and fluent
time I spent hearing sounds I liked.

The feeling of disappointment I tasted
when worldly
    stuff
    faded
        like melting ice cubes
      in highballs in
        glasses with
        lipstick stains

the false
    māyā cured by Your
      sādhu who told me
there was beauty only in You
and the fields of Vraja.

12:15 P.M.

Is it my last time in Geaglum? You never know. "Life," he said, "our world, is paper thin, like the walls of a Japanese house. They can be poked and ripped. Then we will be left with maybe a kernel of self, if we're lucky."

We know we would retain the self, because that's the Kṛṣṇa conscious understanding. Kṛṣṇa conscious people withstand disasters because Kṛṣṇa often spares them even externally, but even when He allows them to suffer for their own purification, He doesn't make the suffering so severe that they cannot handle it. "I carry what they have and provide what they lack," Kṛṣṇa says. That's only for His pure devotee? What are we? Feeling hollowness and lack. That's a symptom of a pure devotee, or someone wishing they were. Round and round.

3:30 P.M.

Despite head pressure, I went on an afternoon walk with M. We met no one else. Damp and cool—end of autumn weather. I felt as if I were saying good-bye to the woods. I showed Madhu where someone chopped down the forest trees and I talked about yesterday's meeting with my Godbrother. Hare Kṛṣṇa. It was good to get out of the room where I was starting to monitor my aches.

Hare Kṛṣṇa. *The Desert Way* suggests we practice what is difficult in order to find true spiritual life and get beyond ego. Śrīla Prabhupāda taught that Kṛṣṇa consciousness is *susukham*, joyfully performed, although he has also spoken (in NOD) of the tears that are the price of spiritual perfection. Bhaktisiddhānta Sarasvatī said we should "soak our couch with tears." Piteously implore Kṛṣṇa for His mercy. Repent our failures. To realize we are blundering is good for our advancement. Underlying that, however, we have to feel a basic trust and well being, a satisfaction of self (*yenātmā suprasīdati*).

I can't expect *The Desert Way* or any other kind of psychoanalysis to line up with Kṛṣṇa consciousness exactly.

Tick-tock. Try to read more this afternoon, if possible. It is possible as long as the ache doesn't move into the right eye.

"I hear you're spending a lot of time in Ireland."

"Yes, here I am able to be a semi-invalid but still live with devotees." (They don't demand of me.)

"The Irish seem to be simple people."

"Yes, no big controversies."

No big rodeos either, and no roundups or Thanksgiving days, but plenty of sinful karma from all this animal slaughter.

"I'd like to get rid of Tin Pan Alley in my music," he said. "We Americans . . . " They performed a play for Śrīla Prabhupāda's disappearance day at the Manor. One young man played Tamāl Krishna Mahārāja—he even had the mole on his forehead "and spoke with an American twang."

Chestnuts don't go moldy. I'll leave them behind in jars. Go off and lecture by repeating what the *śāstras* say, according to your realization. You cannot contradict it. Whoever hears you with sincerity, eagerness, and submission will benefit. I shouldn't go a day without *kṛṣṇa-kathā*, and we shouldn't hear merely out of duty but with an anxiety to hear. This is the prescribed path. I'm aware that I stay with my reading by choice, but that choice is made from the heart and desperately (I'll discover that more in hours of crisis). I beg not to be kicked away. When I say I choose Kṛṣṇa consciousness, I know I'm not doing *bhakti* a favor, but just that I am not practicing it casually.

It's true I tend to take my everyday routine for granted. Still, I do appreciate the peace my life affords me. The sun rises over the same lake and sets. There are a few differences between the seasons. Neither the weather nor my life makes severe demands upon me. I hope not to abuse my time.

And waves of creativity come. The harsh, tragic, suffering ahead we all fear. I pray to be strong enough to face it. We stopped on our walk, and M. patted Prahlāda's friendly cow, whose bell tinkled.

5:18 P.M.

Not much left in me for this day. "Are you doing any better?" Madhu asked. Not really, and no, I'm not up to memorizing verses just now.

O Kṛṣṇa, Kṛṣṇa. Read again *Bhagavad-gītā's catur-ślokī*. In 10.8 Kṛṣṇa says that He is the source of all the worlds. How could a person be the source of everything? He has inconceivable power. If people struggle with this concept, I think it's just as unlikely to believe that there is an impersonal force behind everything, or no intelligent force at all.

But why does He make us suffer?

He doesn't. We create our own suffering. Now that we are in this difficult situation, we can become free by practicing Kṛṣṇa consciousness. Our present suffering could be our last. Accept authority.

Doubts, doubts: "Prabhupāda could be confident of the *ācāryas* and *śāstras* because he was from India."

Even if we accept that argument, we can also be "from India." India is the source of religion and great, ancient traditions. The *Upaniṣads*, *Vedas*, the *yogīs*, the epics, *Bhagavad-gītā*—and Kṛṣṇa—all come from there. Lord Caitanya too. I have been brought into it even though I wasn't raised in it. We Westerners must struggle to adjust to it all—the culture that goes along with the faith—and learn to dovetail who we are with who we would like to become. No one asked us to become Hindus over it.

How does pain figure in God consciousness?

You already know that answer, although official answers aren't always "the answer." Answers must be realized.

So, my friend, be nice to others and I'll see you tomorrow.

November 23

12:16 A.M.

Most of my dreams seem to have the simple message that material life is entanglement and delay, and that we are always stuck in some universal bureaucracy. Reminds me of Kafka's two big novels. In one dream, the NYC subway tokens I was issued were defective. I was told to turn them in so that I could receive dining privileges. But that turned out not to be free either. I went into the cafeteria with the defective tokens, but didn't have enough money to pay for my meal. I was also helping an old woman in need of care. What to speak of not moving speedily to our destination, we were twice delayed, once by the tokens and once in the cafeteria. Hopeless.

I woke from the dream thinking that this is the sort of delay we experience every day. At present, our lives may seem relatively free of confusion and the sense of displacement, and perhaps no one is mistreating us. Perhaps we are not even being abused by the system. Still, such dreams warn me about the true nature of material life, and if I don't appear to be experiencing such discomfort and confusion now, I will experience it in the future. I *must*, because that's the nature of this world.

Does this information impel you to feel intense contrition for having come into this material world in the first place? That's the first step in developing the desire to get out. Usually, we are so attached to body and mind that we can't feel such things deeply. We have already expended too much of our energy in serving the senses. The only thing that can save us is to hear intensively about Kṛṣṇa. We're usually lucky if we can maintain any kind of reading schedule, without letting it diminish. We can also chant with love and petition. But we don't. We simply refuse. Alan Jones writes, "When do tears come for the attentive believer? They begin to flow at the moment when we see the contradiction between what we hope for and what we actually are; when we see the deep gulf between the Love that calls us and our response to it." (*Soul Making*, p. 90)

I read again of Kṛṣṇa's opulence as He briefly describes Himself in the opening verses of the tenth chapter of *Bhagavad-gītā*. Śrīla Prabhupāda states, "If one knows factually how God is great, then naturally he becomes a surrendered soul and engages himself in the devotional service of the Lord. When one factually knows the opulences of the Supreme, there is no alternative but to surrender to Him." (Bg. 10.7, purport)

Although I read, I'm not moved. I can barely pay attention to what is being said. My mind wanders. I did appreciate the exercise, which I continued through June and July, of reading *Bhāgavatam* throughout the day and writing down notes. At least I was trying to concentrate more when I did that. It seemed more important than my other literary endeavors.

It's a fact that I'm not anxious to hear *kṛṣṇa-kathā*. At least my intelligence is alert enough to know the folly of this, so I turn to *śāstra* again and again.

Especially since I'm not able to do other services—or as a *sannyāsī* I'm free of so many duties—I should not minimize the power and opulence of *śravaṇaṁ kīrtanam*. I can achieve much by reading the scripture. "This factual knowledge can be known from the descriptions in *Śrīmad-Bhāgavatam* and *Bhagavad-gītā* and similar literatures." (Bg. 10.7, purport) I still need to practice self-examination, or else my reading of scripture becomes superficial or reduced, like poor chanting. When I see such poor performances from myself, I need to ask where my love is. Only then will I face it.

4:15 A.M.

Thinking of calling this volume *Parting from Peaceful Geaglum*. That means something. It is peaceful here, and I know I cannot always have such peace in this world. The scenery, the solitude, the going to the shed, the doing as I like, the freedom from having to lecture more than once a week—it is certainly a place of peace for me. I am leaving because we are going to the Caribbean via New York City to preach. *Parting from Peaceful Geaglum* would be a fitting title, unless I can find something more central and deep.

Geaglum is a mundane, Northern Irish name, probably named after some rich farmer or politician. I pun on the name and refer to it as "gay-glum," so that we don't forget the dualities that exist even here. The place is actually called Geaglum Quay, pronounced "key," or as in the Sanskrit "*kī*." Geaglum is meant for spiritual life.

Life in the mode of goodness here is quiet but not dull. There are probably many semi-hermits in Ireland—old people who stay mostly indoors, as I do. Staying indoors doesn't make their lives spiritual, but many of them do live spiritual existences, eating simply, abstaining from sex and alcohol, reading scripture, and praying. Ireland is conducive to that kind of a life. I find that to be true for myself.

I'm typing, and Śrīla Prabhupāda is looking over my shoulder. Rādhā and Kṛṣṇa are here! They are dressed nicely in pink and maroon. Śrīmatī Rādhārāṇī is the daughter of Vṛṣabhānu Mahārāja. Follow the path of the Gauḍīya Vaiṣṇava saints in your worship. They aspire to one day receive a spiritual body and serve the Divine Couple beside their spiritual masters in *their* spiritual bodies. I won't find even a hint of that in Alan Jones, although what he says may be a valid prerequisite for cleansing the heart and freeing ourselves from material religion.

I want to make art, not just live in religion, theology, and philosophy. What do I mean by art? I want to find and express the compelling emotions that allow us to love God. I draw on memories and desires in an intuitive way, to move us. Art is not so easily defined. Hare Kṛṣṇa. It comes up when we act sincerely and the words have an eloquence free from affectation. I can't describe it more than that.

Now folks, let's drink our bitter lemon drink while it's still hot. Let's dance the silence of a pious monk. We will rest too, so that this fellow can fulfill his duty and give the lecture at 8:00 A.M. I will read from *Caitanya-caritāmṛta*, not exactly improvising my lecture, but I haven't overly planned. The section I chose starts with praise of pilgrimage, and the purports tell us which railroads to take to get to particular spots. After that, we will speak about Lord Caitanya's contemporaries and how we can still see Him today if our eyes are tinged with devotion. Then there's the verse where the Kūrma Brāhmaṇa states that he wants to get out of the miseries of birth and death. He begs to renounce his family and travel with Lord Caitanya. Here I may comment on how a pleasurable life can be disrupted by tragedy. Peace is not really the source of pleasure, and neither is family life, so Vedic society makes renunciation compulsory. In any case, we cannot be happy. Having come to the temporary miserable world, we should engage in Kṛṣṇa's devotional service. Hare Kṛṣṇa. To be in the temple room is a gift. The experience will be up and then down, but I'll be able to return and reenter this private world.

5:30 A.M.

Various scriptures prove that Nārāyaṇa is the source of all. Lord Caitanya teaches that Lord Kṛṣṇa is the source of Nārāyaṇa. Who am I to resist or doubt Lord Caitanya? I just heard Śrīla Prabhupāda explaining (in a 1969 lecture) how *brahma śabda* is, as evidence, superior to direct sense perception (*pratyakṣa*) or hypothesis (*anumāna*). He convinced me. The previous sages researched and received knowledge, and so it has already been presented. We can save ourselves trouble and confusion by simply accepting it. To the degree that *pratyakṣa* and *anumāna* are useful, the compilers of *śāstra* used them to convince us, but ultimately, a simple hearing of *śāstra* is enough. We must trust guru and *śāstra* as a child trusts his father when the father offers him food, or as we trust a licensed restaurant not to poison us. In spiritual matters there is no other way to receive transcendental knowledge except as it descends. I like that image of men in a tree carefully handing down the ripened mangoes. Are we there to receive them?

NOON

Mahā-mantra dāsī returned from Vṛndāvana carrying a package for me. I picked it up at the temple room when I went to give the *Caitanya-caritāmṛta* lecture. Then I went into my room alone and opened it. It contained both Rādhā and Kṛṣṇa! They are beautiful, brilliant, effulgent, with fine features. I am wondering who in Vṛndāvana I should thank for this wonderful gift?

I have packed up the "training" Rādhā and Kṛṣṇa for return to America. Now my own Rādhā and Kṛṣṇa are kindly standing together on the altar, beautifully dressed in one of the eight sets of clothes I've been given. At first I was thinking to hold an *abhiṣeka* as a gesture "installation," but I think I will just ease into Their worship more simply and humbly. Soon

They will receive Their first meal here in Geaglum, Their new home. Maybe I will call Them Śrī Śrī Rādhā-Govinda after the presiding Deities here.

2:35 P.M.

Thank you, Rādhā-Govinda, for coming to me here in North Ireland. It's not Vṛndāvana. It must be exciting in Vṛndāvana, hearing the sounds so close to the original Vraja, to experience the *bhāva* and the *rasa.* O Govardhana, you have given me mercy. You know when I come to You, I become a target for so many people and controversies. I stay here, remembering You, Your mercy upon me, and living alone. I am not on the eve of the Christmas marathon nor in Vṛndāvana with its lanes, cows, peacocks, holy places, *bhajanas* to Rādhā and Kṛṣṇa pouring out from the loudspeakers, Vraja-Kṛṣṇa's closeness under the veneer. No, I live in solitude at Inis Rath, and not even at Inis Rath, but on a piece of mainland facing the lake island.

But I'll soon be leaving here. I won't even have two weeks with my new Rādhā-Kṛṣṇa Deities. I'll just be getting to know Them when I have to leave. I know They'll call me back. O Rādhā, O golden-complexioned one, O dark Kṛṣṇa . . .

Kṛṣṇa is the source of all. Those who know it worship Him with all their hearts. They enliven one another discussing His qualities and pastimes. Here's how He reciprocates with them: "To those who are constantly devoted to serving Me with love, I give the understanding by which they can come to Me." (Bg. 10.10)

People read *Bhagavad-gītā* without Kṛṣṇa. Śrīla Prabhupāda insists that Kṛṣṇa is to be known by *Bhagavad-gītā*. Take His words—He speaks them directly. *Buddhi-yoga:* He grants us the intelligence to serve Him with devotion.

I can't expect to remember all this from one life to another, so what is the best way for me to meet this approaching death? I want to discuss it and *pray*. I wish I could wish I could pray.

LUGLU

Today I received Rādhā and Kṛṣṇa from
Vṛndāvana with
    dust and
mahā sweet balls—
what are they called?
Gulabs? No,
    luglus!

Luglus too sweet for
me—harsh Indian sugar
    and now you see
    I can't see
    the inner Vraja.

"Yeah 'cause you gave up your
connection with—"
No, no
I'm Prabhupāda's *celā*
I'm one of the far-out
    Swami's
boys who prayed for him to recover
and whose sons' and daughters' prayers
saved him, he said, our love.
He loved our love and I love to hear it
even now, thirty years later.
In NYC we loved him and
shaved and dressed in *dhotīs/ sārīs*
it
didn't
take us long.

The Ganges takes a long time
to purify, but not the pure devotee.
He got us right away, moaning for Kṛṣṇa, like
that crazy guy in SF on Frederick Street:
"I am God!"

Hayagrīva spun in circles
cymbals on his fingers
and I gave it all up—my LPs, my
stray hall cats, the Swami
crashing through our lives our
love
reeling us in as he
feed us *luglus.* ‖

3:15 P.M.

No headache all day. I spoke with drama in class. One devotee, tanned, had just returned from Vṛndāvana.

Kṛṣṇa is effulgent. I glance at Him, amazed.

Rain on roof. Wind.

I've got it easy in
easy time
with rain and relish
of being alone.

Departing from peace to enter the stress of the preacher. Glad, too, that I'm going.

They like to listen in Trinidad, and that's their good qualification, even if they can't take action.

Don't tell them that—it's not really my opinion anyway. I heard it from another.

Samosās for lunch today. I heard my brother on tape as I ate. He was speaking of the importance of what the sages taught at Naimiṣāraṇya. Who, caught in the meshes (not black mesh stockings of cabaret dancers, but the iron meshes of karma) will not hear the pastimes of the all-good Personality of Godhead?

Swami asked his Godnephew in India to pack up his books and mail them, with *mṛdaṅgas, karatālas,* beads, Rādhā-Kṛṣṇa *mūrtis*—and hurry up! We need weapons on the American front. He was demanding. When his correspondent wrote back, "I regret," Swamijī replied, "Yes, I regret too." He wanted action. Still does.

"Mercy," he begged.

"You and I can disagree. We are like father and son, and there is no offense."

That's the testimony. They were close and I should not step in like a fool and say otherwise. But if I choose to stay in the ranks of ISKCON's boys and girls who need only one guru ("If I sent someone else and he said even one thing different . . . "), then that's not wrong.

MY ROMANCE (WHAT DOES IT MEAN?)

𝄞 I want to be a devotee. That
is my romance, but

I once romanced
in a taxi on
the ferry
        and now I must dream of it—

the return to Staten Island
the Navy
and I can't get out
or be happy
and no one helps.
It means I am a devotee
who can't get to perfection
or even to first base

that I am skinny
fasting and praying because
I wish I could be more transparent
        and give you the best
guru's
        true wisdom

tear away the veil of all
questions and comments. But
this old romance
forces me
to be myself. ‖

4:00 P.M.

I was caught in the rain on my way back from the shed. That's a pleasure too. The wild grass is trampled from my once-a-day walks out here. The place where I walk has yellowed. Otherwise everything is green. Except the sky, which is very dark, and the trees' gnarly branches like crooked fingers against the sky. Clouds torn and drifting. Heading back to a warm room in a protected house. Kṛṣṇa's mercy.

November 24

12:12 A.M.

A Kṛṣṇa conscious person should go forward with firmness and determination. Avoid all unauthorized commentaries on *Bhagavad-gītā*. Just by the evidence he gives, go forward. "There is no supreme controller other than Kṛṣṇa." (Bg. 10.8, purport)

"Is this the one Supreme God? Is this the same God the Christians worship?"

Yes, it is. Other questions?

"Why am I shriveling up? Is that symtomatic of something?"

Hare Kṛṣṇa, Hare Kṛṣṇa.

I heard that. Your *japa* was accidentally recorded. It sounds like you are skipping over syllables. But it may be said that Śrīla Prabhupāda also sounds like he's skipping. I don't worry about that too much as long as I think I'm saying the thirty-two syllables as they pass in rhythm through my mind's attention.

We accept, we consent, we are silent and don't vocalize objections when Śrīla Prabhupāda writes that Kṛṣṇa is God. Of course, that is not enough to make us Kṛṣṇa conscious.

SK said he was afraid to be alone with the word of God, but he tried anyway. He was humble and honest, and at least he didn't claim that being a scholar interpreting scriptures is something great. I read in *Fear and Trembling* of the demands that God makes on us. Don't glibly think we devotees already live up to them.

We have our own list of Kṛṣṇa's demands. "The wise who perfectly know this engage in My devotional service and worship Me with all their hearts. The thoughts of My pure devotees dwell in Me, their lives are fully devoted to My service, and they derive great satisfaction and bliss from always enlightening one another and conversing about Me." (Bg. 10.8–9)

My mind wanders even while I write this down. Then let me write about the wandering. Face the doubts and tepidness. Read more. Pray now. Please let me be more open to Your holy name. I see my shortcomings. I am tiny and cowardly, exhausted and wishing I could do more. Dependent on the Lord to revive me.

We read of heroic devotees but can't become one. Manu asked in effect, "Is it enough that I be honest?"

"Yes," as if (I assume) that's what I'm doing.

Underachievers, most of us. Still, it's a great achievement to have come to Kṛṣṇa consciousness. We need to share our struggle and in that way help ourselves.

In his purport to Bg. 10.10, Śrīla Prabhupāda writes that Kṛṣṇa will help the devotee from within. To receive that help, "He should perform some sort of work for Kṛṣṇa, and that work should be with love."

4.28 A.M.

It takes longer to dress Rādhā-Govinda now that I have so many ornaments and dresses. I have a hard time fitting Śrīmatī

Rādhārāṇī's crown. It tends to slip. I hope Their clothes are fitting with the Vraja mood; they're so opulent. The main ornament of Vraja is *prema* in its various manifestations, and Śrīmatī Rādhārāṇī is a simple cowherd girl. Still, we hear of Her wearing gorgeous ornaments, and I hope She will not mind that Her crown is so large. I also hope I can receive a drop of the nectar of serving Them in Vṛndāvana through this Deity worship. They are my king and queen, the Lords of the kingdom of love. The ornaments I have, in fact, do not enhance Their glorious natures.

Śrīla Prabhupāda sits beside Them. He's the spiritual master sitting on the *vyāsāsana*, and it is he who has allowed me to serve Them. He guides me as in the "*Gurvāṣṭakam*" verse 3, *śrī vigra-hara* . . . and also the fifth, beginning "*śrī rādhikā*." He wears a bright saffron wool cap today. That too came from Vṛndāvana.

I know I cannot carry these Rādhā-Kṛṣṇa Deities when I travel. They belong in one place. I would like to come back to Them soon, so I'll carry Their photo with me. Hare Kṛṣṇa.

What else? What else is there? Simply the holy name. I don't need to say this. You already know. I write for my purification.

One devotee asked Prabhupāda how he could become a servant of one who serves the *gopīs*. Śrīla Prabhupāda replied that the *gopīs* are on the liberated platform. We have to first become liberated before we can serve them. Still, to serve the *gopīs* is a good idea, Prabhupāda said, even if we can't do it immediately, and certainly not by imitation. Do the routine work, including serving the Deity, chanting, and hearing, and the time will come when everything will be revealed. Automatically.

Answered letters. Read books. What else is there to do but hear about Kṛṣṇa and then tell others what you heard? And if there are difficulties, turn to Kṛṣṇa more. Don't let all your energy go into simply coping. Use it to help yourself and others by remembering Kṛṣṇa. That is Kṛṣṇa consciousness.

Rādhānātha's father and his father's second wife are here visiting. M. played music for them last night. They want to see me for at least a few minutes, a handshake or something. I will satisfy Rādhānātha in that way. But no extended meetings.

Today, Monday, Rādhā-Govinda wear light green trimmed in gold. Each day I offer a different color scheme—seven days, seven outfits—and at night a bluish dress. Mercy upon me.

Parting from peaceful Geaglum, parting my hair, parting of the ways—I play the part of a laborer or sweatshop boss or writer with delicate hands and a low brow. Part of me wants to go to Goloka. I am part and parcel of Kṛṣṇa. I part from Inis Rath and go to preach. All temporary partings, or most of them. Therefore I have not used words such as "farewell" or "good-bye." Just a two-month separation from here. O Kṛṣṇa.

5:58 A.M.

Like to spend time discussing *Soul Making* with Bhūrijana Prabhu, but I can't spare the time and neither can he. He's in Australia with his family preparing for his three *Śrīmad-Bhāgavatam* overview lectures per week. I'm here in Ireland (or traveling soon). When I'm in Ireland I'm alone most of the time and can find time to read a book like *Soul Making*, but I say my health and lack of sociability (they go together) make it difficult for me to endure much company. I like some of the points in *Soul Making*, which include the concept that we should preserve "pity, grief, and joy" within ourselves and honestly face God as we read our *śāstra*. We have to name our fear, our shortcomings, our cowardice, and also our love.

8.45 A.M.

Still running on clear time. I walked out the door and realized I'd forgotten my dictaphone. I ran back in and Madhu already had his melodeon strapped on and was playing away, absorbed. I said, "I forgot my—accordion."

Madhu asked if I had named my Rādhā-Kṛṣṇa Deities yet. I said I hadn't decided, but was thinking of Rādhā-Govinda. He said he had also thought of that name. My reasoning is that I don't dare—it would seem presumptuous—to choose a name. Who am I to say I was inspired that the Deity should be named Rādhā-Ramaṇa or Rādhā-Mādhava or Rādhā-Śyāmasundara? In the absence of such God-given inspiration, Rādhā-Govinda seems right because we are living in Their *dhāma*. I have already been worshiping a picture of Inis Rath's Rādhā-Govinda on my altar, so why not? The name provides perfect shelter. I am also reminded of Rādhā-Govinda in New York, whom I never worshipped on Their altar, Rādhā-Govinda in Calcutta, whom I would never dare to approach because of the India factor, and Rādhā-Govinda of Denver, so tall and stately. Why not Rādhā-Govinda of Satsvarūpa dāsa? And instead of calling this volume *Parting from Peaceful Geaglum*, I'll call it *Rādhā-Govinda, We Hardly Knew Ya*.

As I was walking back from the property's edge, I saw Ānandamāyā's red car leave her house. She must be on her way to work. I raised my hand as her car approached, and she slowed down and made *praṇāmas* with her hands. I could see she was wearing what looked like a starched white collar. It reminded me of the collars worn by choir singers or church people. Inis Rath and your people, I hardly knew ya.

10:15 A.M.

Kṛṣṇa helps the devotee from within his heart if the devotee is sincere. Do I say, "Well, I'm not sincere, so Kṛṣṇa doesn't help me?" Do I think He doesn't destroy my ignorance or give me the understanding by which I can come to Him? Or do I accept the śāstric statement simply: "Yes, it's true. God informs me from within the heart. I do not feel His absence."

I don't always know which is right. What *is* my position? Am I God conscious, or is it mere intelligence, piety, and obedience that encourage me to chant my rounds and try to read the scriptures? Maybe I'm only beginning Kṛṣṇa consciousness. When I'm on the *vyāsāsana*, if someone asks such questions, I answer positively. Maybe I should take a sabbatical from lecturing until I know something for sure. But I have duty. I'm just a mouthpiece anyway. What I repeat proves that I experience at least a shadow of true *śraddhā*.

2:35 P.M.

Woke from my nap thinking about racism. Why should such thoughts affect me now? They feel like a distraction from Kṛṣṇa consciousness to think about all the repercussions and the anger, especially, that is expressed, by the dominated race. Such distractions tend to bring with them emptiness and even depression. If we indulge in following such thoughts, the result is acid indigestion of the spirit. Why can't we conquer racism with broad-hearted Kṛṣṇa consciousness? If that's not possible, we still need to incorporate everything to spearhead the Kṛṣṇa consciousness of our own thoughts and acts.

Walking out to the shed, this day cold and gray. A few flies struggling against the windowpanes. No interest lately in drawing or painting. Okay, then don't force it.

Kṛṣṇa is alive, real, and all-powerful God. We can't see Him unless we are qualified. That's just the way it is.

Had a small, friendly talk today with Rādhānātha's father, and I felt it brought me afterwards to a more attentive Kṛṣṇa consciousness. Of course, I didn't try to preach in such a situation—just showed him that we are human, can joke and relax, etc. He was open-minded. I told him that Madhu's autobiographical essay was called "From Punk to Monk."

Śrīla Prabhupāda in Seattle, 1969, telling them, "We are all servants; serve God or dog. Better to serve God and go back to Godhead." "It is only by devotional service to Kṛṣṇa that one can understand his position and get rid of this material body." (Bg. 10.13, purport) Arjuna was not flattering Kṛṣṇa when he addressed Him as the Supreme Personality of Godhead. He cited authorities who also accepted Kṛṣṇa as the Supreme.

A cow is lowing and sounds miserable or at least beastly, bovine, lamenting. For food, I suppose. Rain tinkling, then silence. I turned on the heater, but the windows fogged up, so I turned it off again. It's not so easygoing or pleasant out here in the afternoon at this time of year. One and a half hours is all.

TRYING TO MAKE IT CLEAR (FAST)

1

𝄞 I have limited time but
after all, I am the Lord's boy
and I can catch these notes
fast.

There is no way there is
no way
I said hey I
want to be a man
too
and accept *all* the folks in my
house. The police,
those bigots, say No
you are in trouble if you do.

Stay alone, he said
Then back to the house for
me
and I am dedicated
I said
and
Let my people go
we Hare Kṛṣṇas
already persecute ourselves
through our schisms
and need no extra help.

Philly
New York
D.C.
everywhere we go

we have farms and cows
do no harm have
little steam it seems but

plenty of complaints against our leaders,
against those
who stick to themselves and eat apart.
We want everyone *together*
he said

He said no one cares
if they offend pure devotees—
who? We need bucks, education
we need *you.*

I love the sound
up and down how they traded
by fours the
chanting

and you know, I can't get any clearer
than this:
we boys and girls
in clover

souls eternal
trapped
can only get out
through devotion

and if we can't quite believe
(not yet) please help us
give us knowledge and soup and
fun and sorrow and tell us to
wait without grief.

2

Look at my navel?
Not me I've got
Rādhā-Kṛṣṇa to glance at
after lunch—now They can
see where They agreed to
come—this voracious bear cub
wolfs it down before Their eyes
but to the side.

O Kṛṣṇa and Rādhā, that's
who I am and still I beg
be close to me, be mine.

"I CAN'T GET STARTED"

I can't get started
and I'm sorrowful about that
trying to do what they are doing

I complain in blues and can't
get started but when the master plays . . .
I played in Prabhupāda's presence
when he said "Lecture."
He'd cut us off. I said
Kṛṣṇa stole butter and Prabhupāda smiled.
Now my sons speak in front of him all
in separation
as we die off/ like the flies
in the shed.

Lecturing I said
Kṛṣṇa consciousness is a good thing
told a story and quoted *śāstra*.
What else do I know?
But in '66 I came
to him in NYC
and it was good
and still is. He
let us play drums and flutes and I still
remember.

In his stretched turtlenecks
what did we know about him?
We thought of Tompkins Square Park
and giving up and
rules
and brahmin spaghetti
but we didn't know his mind
how he could think
of Vṛndāvana sweetness and wishing
to wear a torn quilt, bathing in the Yamunā
yet live with us.
I just can't get started
but by his grace. ||

3:55 P.M., SHED

Completely overcast. Dark as if at dusk. Nobody knows . . . that I wrote a poem. Kṛṣṇa gave me the energy to do it and I simply accept His gift and keep going, hoping to make at least a small contribution to His mission according to the capacity He gives me. I compensate for my failings and try to find a way to serve despite them.

Wet leaves, wet grass—who says Kṛṣṇa is absent? Who says we can't find any sign of Him? Prabhupāda says that this nice thing we feel, this direction we get, is a form of Kṛṣṇa. He assures us, so why should I deny it? Following my Swami is also a method of realizing God.

Most religions place little emphasis on the role of the guru. There are so many gurus who inspire our spirituality—the fat lady, the man we met on the subway, the impoverished, an animal, a stranger who knocks at the door. Yes, they're gurus, and the *Bhāgavatam* even refers to bumblebee and python gurus. A pure devotee sees Kṛṣṇa everywhere.

But in the Vaiṣṇava *sampradāya* we prefer to speak about that heavy person who comes in disciplic succession and to whom we must surrender our whimsy—that person before whom we always remain the fool. When we submit, he teaches us the Vedic understanding. He has faith in the experience of what he has heard from his own spiritual master, and he can give that to a willing and loving disciple. This is quite a bit further along than most people in this world consider guru, and although I have respect for their attempts in spiritual life, and in fact some of them make me feel infantile and aware of my glib confidence, I must say that without the blessings of the genuine spiritual master in *paramparā*, they can only go so far along the path.

5.27 P.M.

Choosing what day we will actually leave. M. has an interview at the U.S. Embassy in Dublin on the 3rd, so we'll leave either the afternoon of the 2nd or the morning of the 3rd. I hardly got to know ya here, Inis Rath. Well, I have to leave at *some* time.

We'll stay for a few days at Bhadra and Sile's in Dublin, away from the quiet peace of Geaglum, but I plan to carry the peace inside me. I'll go on reading and writing while I'm there.

O Rādhā-Govinda, I will miss You. I'll have to wait to see You until I can return in two months. In the meantime, I pray to live with You and never leave You. Vṛndāvana has come to me. Rādhā-Govinda, You are the charming Supreme Personality of Godhead in Your original form, and You have made Yourself accessible to me in Your *arcā-vigraha* form. Please accept my service.

November 25

12:05 A.M.

The reality of our leaving here is beginning to dawn on both M. and me. We have started packing mentally, and I have even started to physically gather some of my things for the trip. Our remaining days here will be charged with such thoughts of what to bring and how to get there.

Arjuna proclaims that Lord Kṛṣṇa is the Supreme Personality of Godhead. The *Vedas* also proclaim it. People foolishly think they are independent of the Supreme Lord. Devotional service removes our ignorance. For me, I need a lively conviction in the absolute nature of Vedic evidence. Kṛṣṇa is God because the *Vedas* say so. The *Vedas* also teach the nature of matter and spirit. Follow their direction. Put aside the relative thoughts, "I am born and brought up in Western culture, so why should I accept Hindu teachings?" or, "Hare Kṛṣṇa is just a cult."

Soon I'll be regularly lecturing, citing Vedic evidence and making the arguments and analogies we all know so well. We have been hearing about Kṛṣṇa for decades. My disciples too. As I speak, I hope to bypass doubts and increase my conviction and the conviction of my audience. Our reward will be freedom from doubt and the feeling that we are rightly situated. I feel like a train revving up and preparing to clack down the rail.

sarvam etad ṛtaṁ manye
yan māṁ vadasi keśava
na hi te bhagavan vyaktiṁ
vidur devā na dānavāḥ

> O Kṛṣṇa, I totally accept as truth all that You have told me. Neither the demigods nor the demons, O Lord, can understand Your personality.
>
> —Bg. 10.14

"Mental speculation that leads one away from the Supreme Lord is a serious sin . . . " (Bg. 10.15 purport)

Arjuna asks Kṛṣṇa to explain some of His opulence so that a common person can learn to think of Him constantly. "In what various forms are You to be remembered, O Supreme Personality of Godhead?" (Bg. 10.17) Those who don't love Kṛṣṇa cannot always think of Him in His internal energy. If we can learn to remember Kṛṣṇa even in this world, we will eventually be able to remember Him in His pastimes in the spiritual world.

Can I fit a copy of *Bhagavad-gītā As It Is* into my carry-on luggage? Yes, I will make room for it. That one book will be my main reading as I travel and will satisfy all my needs. Hare Kṛṣṇa. I want to read it carefully and with prayerful intent.

KEEP MOVING OUT OF THE FALSE AND FOG

(You want to express your worship, personally, for others.)

𝄞 You walk into a place where artists are performing. You hear dissonance and wonder whom to trust.

"Mental speculation leading away from God is a serious sin, and one who doesn't know Kṛṣṇa . . . "

You stand up on the train bench and lecture, but no one wants to hear. They think you're a crazy fanatic.

You sit down.

After all, you're a passenger too, and you suffer the passenger's plight. Got your ticket? What if your companion dies of heart failure or simply disappears into the city without you? How will you live without him?

Who will take you where you need to go?

Addicted to safety and security, we passengers.

Well, *that's* a pretty tune—as if each of you are alone. Is
that the sad truth? I mean,
do we all simply meander and
peter away?

The cowherd boys assured one another that Aghāsura was only pretending to be a demon—he was really a statue
with a fishy smell. No matter. Kṛṣṇa will save us
Kṛṣṇa will save us all. Why can't I be so merry
as I walk into the snake's belly?

Violins and beggars, Rilke and
empty pockets. Charlie Chaplin and muggings.
Police and entanglements. Find safety somewhere
(in Stroudsburg?) and eat and sleep in peace?
Safety?

Get yourself convinced. Keep moving out of the false and fog. ‖

4:25 A.M.

Today, Tuesday, Rādhā-Govinda are dressed in soft yellow dresses and matching crowns. I don't have the artistic touch of a *sakhī* or *gopa* in the way I dress, and have almost no realization of what it is I am doing, but still it is nice, and Rādhā-Govinda reciprocate. What a sublime life. No *jñāna*, no karma, no trace of Western psychology or religion or speculation—just place the ornaments as beautifully as possible with clumsy fingers trying to make it right.

M. came in with my hot lemon drink and didn't bow down to Them. I wrote him a note about it. I want him to enter Their room consciously. Hare Kṛṣṇa.

Prabhupāda wants us to train ourselves to serve Rādhā-Kṛṣṇa in the spiritual world. Deity worship makes it feel more real because This worshipable couple is so accommodating and regal, dressed with ornaments straight from Vṛndāvana. If only I can touch Them in the right way, and offer my fruit, leaf, and water with devotion. Prabhupāda says we should not offer directly to Kṛṣṇa, but to Śrīmatī Rādhārāṇī, who will offer to Kṛṣṇa. Of course, I offer everything through my spiritual master. He is dressed in a gray knit *cādar* today, protected from the cool air.

The altar is a place of meditation and centering. Alan Jones says one should pray without images, but our altar is filled with the spiritual images for which the soul yearns. Otherwise, we tend toward impersonalism in our prayers.

Mr. Writer went to town riding on a pony; dressed the Lords and then said here, "I am not a phony." Yankee doodle dandy come in

handy with your
prose and carping
and adventures of a mild sort
sustained by the economies of great Western countries,
with visas and passports and
all that and

my money donated.
Ride on, hour by hour, remembering
what it's like to remember Kṛṣṇa although
I cannot.

Someone wrote me a note: "I am in downtown Vṛndāvana. I met devotees going to America. I am giving them this for you." The note was to tell me that I ought to consider their guru and not only Śrīla Prabhupāda, but that phrase, "Writing this from downtown Vṛndāvana," made me think of the excitement devotees feel when they are there and how they think they are getting inside nectar, preparing themselves for the eternal abode, Goloka Vṛndāvana. Why do I insist on living on some lump of wet earth in North Ireland?

Because I can be introspective here, and recollect with Rādhā and Kṛṣṇa better than in Vṛndāvana with all its stimulus (much of it not Vraja-centered) and controversies.

Hear the whipping of the wind and rain. Thinking of Kṛṣṇa out in the rain—the time He went to collect wood for His spiritual master. Also, how Vasudeva carried his newborn child across the raging Yamunā. O Kṛṣṇa. The river was flooding the night Bilvamaṅgala Ṭhākura went to see the prostitute. And one night, while the secretary of the Muslim ruler—the secretary who later became Rūpa Gosvāmī . . . Even bad weather reminds me of Kṛṣṇa, who is our protector against the destructive elements that threaten His devotees.

O Kṛṣṇa. You say, "The devotees are in My heart and I am in the hearts of the devotees." We don't think of anything else but each other. We are not whistling in the dark.

I was in a *brahmacārī-āśrama* in my dream. I was cleaning, and Viṣṇujana was with me. I asked him, "Where are you now?" I was aware that he had passed away and that he had suddenly returned. He said he was going to be tested before he could be released. He said the Board tests people. When he has satisfied them, they will release him.

Then Viṣṇujana told me there would *harināma* in the afternoon, and he asked me to join him afterwards in his evening duties. He said that because we were so busy all day, we had little time for chanting. I suddenly caught a glance of myself in the mirror and saw how old I had become.

10:16 A.M.

"Please tell me in detail of Your divine opulences by which You prevade all these worlds." (Bg. 10.16) We can help the common people by telling of Kṛṣṇa's opulence and accessible nature. We can think of Him constantly (*kīrtaniyaḥ sadā hariḥ*) and help others to do so too.

Arjuna: "I am never satiated in hearing about You, for the more I hear the more I want to taste the nectar of Your words." (Bg. 10.18)

Trust in guru and *śāstra* is a rare quality in the West, and it is not found at all in Western educational culture. We have heard only about "idols with feet of clay." Yes, Kṛṣṇa is all-opulent, and even He will not bother to recount it all: "For My opulence is limitless." (Bg. 10.19)

8:55 A.M., MORNING WALK.

It's raining and I thought to wear my blue rain pants, but the devotees will see me and may criticize that I'm not in a *dhotī*. Madhu said it wasn't raining *that* hard, so I decided to go out anyway. It was quiet and peaceful and the rain was soft.

Arjuna says he never tires of hearing Kṛṣṇa's ambrosial words. I should also never tire of writing them down. It's not that I am another Kṛṣṇa who speaks nectar, but to steer to Kṛṣṇa with His own words, and to allow His words to flow through me is a wonderful service. I should never give it up.

Raindrops filling puddles with their expanding circles. Yes, these are our last days here. Geaglum offered security, which included, I suppose, a sort of forgetfulness of time and death—or at least a gentler way of relating to them. Time to let go.

2:35 P.M.

Running on an Esgic today (artificial pain relief). M. says I'll have to catch it later. Used my freedom to edit, read something aloud, record, work, and then come out to the shed. I was actually as busy as other people, but I'm not sure what it adds up to.

Kṛṣṇa says, "I am the Supersoul, O Arjuna, seated in the hearts of all living entities." (Bg. 10.20)

Cold start? Turn on the heater? Live with the last flies? Kṛṣṇa is Supersoul. I know. He's in the heart as well as in His own abode. I can pray to Him to live openly in my heart. Kṛṣṇa calls Arjuna Guḍākeśa, "one who has conquered ignorance or sleep." I have to also conquer ignorance in order to hear Kṛṣṇa submissively.

Dead spider lying on its back, legs curled up. Pens in blue jar. They too are dead matter, but the Supersoul lives in them somehow. Back to the *bhakti*-filled verses of the eleventh chapter.

O Keśava, it's right that even the best demigods worship You. Somehow I'm going to carry this *Bhagavad-gītā* with its zippered cover in my carry-on luggage so I can continue to turn to it to overcome my feelings of the foreign and unreal. I have so much to ease past.

THE TOUCH OF GOD AND GOD'S PURE DEVOTEE

(Tired of him, tired of me? These parenthetical remarks haven't been lasting lately. They get knocked down like flies. What lasts? The process, the blue infinite Kṛṣṇa).

1

𝄞 Wail a fat sound he said
I'm going to try to
read *Bhagavad-gītā*

Kṛṣṇa is God and associated with
wide rooms

pianos
Bengalis especially
Lord Caitanya

and perfect ISKCON prefects
Hare Kṛṣṇas in
North India
    but eternally only known
to the very perfect

you want something new he
said but I thought
Don't put down artists
and revere the old masters

the devotees like new
but old

no Phalgu Bābās—the guy
who tricked with his yogic feats
and perhaps seduced women told
Bhaktivinoda Ṭhākura (on film)
    "I get great pleasure doing
this when
    people bow to me."

He got smashed by true
Śrīmad-Bhāgavatam reading with no
demonic thrills

2
I touch and you become touched.
I too need the touch
of a pure devotee.

then I can claim
to rescue these magic shows
arts and fairs
into the pure light of Kṛṣṇa consciousness
by earnest prayer. ‖

3:15 P.M.

Sitting as if praying, my feet are cold. It's too dark to read comfortably. Drawing? No. That's off, although I could stoke it up like a fire if I made an effort. The teacher in *Life, Paint, and Passion* pushed so hard on the point of process that I finally burned out. It had the opposite effect on me. I drew something as if I was "supposed" to let anything come, then stopped. The author of that book might call that resistance and encourage me to push on, but I saw it as a waste of my dwindling time.

As if praying. I go back inside after about an hour total. I know M. could use more time playing his bouzouki and melodeon (he can only do that when I leave for the shed), but it's too dark and cold out there.

A RAINY DAY (AGAIN)

𝄞 I'm alone it's/ a cold gray day
and I'm the one
who has to leave.

I like a lonelier
sound a
pretty melodic ballad
where no words fail

but where someone tried/ died a little
wanted Kṛṣṇa
Kṛṣṇa

and found another rainy day.
When I look out I see
      barbed wire formed
into a simple fence
for cows a green field,
a scene I've witnessed every day for
weeks—most of the year.

I love it—
      attached (we say)

but I will leave to
sing my ballad
of rainy days
and a sometimes rough lake.
Here the rain was light the
sky overcast/ and visitors came, someone's
father advising his son
Don't rush into marriage.

Here's Kṛṣṇa's *cādar*
Kṛṣṇa's
rain
which didn't stop me
from being faithful.

O sweet music may you
please God and
play with
      introspect
in *bhakti.* ‖

3:35 P.M., OUTSIDE THE SHED.

I lasted only an hour today, but it was delicious. My eyes bathed in the sight of rain-bedecked grass. The plants that used to be puffballs are now dead. The year is mostly gone. What do I have to show for it? A lot.

Carrying the 18"x24" Bristol board pads back to the house. Notice the jagged thorns? Madhu's music is merry, in the mode of goodness, and brightens a dark day, and so does he.

What is life? I see a little kid like Jayānanda walking ahead of me—what does he know? Maybe in his bones he knows Kṛṣṇa. We're on loan here and can only lift something out, a story, a life, get to know the people in it. In the meantime, we're stuck with our big places, our big land, our big sky, and our wild senses and mind. We're obsessed with our illusions and addictions, so we really can't see what's happening. The *śāstras* spell it out. That's why I took to Kṛṣṇa consciousness. Why am I lacking appreciation for it?

But as Śrīla Bhaktivinoda Ṭhākura says, the creation is strange. A big fat crow landed on a bare branch and reminded me of Basho, the great artist. Artists . . . and those who defy God. There are so many people and events conspiring to make us nondevotees, but the sages see clearly. Pure devotees see the best of all. *Śṛṇvatāṁ sva-kathāḥ kṛṣṇaḥ*. Keep chanting and hearing from the source.

6:45 P.M.

Mail arrived. I stutter mentally, say things of which I'm unsure. One disciple writes me that she feels distant from me; I used to chant *japa* with them and meet with them individually.

"Don't you know it's my headaches?" I say you regard me as a problem-solver, but why don't you see me more as a person?

Another argues with me continuously about the origin of the *jīva*. This time I gave him Śrīla Prabhupāda's example of the crow and *tāl* fruit. Where we came from is not as important as how to free ourselves from *māyā*. I made those replies.

Rādhā-Govinda, goodnight. Prabhupāda, goodnight. I'll see you at midnight. My heart beats "mightily," but I know we all must die. Tomorrow I'll see how much rope *prakṛti* gives me.

November 26

12:10 A.M.

The traveling and preaching will be good for me. Lecturing will enable me to enter *Bhagavad-gītā* and *Śrīmad-Bhāgavatam* with greater focus.

Arjuna prays to the universal form. Remember that eerie choir in the FATE museum, with their diorama of Viśvarūpa? The lights flashed in the dark room, and we watched the visual effects while listening to Bharadvāja's dramatic voice. It was effective, but I don't think *that* was the universal form! We walked out from seeing the display into the sunshine on Watseka Avenue, and for a few moments we had to adjust to that other reality. The universal form was a complete knock-out, and even a great warrior like Arjuna was afraid.

The philosopher Carlyle allegedly overheard a woman in conversation saying, "I accept the universe." He replied, "Gad, she had better!" Who are we to be condescending toward the all-powerful Supreme Personality of Godhead and say, "We have decided to accept Kṛṣṇa as God, at least theoretically"? Gad, we had better!

Use whatever you can in His service. If pettiness arises, if fear comes . . . Arjuna asked forgiveness for his familiarity with Kṛṣṇa—"informal gestures which arise out of friendship." Despite His opulence, Kṛṣṇa played with Arjuna as a friend. That relationship is eternally fixed. I wish to revive my own eternal relationship, whatever it is. Śrīla Prabhupāda said such revival is for the liberated. We may have to wait for it, but we can yearn for it in the meantime.

"No one is greater than You," Arjuna says. The words float before me, and yet it's hard to control my mind. Still thinking of letters and my replies. At least I'm taking *Bhagavad-gītā* with me as my companion on the preaching tour. Arjuna worships Kṛṣṇa as the father of the cosmos and the supreme spiritual master. Any bona fide spiritual master must be a descendent of the disciplic succession. Instead of becoming embroiled in ISKCON quarrels about the spiritual master's qualification and whether or not Śrīla Prabhupāda appointed certain people to act in that capacity, we can meditate on what it actually means to be a representative of Kṛṣṇa in *paramparā.* For better or for worse, we have each accepted the position to represent Prabhupāda, and at the same time, we each seem to want to be ourselves. We are eternal servants of Kṛṣṇa and have still to discover the depths of what that means. That we don't yet know does not stop us from representing Śrīla Prabhupāda's teachings as purely as possible. "As a father tolerates the impudence of his son, or a friend tolerates the impertinence of a friend, or a wife tolerates the familiarity of her partner, please tolerate the wrongs I may have done You." (Bg. 11.44)

MEDLEY FOR KṚṢṆA

𝄞 Listen, sympathetic, to tender
perfect bell tones/ accept this sound because
someone wrote this song in Tin
Pan Alley style, thinking

he was a master sentimentalist a
master musician to handle it—that sound
for all us grassroots populists who
look for songs of love
as we go about our daily execution.

Arjuna remembered that he and Kṛṣṇa
were once friends, sat on
the same bed, joked, but now,
Arjuna thinks, I'm afraid I abused our
friendship because I didn't know
You were so great.

(Remember we attended Penny's
wedding and a few year's later
in the same church her funeral?)

(Remember too the basketball game where you stole
a guy's white silk scarf and later
gave it back?)

O Kṛṣṇa, how could I have known that You
were always with me, Supersoul—even
when my pen ran out of ink and
even on the Navy ship?
You are my sweetest
best friend. ‖

4:28 A.M.

On Wednesdays Govinda and Rādhā wear purple. Madhu just came in, took off his slippers, and made *daṇḍavats* on the floor, staying there awhile to pray. The Deities are not brass dolls. I struggle a bit trying to get everything to fit. There is that aspect too in Deity worship. Not that automatically They float before you all lovely. You have to decorate Them, do the work. By Their grace it comes out all right. As I decorate Them I listen to Narottama dāsa Ṭhākura's prayers, where he asks, "When will the day come when I can serve the Divine Couple? When, with my spiritual master in his form as a *gopī* beside me, will I give water to the Divine Couple," etc. He wants to serve Rūpa-mañjarī. After, I sing "*Gurvāṣṭakam*" while I dress Prabhupāda in his warm *cādar* and hat.

Still have a few more letters to answer. After all that, I'll sink into the chair.

"May I come and be with you?" someone asked. Someone else said, "Please accept me as a disciple." I don't even know him. I didn't tell him to come from California for the four days of meetings in Baltimore. That would be too much to ask. Instead, I put him off, indicating that I probably won't initiate him. Is that right? Do I expect him to be clever enough to figure out how he could get initiated? A disciple could tell him the ropes, how to get around my refusals. I can't tell him.

Prabhupāda lecturing in Seattle. He asks a young woman disciple to come forward, sit down, and read from the *Teachings of Lord Caitanya*. He had just received an advanced copy from the printer. They start on page 29, where Sanātana Gosvāmī approaches Lord Caitanya and says, "Who am I?"

"When will I be able to serve the Divine Couple?" the Vaiṣṇava *kavi* sings. Some of his songs describe his fallen nature. It is the tradition to express these things, but he actually feels them.

News in typed form arrives once a month. News of police brutality. Leader of China comes to Washington, D.C., but doesn't get along well, shows how much distance there is between China and the U.S. The stock market crashes way down and then comes up again. What does it all mean? Debts, investigations, African borders not safe. One nation doesn't respect another. In Bosnia new conflicts shaping up. President's wife coming on strong again. The President being questioned about how he raised funds for his campaign. In Russia, Communism is dead. Communism is still alive in Cuba, though. Whatever is reported in the news today could change by tomorrow. Many Democrats feel the Republicans now have an upper hand in the debate about abortion because the Republicans are focusing on late-pregnancy abortions. They passed the bill against it, but the President vetoed it once and will probably veto their second bill. He comes off looking murderous: it's all right to kill.

I write a daily newspaper too, but not exactly the same one Bhaktisiddhānta Sarasvatī spoke of where we could draw news every moment from the unlimited spiritual world. I draw mine from within myself as a spider pulls threads to weave a web. I could call it a "Personals Column for Members of the Hare Kṛṣṇa Movement." I try to focus it on inner life for those who have had enough outer news.

In the end, the Hare Kṛṣṇa movement's news is the same old chanting on the same old beads. Winter is coming on, did you know?

8:50 A.M.

Out walking. Letters spinning through my head—what they said to me and what I said back. I want to be a giver, not just a taker. Sometimes my correspondents are bitter about how ISKCON has mistreated them. I say what I can, but mostly I try to listen. I am not really a problem-solver. I find I give the most to those who give to me. It's with them that I find occasions to share deeper Kṛṣṇa conscious thoughts. Those who give can create giving in others.

The infinite analogy of that extends to Kṛṣṇa. Kṛṣṇa gives to everyone in a general, impartial way, but to those who give to Him and His devotees, He gives Himself.

If I get a headache today, there'll be no allopathic cushion; I'll have to use the bed cushions. The fact is, however, I have set up a daily expectation for myself. If I don't get what I consider a good quota of pages written, or enough reading in, then I feel I have not seized the day. Why be so product-oriented? Where is the time to just be, to harvest silent moments and turn them into prayer? Does everything have to be focused on getting something done? I tend to measure my days by how much gets dictated and how many pages get written or read. I work to whittle down the pile of incoming letters until none are left.

9:28 A.M.

It's difficult to see the universal form of Kṛṣṇa, but it's even more difficult to see Him in His original two-handed form. We can look at Brijbasi prints or calendars and there He is, Gopīnātha, standing by the Yamunā with His flute in His hand. But we cannot *see* Him there unless our eyes are anointed with devotion.

Kṛṣṇa, His two-handed form. Not "Krishna Iron Works" or "Krishna Bengali Sweets" or Krishnamurti, the impersonal philosopher-mystic. The Supreme Lord Kṛṣṇa is known to the *ācāryas,* especially since Lord Caitanya and His Gosvāmī disciples have introduced Him. We are in that line, but we are not automatic recipients of something we have not learned to want with all our heart. That wanting takes time. "My dear Arjuna, only by undivided devotional service [*bhaktyā tv ananyayā*] can I be understood as I am, standing before you, and can thus be seen directly. Only in this way can you enter into the mysteries of My understanding." (Bg. 11.54)

2:41 P.M.

Did you forget something? No, got my key, my recorder, and my shed bag. Didn't forget Kṛṣṇa either. Bhakta M. wrote that he's praying hard. I thought, "That's something he'll learn—that it's *impossible* to pray." Then I thought, "Just because *I* can't pray doesn't mean a young man can't pray."

Finished *Soul Making*. It got too Christian at the end, discussing the Trinity. But I'll carry it with me and use it when I attempt to write to my Godbrother about it.

I liked his point about the three conversions, and I thought of it in terms of our experience in ISKCON. After the first happy discovery of Kṛṣṇa consciousness, we enter a kind of dark night. We usually go through an experience of feeling betrayed. We may have thought this was a wonderful movement. We thought, with Śrīla Prabhupāda at the helm, we would sweep the world with our all-attractive Absolute Truth. Then Prabhupāda left and we collapsed. Now we serve in separation and have had to find Prabhupāda in a more internal way, looking more realistically at our ideals. *Soul Making* pushed me when it said we can't make it alone; God must be found in association with others. True enough.

To know Kṛṣṇa we have to follow the process of devotional service under the spiritual master's direction. Just chased a loud bee out the window, pushing it gently with a gloved hand. Then I saw that the sky had become completely gray for the first time in several days. *Yasya deve parā bhaktir*. We must have faith to receive revelation of Kṛṣṇa. Temple worship helps. I left Govinda and Rādhā without *cādars* in the room. Heat was pouring from the electrical heater.

The four-handed form of God and His two-handed form are completely different from the temporary universal forms Arjuna saw. One should worship the personal form of Kṛṣṇa as the Supreme Personality of Godhead, the source of all the other forms (which are the source of the universes and all life).

Govindam ādi-puruṣaṁ tam ahaṁ bhajāmi. God's original form. Write it down. Stop complaining, "I'm dry, I'm no good, no drop of devotion."

So he sighed and wanted to give up ego, but he didn't know how, didn't have the courage or inspiration to make such a change. He was afraid of cataclysmic changes. A semi-invalid wants peace, even as he prepares to travel.

A devotee introduced me to her understanding of Active Imagination. I may be too down-to-earth to sustain a character or to write in trance, but I became interested to think about it.

3:28 P.M.

It doesn't matter what you do? Yes, it matters very much. Every activity and endeavor should be centered on Kṛṣṇa. Hare Kṛṣṇa. If you don't have work, then chant Hare Kṛṣṇa, Śrīla Prabhupāda used to say. He expected us to work hard to spread Kṛṣṇa consciousness worldwide (they say globally now instead of worldwide). Must be relevant.

What am *I* contributing? Stock answers.

Hurt that they attack me—enemies of ISKCON criticize me as the demonic author of SPL who blasphemes Śrīla Prabhupāda and maybe poisoned him, who became a false guru without authorization.

PRAYING IN THE SHED

𝄞 Namby
Pamby
went to town
in a rig that spilled
jewels. Kṛṣṇa baby took
them in His hands and gave
a barrelful to the fruit
vendor, who liked Him.

O infallible Kṛṣṇa with Rādhā
please let me . . .
        What?
I can't even say.

Simply let me be satisfied.
When the tide carries me along
let me remember You and with
certainty cling to the *mahā-*
mantra. Let me report for the final
roll call
        with those already gone
                and answered. ‖

PRAYING IN THE SHED

𝄞 I want/ he wants
this way to the skipping rope
the chalk
        Kṛṣṇa is the
center of my Life.

I read and it was too fast
to absolve
        problems
because I had to go as fast as possible.

Charles was the first one
to pray like this. ‖

4:00 P.M., OUTSIDE THE SHED

Lean shoulder and head against the little shed. A prominence of golden sunlight behind one cloud. Otherwise there are gray-blue smoke clouds, and behind all the clouds, clear blue. Believe it or not. The water is as flat as a plate, and the island is small and contained with a golden reed edge. In winter I can sometimes see the chimney of the boathouse from over here because the trees are so thin. I think I broke through some of my dryness. Now back to that wet path—so wet it makes my wellies shine. O Kṛṣṇa, Hare Kṛṣṇa.

5:35 P.M.

Yes, sirs, the rain has stopped. Kṛṣṇa science startles London. Bhavna Patel has three options: live at home, live in the temple, or live in a flat. I didn't choose one for her, but told her to be a devotee wherever she lives.

Life bubbles through the frothing blood. We keep our blood inside these slimy bags. Did you know that someone actually signed a letter to me, "Slimy Bag"?

Kṛṣṇa science startles London. I already said that. M. is going to England. I'll be here counting my duties on my fingers. I plan to keep it simple—that's why I came here in the first place.

Only details left now before we travel, and I don't want to burden this book with details. Devotional service means "One should transfer his energy entirely to Kṛṣṇa conscious activities."

PUKKA PAD SHORTIES: AN ACTIVE IMAGINATION STORY INSTALLMENT #1

Bonny went to put Rādhā-Govinda to bed. He-she was in a hurry, so didn't have time to write of the inner world.

Anyway, he-she is at least three people and all of them are dizzy.

Dizzy?

You know, off balance.

So that's the first installment. It does not have a pure narrative thread.

November 27

12:05 A.M.

The *Bhagavad-gītā* teaches that the art of going back to Godhead is a serious proposal. Śrīla Prabhupāda states that 11.55 is the essence of it. If we admit or agree that we are eternal and meant for life in the spiritual world, then we will have to act accordingly. We can work for it according to the rules of *kṛṣṇa-karma*, working for Kṛṣṇa. For example, we may write a poem. However, we may first have to research how poets write poetry. The point is, that our work should be performed only for Kṛṣṇa's cause, for Kṛṣṇa's pleasure. "One should not be attached to the result of his work, but the result should be offered to Kṛṣṇa, and one should accept as *prasādam* the remnants of offerings to Kṛṣṇa." (Bg. 11.55, purport)

Or, we can simply consider Kṛṣṇa the goal of our lives (*mat-parāmah*). Such a person is attracted only to being transferred to the spiritual sky, and within the spiritual sky "he wants to enter the highest spiritual planet, namely Kṛṣṇaloka, Goloka Vṛndāvana." Of course, to do this one has to become "*mad-bhakta*," a real devotee of Kṛṣṇa, by fully engaging in devotional service in all or at least one of the nine processes.

In Bg. 11.55 Kṛṣṇa also recommends *saṅga-varjitaḥ*, "disassociation from persons who are against Kṛṣṇa."

I hear a few noises and am reminded how precious is peace. To be able to read *Bhagavad-gītā* with a relatively clear mind is a gift. It is *puṇya-śravaṇa-kīrtanaḥ*, pious activity. Twenty years after Śrīla Prabhupāda's disappearance, we are still reading his books, still learning the ABCs.

The pure devotee is neither a *karmī* nor a *jñānī*. He doesn't think of Kṛṣṇa unfavorably, as Kaṁsa did. Kaṁsa attained salvation, however, despite his negative approach, because he thought incessantly of Kṛṣṇa. "The pure devotee does not even want salvation. He does not want to be transferred even to the highest planet, Goloka Vṛndāvana. His only objective is to serve Kṛṣṇa wherever he may be."

Another item taught in this verse is that a devotee is friendly to everyone. Śrīla Prabhupāda defines this as a devotee being prepared to risk his life to spread God consciousness. "The favorite example is Lord Jesus Christ." This purport then glows with praise for the preacher: "Why such risk?" Kṛṣṇa is more merciful to those who risk their lives for His sake than we can ever imagine. "Therefore it is certain that such persons must reach the supreme planet after leaving the body."

4:20 A.M.

On Thursdays Rādhā-Govinda wear light tan with gold trim. Their crowns are gold with red and green trim, and their necklaces are the same. Kṛṣṇa has a long golden flute with a peacock on the end and a dangling white pearl. They are beautiful, both of Them, and gracious to allow me to dress Them. My stubby fingers. My chaste restraint. Rādhārāṇī's hand, my eye upon Prabhupāda for approval. His granting it. Prabhupāda is wearing an old tan *cādar* with a smaller pink one on top. He also wears a pink-saffron knit hat.

Narottama dāsa Ṭhākura describes the names and pastimes of the Lord and His devotees. Whoever has *niṣṭhā*, his faith in Lord Nityānanda which he says is required if we want to love Rādhā and Kṛṣṇa—and whoever chants Gaura's name is a devotee. Narottama dāsa seeks such a person's association. He asks for the mercy of Gaura-Nitāi and says his claim is first as he is the most fallen. "Fie upon Narottama," he sings. He wants to be a devotee, happy in the shelter of Gaura-Nitāi. Then he can attain the service of Rādhā and Kṛṣṇa.

Yesterday I met Prahlāda feeding his cow bales of hay. She was eating peacefully. I asked, "Is the cow in heat?"

"You heard her bellowing?" He said she's out of heat now, and he missed his chance to have her inseminated. He plans to try again in three weeks. He said unless a cow is giving milk for the Deities and devotees, he feels dissatisfied taking care of her. She has no purpose—just eats, he said, unless there is milk. I asked him about his *japa*. He has had a personal quota increase of one round per year for many years now. He's now up to forty. He said it takes him a long time to chant, and admitted that it's still difficult to control his mind.

"With forty rounds you have more chance that a few of them will be attentive," I said, and then we parted. Irish and American *sādhus*. But who is the *sādhu*?

"My mind doesn't let me chant," someone wrote me. I always advise such people not to despair and to keep trying.

Śrīla Prabhupāda said that no bona fide spiritual teacher says, "Stay here and form a United Nations and you'll be peaceful in this world." No, they all speak of that other world where we will go. They may call it *nirvāṇa* or Brahman or the kingdom of God or Goloka, but every bona fide teacher states that this world is filled with birth, death, disease, and old age and that we shouldn't remain here.

In the bathroom I heard another lecture by Prabhupāda, but the sound was too distant, a formal lecture in a hall, to nondevotees in San Francisco. Very basic. I chose another one instead.

Hare Kṛṣṇa. The collie with his long snout and thin eyes looks a bit scabby. He stays out in all weathers. The cow has a shed to which she retires. The goats too. Cows need protection. So do people.

Rādhā and Kṛṣṇa kindly stand for me. Rādhā's hand is extended to Kṛṣṇa. She's holding a betel nut. We have no *tulasīs* here, or I would put a *tulasī* leaf in Her hand or at His feet. Hare Kṛṣṇa. Someone please give this garland to Śrīmatī Rādhārāṇī. Now let us talk of Kṛṣṇa playing His flute. I don't know what pious activities this flute performed in the past so that it now receives all the nectar from Kṛṣṇa's lips—nectar which is meant for the *gopīs*. The Christians don't know the answer and neither do I, but I keep listening and attempt to stay in *kṛṣṇa-bhāvanāmṛta*.

PUKKA PAD SHORTIES, INSTALLMENT #2

The main character only had a few minutes. He-she is a devotee, we know, because he-she was busy in the last episode putting Rādhā-Govinda to bed. Now a woman invites him-her into her own imaginative story, but he is afraid of getting caught in another's trip.

In *her* story, our hero appears wearing saffron robes and he is a he. He asks, "How do these imaginative stories work?"

That other author has an alter ego (or whatever) who lives in a *kuṭīr*. She says, "We go into a trance at unexpected times and talk to one another. That's all there is to it."

He disappears from her story.

He's on his own now, following the Alone Idea. He sends his men out to investigate the area, and "while you are there, see if you can get me Ascension."

The story begins to fade and he struggles to reenter it. He dreams but judges the dreams unworthy. In Active Imagination he hears that he can allow the conscious mind to play with and accept the unconscious stuff. It's all very symbolic, you know.

Black face, white hands of
clock—he doesn't actually want to be in
anyone's dreams but he has no power
to stop it. He tells the people
to dream
on.

9:00 A.M.

On my way out the door for a morning walk I told Madhu what I'd been reading to prepare for Sunday's *Caitanya-caritāmṛta* class: Lord Caitanya instructing the Kūrma Brāhmaṇa. The emphasis is strong that one may stay at home as a *gṛhastha* and still become a first-class devotee and preacher. Some *sahajiyās* take advantage of this instruction, however, and criticize renounced preachers who write books. It's all right to become renounced and leave home if it is done properly and with the correct motive. I mentioned this to Madhu because he's feeling regrets about having left his own family years ago in a way that caused his family members to resent him and Kṛṣṇa consciousness. I said that it seems like we are always making mistakes. He made the mistake of becoming a materialistic householder. Then when he discovered Kṛṣṇa consciousness, he made the mistake of leaving his home life abruptly. We can only ask Kṛṣṇa to forgive us for our constant mistakes.

Madhu laughed and said, "That's one way to look at life—we're always making mistakes!"

I can't say that it was a mistake for me to take on responsibility in ISKCON. Prabhupāda wanted it, and one was quickly recognized by him for doing it. He told us to go somewhere and open a temple. Later I left home, became a *sannyāsī*, was placed on the GBC by Prabhupāda, and entered the perfect set-up to become one of the "Eleven Appointed Gurus."

And so I reigned. Now I'm infamous. But one thing after another followed from my having initially agreed to accept responsibility. I would have had to have been much more humble and discriminative than I actually was—and am—to avoid the pitfalls. I would have had to say, "I've taken this much responsibility for Prabhupāda and I've received honor for it, but now I will not accept any further recognition." We easily get carried away and run under one banner, "Become a preacher!" and we forget other things, trample on people's rights, learn to manipulate others to carry on the mission, and become bewildered by wealth and women. Then after we are thoroughly messed up we ask, "What happened? I was just trying to be a preacher."

The path of devotional service is like a razor's edge. It would be another mistake to now recoil from preaching or participation in the *saṅkīrtana* movement, or think I can become "holier than thou" by seclusion.

10:23 A.M.

Rain smeared and dripping down the windowpanes. M. will leave around 2:00 P.M. for Dublin and England. I'll be alone, as I like it, to do the usual. I still plan to give the Sunday morning lecture on the *Caitanya-caritāmṛta*.

Received a batch of "Improvisations" to edit. I like them—each one a trip through emotion and pulling at my own Kṛṣṇa conscious attempt to live my life in poetry, music, and art.

Time for Prabhupāda's *pūjā*. The room too chilly.

PUKKA PAD SHORTIES, INSTALLMENT #3

Two men get into a white rowboat. They'll go from Inis Rath to Geaglum—just a few minutes' worth of rowing is all it takes.

One asks, "Where have you been?"

The reply . . . "Ha, a million gags, a whole joke book I could make in reply."

Remember the time you and Murray got high and took turns writing on the typewriter? I wrote a cynical line, "Who is your tailor?"—sticking to externals. On Murray's turn he indicated the bedroom. He was trying to be daring. I didn't want that and neither did he, so we moved on to something else. Then he said he had learned that there could be love without sex. I was his friend; I offered him love. At the end of the day when we returned to Manhattan he quipped, "Life is cheap." By that he demeaned the day's experience of a simple friendship.

"Too many old stories," says the man in the boat. "I want to hear an up-to-date account of your transcendental life. Did you pray today?"

"I sat in a chair and tried."

Both men in the rowboat want God, but they still don't know who they are. They live with a portrait in pieces.

Did the Swami take away my life?

I gave him my youth. He told Kīrt, "You have nothing to renounce. Everything already belongs to God." And he took it all, as Kṛṣṇa's representative. In return he gave us *dāl* and vegetables and *capātīs* and loving service to Kṛṣṇa, *kīrtana*, Lord Caitanya, and employment in his service, which was to execute his spiritual master's mission. I have no regrets, although I acknowledge what I gave. In return I received status, privilege in a little world, and an airtight, watertight, philosophy. I got to follow the Swami.

The two men in the boat—what happened to them? Did they fall out and swim? Die peacefully? Give more advice? (It had better be in *paramparā*.)

No, the two men reached the shore while I was telling you that part about what I gave to Prabhupāda. One of them was Baladeva, a kind friend, and the other was Madhu, a minstrel with an aging Irish face. The third was me, his grace disgrace, although I didn't mention my presence earlier.

We parted like a tree branch and the land held us up. O Kṛṣṇa, You are everywhere, even in a friendly talk in a land wet from constant rain.

"Is this Active Imagination?"

Not yet.

O Kṛṣṇa, please help us all—we depend on You.

2:20 P.M.

As Madhu was leaving, his head freshly shaved, I said, "When you return we will get into high gear."

"I'm already in high gear!" he said.

"Well, I'm not." Sitting in the easy chair with three quiet days ahead of me. It will change soon enough.

Land of green, matted, long, wet grass. I see a man starting across Lough Erne in a rowboat, his strokes strong. O Kṛṣṇa, let me turn to *Bhagavad-gītā*. Kṛṣṇa recommends we think of Him constantly. I glanced at some verses after lunch and thought at first that Kṛṣṇa was demanding so much. I'm already over that. He gives us so many ways to approach Him more gradually, but He never waffles. If we want to be happy, free of anxiety, we must fix our minds upon Him in devotional service. "But those who worship Me, giving up all their activities unto Me and being devoted to Me without deviation, engaged in devotional service and always meditating upon Me, having fixed their minds upon Me, O son of Pṛthā—for them I am the swift deliverer from the ocean of birth and death." (Bg. 12.6–7)

Kṛṣṇa gives us the choice to serve Him or to serve *māyā*. A devotee's life mission is to please Kṛṣṇa, "and he can sacrifice everything for Kṛṣṇa's satisfaction . . . " The simple process of continuing our occupation while dedicating our activities to Kṛṣṇa and chanting the holy names will gain us entrance to the spiritual world. We don't have to be expert mystic *yogīs*, because Kṛṣṇa will take care of us. That old ISKCON illustration shows the devotee swimming alone in the ocean. Lord Kṛṣṇa comes on Garuḍa (like a helicopter on a dangerous mission) to pick the devotee up by the hand (not the *śikhā*, as is commonly thought).

SOMETHING SWEET, SOMETHING TENDER

𝄞 There was a time when I knew I had to go to
Kṛṣṇa in the book/ O Kṛṣṇa, You are difficult
to know. You reveal Yourself to Your pure devotee but
I guess I'm just not one of them. A comic instead and
this weather keeps raining on and off.

For me the sweet and tender is no wife or kids or
people in my class and me a college prof.
It's how I feel when I approach God.

My words are hackneyed and unreal and
I can't even tell you it all. I want
a love relationship with Kṛṣṇa but don't know
how to attain it. The bittersweet truth. He says
think of Him always.
Is that too much of Him to ask?
No, I reasoned it out.

Where is my feeling that
different thing? I try to express it in
different ways. I explore and
talk to myself, squeak sounds out like what never comes out
of a normal person—tears (a gift) but
not that either.
I'm flying too low.
Kṛṣṇa says think of Him and Prabhupāda clarifies:
it can't be done
in any other way except through devotional service.
If you choose otherwise, go to hell.
A black horse, a brown cow, a gray-hooded
crow and insects dying in shed. I have heard
there are rats in the temple—each a soul
and me wishing
I was a *niṣṭhā-bhakta*

ready
to help others
sweet and tender. ‖

LOVER

𝄞 I want to love, we *all* do
but love only Kṛṣṇa.
    Loving God is the work of a
lifetime because
    He's the Supreme Lover
and all art
    is meant for His praise.

Raspy-voice it or angelic
lilt it if   you're
a harpist
but you have the right
    to say what's true
    and to know
He's the
taster of *rasa*.

He's a lover even of demons
He kills
in play
and when He leaves His
dearmosts in separation—
those who want only
to please Him

His music sound was heard and
no one knew what
to say
    because other music is a string of
zeros unless *He*

accepts it and it's
for Him
offered with love

to the Lover
Supreme. ‖

3:55 P.M., OUTSIDE THE SHED

There is a tractor or other machine in the woods nearby. I tried to ignore it as I walked past. This was the first time in about four days that I have drawn and painted. It felt good, this living in process, living with the constant prayer that Kṛṣṇa will accept my meaning.

November 28

12:05 A.M.

Regarding the "swift deliverer" verses, (Bg. 12.6–7), I like the repeated use of "Me"—"worship Me," "devoted to Me," "meditating upon Me," "fixed their minds upon Me." Kṛṣṇa is insistent, expecting and encouraging total dependence on Him. I am always sorry I don't do what He asks, but I like the concept of doing it. Devotees should be careful not to become depressed by their failure to follow an instruction, especially to the point where they actually come to think following the instruction is impossible. We are, after all, only *aspiring* devotees. That we are aspiring is the source of our hope.

Many of us are attracted to good, early morning *japa*. "Such transcendental chanting attracts the devotee to the Personality of Godhead." That also gives me hope. Śrīla Prabhupāda writes, "Simply by chanting the holy name of Kṛṣṇa—Hare Kṛṣṇa, Hare Kṛṣṇa, Kṛṣṇa Kṛṣṇa, Hare Hare/ Hare Rāma, Hare Rāma, Rāma Rāma, Hare Hare—a devotee of the Lord can approach the supreme destination easily and happily, but this destination cannot be approached by any other process of religion."

Śrīla Prabhupāda's presentation is enough for me. What is missing? I don't require even other Gauḍīya Vaiṣṇava commentaries. Prabhupāda already studied them and distilled them for us.

PREACHING TO MY MIND AND TO OTHERS AFTER A DREAM OF BEING LOST IN THE SUBWAYS

1

𝄞 I was lost in the subways/ but even
then I didn't think of Kṛṣṇa—
lost
distracted that
outer demand Oh
chant, chant, chant,
a constant prayer
the only thing practical.

I'm telling you but you can't do that either. Need a quiet place where you can do your needful work at a pace. Don't dwell-indulge in
that despair
stay out lost in subways

pray in a peaceful grotto
of the mind
Please tell me why do you
want to gut it?

We want to be men
not divided against ourselves—I'm
preaching to my mind but not
as Raghunātha Gosvāmī did.
    I'm asking what I want and why
I'm lost in that underground stretch
the man who never returns
to Staten Island the man who wishes
he could keep going, telling people about Kṛṣṇa.
But I can't because I
am a beggar, homeless in dreams
robbed and killed underground
lost.

2

O Mind, I can't give you the peace you want. In the 1960s we went berserk. Now peace—a fence around my mind around
my growing creeper. Then it was too much suffering.

O Mind, I am a complicated fellow, polluted, can't wear
the brown robes of a Franciscan or the ochre robes of a Gauḍīya—
too smudged with dirt.

O Prabhupāda, you see me lost in the subways
of my mind, and when a Godbrother joined me in my dream,
we both got lost.

Am I such a blind uncle going home?
I'm chanting Hare Kṛṣṇa
and trust I can be saved.

4:43 A.M.

On Fridays, Rādhā-Govinda wear white dresses trimmed in gold, pink, yellow, and light green. They have *very* tall crowns. One might say these outfits are too *aiśvarya*, but I suppose there are some regal settings even in Vṛndāvana. They know how to make jewelry and crowns in Vraja, and how to worship Rādhā and Kṛṣṇa as the king and queen of transcendental, amorous pastimes. Still, I prefer something more simple for Them to wear, a *sārī* and *dhotī*, something that shows His feet.

It takes a lot of blu-tack to keep Their crowns from falling off, they're so heavy. I feel it's important to play the tape of Narottama dāsa Ṭhākura's prayers as I serve Them. It reminds me of the essence of what I am doing. Eventually his prayers may take hold in my heart and my desire may become the same as his. I don't want to forget Rādhā-Govinda while I travel, although They will remain here. I am asking the devotees to take pictures of Them every day so I can have seven pictures in seven different outfits to worship on the road.

God, the source of all, does not lack form. That is absolute truth. I once met a student at Boston College in 1968 who said it appeared that the Swami had "buffaloed" me. Then who had buffaloed him so that he was now attending Boston College trying to be a something or other? We are *all* bowled over by material nature and influenced by the many different forces and ideals that appear in our lives. I accepted the Swami, who gave me truth. I gave myself to him voluntarily. I now want to be buffaloed by Kṛṣṇa. I want Him to spread His trance of *yogamāyā* over me so I can understand Kṛṣṇa consciousness. I don't care whether that makes me a better person; just let me become a better devotee.

Rādhā-Govinda, You look first-class. My words cannot possibly describe Your beauty or Your kindness for appearing in this form. When I was waiting for You to arrive, I expected only Rādhā to match my little Kṛṣṇa. I didn't know You would both come to steal my heart. You both have come and fulfilled a deeper desire. I didn't want to reject the first Kṛṣṇa who came, but this Kṛṣṇa is similar to the first, and since the other wasn't really mine anyway, I am able to return Him without insult at His feet.

O Rādhā-Govinda, Your crowns are pink, yellow, and green, and I hope they are not too heavy. They were purchased in Vṛndāvana, although they seem larger than how the Divine Couple, in Their *mādhurya* pastimes, would wear them. Hare Kṛṣṇa, Hare Kṛṣṇa—to me They are *prasādam* from the holy *dhāma*.

O Govinda, You move us like a chess player moves pieces on a board. We are Your instruments. Please let me serve as one. You are the Lord of my life.

8:27 A.M.

Read about the internal signs of a devotee (end of twelfth chapter)—how he accepts suffering, how he is not disturbed, how he's fixed in devotion. No letters to answer. A day for my own doings.

PUKKA PAD SHORTIES, INSTALLMENT #4

Out of the midst comes a dragon spitting balls of fire—just a puff dragon cloud, really, and harmlessly white. How serious?

A voice asks, "Why do you bow down in sleep when you read?"

"Don't fault me."

The voice: "Don't you want to know the truth? Are you afraid to suffer?"

"Suffering comes as a token reaction from past bad karma. I tolerate it and continue my devotional service unabated and unconfused. No mystique here. I am interested in devotion, not suffering. There is a Kṛṣṇa conscious understanding of this, and we should not adopt the Christian theology on suffering."

"You are trying to save yourself?" Now the dragon speaks.

"I want to be, and I'm tired of writing so many quotation marks."

So the mist pilfers and flutters away, dragon and all. The spirit in me is in my heart and I have no time to spare. Life is immediate—a simple, physical exercise, with perhaps a few thoughts to move us along. Don't expect more than that. Just worship Kṛṣṇa.

9:00 A.M.

Thinking over travel details. One minute I decide to bring Kierkegaard and the next I decide against it. I favor using my limited luggage weight for *Bhagavad-gītā*. Stay with that. Even if I can only take in a little at a time, siphoning the nectar through a narrow straw, I want to keep sipping at it. Same for prayer.

I value clear thinking, and I want to work on finding clarity while traveling. I mean, clear thinking about spiritual truths.

While reading this morning, between bouts of drowsiness my mind passed over the tenets of what I have learned from Śrīla Prabhupāda about suffering. I felt a desire to live by them and to keep them unsullied.

I also thought about how Prabhupāda boils issues down to the immense value of simple, direct devotional service. Everything else is roundabout and basically a waste of time. Everything else is either karma or *jñāna*. Prabhupāda's sincere disciples follow his straight and narrow path. Sometimes we are embarrassed at our lack of knowledge in other fields or our actual dryness due to our lack of contact with spiritual reality. We are poor. But we have Prabhupāda and his direction on the process, so we cannot lose.

1:09 P.M.

Saw Natalie Goldberg's book on her life as painter. She now takes it seriously, and as she ends her book, says she's ready to enter abstract art. No mention of God.

So? What do I want to be? A poet? A painter? A devotee.

Bhūrijana Prabhu, lecturing on *Śrīmad-Bhāgavatam*, draws out "seriously inquisitive" and "single-pointed attention" from the *ślokas*. Purity of heart is to will one thing, Kṛṣṇa. But I can't only chant or only read. The other expressions can also be part of my whole life in Kṛṣṇa consciousness. Art too. We each have to be sure, however, that our activities do not become ends in themselves and that our minds do not become splayed in the name of learning to be more creative or whatever. Everything we do should have a direct Kṛṣṇa conscious purpose.

I took the crowns off Rādhā and Govinda. They are so tall; they seem to be too much strain to wear.

I'm clear-headed, so I'll go to the shed.

Hare Kṛṣṇa. Filled up on lunch. Spoke to no one so far today. Even if I see someone, I'll speak few words. I have already put all my words into writing.

2:36 P.M.

I'd like to think my identity as a writer is not separate from my identity of being an aspiring devotee or disciple. If I create a duality, then I'll have to answer for it.

And the unconscious is a false nectar god. Just write and draw freely, use it for prayer. That's all. Look for the heart expression of Kṛṣṇa consciousness. Kṛṣṇa consciousness is not meant to be merely an intellectual or mechanical, dehumanized process.

So many words that I can't reject them *all*. On my way out the door, Śyāmānanda arrived with his camera to photograph Rādhā-Govinda. Good. I replaced Their crowns for the photos. O Kṛṣṇa.

Dark and misty. What does Lord Kṛṣṇa say in His *Bhagavad-gītā*? That He's the seed-giving father (*ahaṁ bīja-pradaḥ pitā*). Hear it and heed it. Understand it. Be a student of *śāstra*, because *śāstra* provides knowledge we could never obtain otherwise. *Śāstra* says the living entities are injected into various bodies at the time of creation according to their past desires.

One should know how the modes of nature work, and when "he knows the Supreme Lord, who is transcendental to all these modes, he attains My spiritual nature." (Bg. 14.19) Kṛṣṇa is the real spiritual master. He instructs us all through His instructions to Arjuna. A bona fide spiritual master teaches what Kṛṣṇa says, and we must have faith in that.

I can't explain exactly why I decided to accept Prabhupāda and Kṛṣṇa and the whole line of thought. Certainly I used reason. For example, I had to admit I didn't know everything, that I was tiny, that I was suffering, that I was lost. I also have to admit that the Vedic explanations satisfied my mind and intellect. Perhaps I also had some piety. Even a great sinner or atheist like me could come to understand by guru's grace. As the *Vedas* say, we are each innately spirit soul, so the truth is appealing, especially when it is carried by the spiritually attractive guru. So much of it has to do with spiritual-intellectual satisfaction. Later comes direct experience when we chant. Great hope is awakened, because if the guru is right—if by chanting God's names we can conquer death and rebirth and attain an eternal life of bliss and knowledge—then there's nothing more for which to aspire or to attain. We could never have hoped for anything after we shed our sentimental religions.

I am linked. I pray for my continuance and survival and the growth of my faith, and I hope to "enjoy nectar even in this life." (Bg. 14.20)

VEDIC SCROLL

(Windows clouding over with evaporation. I hope to convert my modes to something transcendental. This is my secret message to uncode.)

𝄞 Ordinary riffs, I heard
    at a cemetery on a hill
    they played "Taps" on a bugle—
Monty Clift in *From Here To*
Eternity.

Dirty books I read, recommended, talk of
what the guy says and what
he . . .
        Yeah, I read it and got
into the literature

of the ordinary riffs.
I had decided to love no matter
what. Tapped my toe and something went
down my back—more to it than that—
familiar, demystified.

Go to the *Vedas*
where the structure will take us
higher

higher higher higher and penetrating,
the man goes into
contortions
        trying to get the most out of it
        O Soul
        trying to get it out the words
telling God "I love You"
and leaving nothing behind. ‖

I WANT TO BE WITH YOU

𝄞 I had to laugh it was
like chickens in the yard
in Trinidad or
India outside the temples

then a goat ran behind a
black man running after him
with a machete

I'm sorry—I heard a group
praying to God we thought
they were all nuts

but wait—there's a way
to sweeten this sonnet
as the other modes are
    all used up

Kṛṣṇa, I just want to be with
You now in this quiet room
    in mantra session

I want to be with You
I want to be with You
please let me be with You
the chanting is the way
please give me peace
    today
I need Your help
this way

The riff. ‖

4:15, OUTSIDE SHED

It's consistently dark and gray from morning until night, day after day. This is, after all, gloomy Ireland. I don't mind. The overgrown grass reminds me of the passages in *Kṛṣṇa* book about the autumn season. The grass is untended, and during the rainy season, the *brāhmaṇas* don't move around. I like to think it is similar to not having to shave your face or make other social gestures—this season at Geaglum. Let the grass mat.

5:15 P.M.

She should bring my clean laundry soon. Light flickers off pen tip or eyeglass lens, reflected. Prabhupāda sitting. I can't draw him any more. Where to go next? I could let voices talk through me and do one of those Pukka Pad Shorties, but I only have an hour and a half left today. Then I will dress Rādhā-Govinda in Their blue nightclothes while Śrīla Prabhupāda sings Them a *bhajana*. I'll take that *bhajana* with me to sleep and hope for something other than those lost, hopeless dreams.

I spoke aloud today while writing an ItM—allowed sounds, grunts, exclamations, and of course, words. I mean, I composed vocally instead of only with the pen.

PUKKA PAD SHORTIES, INSTALLMENT #5

Prabhupāda *mūrti* can talk if he wants. Do I want to keep him silent, afraid he'll blast me (as a Godbrother said he would in his Vyāsa-pūjā homage a few years ago)?

Perhaps my "as if Prabhupāda is speaking" is more comfortable to live with than the real him. What would he say about my ItMs?

Natalie said that when her guru was gone from the world, she had to enter new open spaces alone, so she began to do abstract paintings.

I painted Nṛsiṁhadeva, who roars at demons.

Anyway, I don't want any fiery dialogues this close to bedtime. I'm looking for the blessing of long sleep (five hours) and a good, spiritual dream.

O Dream Source, Dream Producer—no imagination, just Kṛṣṇa.

Thus saying, I squiggle ink onto the page and find the shapes.

I will go to bed, praying for Kṛṣṇa's protection: *kṛṣṇa kṛṣṇa pāhi mām, kṛṣṇa kṛṣṇa rakṣa mām*. Good night.

November 29

12:05 A.M.

Chapter 15 begins with a description of the banyan tree and the point that we must extricate ourselves from its leaves and branches. Few people in this world concern themselves with this important detail. If they at all seek to become detached from passion, it is not with the idea of becoming liberated for a future life or escaping from *saṁsāra*. It doesn't matter. Our duty stands before us.

Knowledge is vital. The search for knowledge must be taken seriously. Imagine what we can do with the knowledge that the tree of material life is entangling and is an illusion; we could seek to free ourselves from it and to enter the real world.

With determination, one must cut down the tree with the weapon of detachment. "Thereafter, one must seek that place from which, having gone, one never returns, and there surrender to that Supreme Personality of Godhead from whom everything began and from whom everything has extended since time immemorial." (Bg. 15.4)

Thoughts this morning:

About Natalie G. becoming an artist and apparently switching her main passion to painting. She says the abstract paintings she admires take a lifetime of dedication to achieve. They seem to her to be The Truth. Seems to think those illuminating paintings can help her detach herself from matter. But can they bring you to a life of devotion to the Personality of Godhead? Can they bring you and others to the eternal spiritual world?

References in the *Bhagavad-gītā* to sense attachment make me suspect myself in different ways. I note the questions, but put them aside. I'm not going to be crippled in what I have accepted as my service. *Yukta-vairāgya.*

"To gain favor of that Personality of Godhead, one has only to surrender, and this is a result of performing devotional service by hearing, chanting, etc." (Bg. 15.4, purport) When we achieve attachment to Kṛṣṇa, we automatically become detached from the material extension.

My mind also goes over the probable scenes of next week—Madhu's return and our final packing, the departures to and from Dublin, the flight to New York City. I go as a preacher to the Caribbean. Swamis go regularly to Trinidad, so I won't be saying anything those other swamis haven't already said. It doesn't matter. Just doing my duty.

THE SINGER'S RUMINATING TALE WHICH ENDS WITH HIM PREACHING TO THE GUY

𝄞 When it's quiet it means you have to listen. There we were in the Brooklyn temple, reading about the tree of the material world. I planned to lecture on it to a tight group of committed devotees. Manhattan formed the perfect example of the tree with all its branches and twigs.

Oh, we're full of stories, we devotees, and we want to give them
to the whole world. Who can take them? The *Bhagavad-gītā* describes *everyone's* predicament, what's actually happening to all of us, where are we going, how we are driven, how the senses demand.
And religion—how we use it to get the things we want we think we
need.
Not just in Manhattan either. The people in Dublin go through it too—how to get money and then how to spend it on a new car or a new partner or a new education or the kids. Those early ideals of universal life are gradually lost and we enter the world of single-minded struggle.
Generalities, I know, but true for each person. And inside? Covered, hurt, scared. The history of wars tells all.
But we live on to enjoy. We live and recover from living.
Sometimes we sing—can't you? I am a singer too, and I like to tell this tale
so folks can see
and escape what is temporary for
what is eternal. No jigs or reels or
polkas from me.
Just a sorrowful ballad to
touch us
deep in the heart.

O people, if you would just chant
God's names—I advocate it
openly
and find this inward practice, this mind absorption
this love. ‖

4:28 A.M.

Today is Saturday and Rādhā-Govinda are wearing bright red outfits trimmed in gold. Their tall red crowns each have a touch of blue—a peacock in the center. Touches of green leaves are embroidered into Their clothes.

I wonder what I will speak on in the Caribbean. Should I plan to cover a certain section of the *Bhāgavatam*, or at least choose something rather than having something assigned to me? They will let me do whatever I want.

Oh, Hare Kṛṣṇa. Dear Kṛṣṇa, please be kind.

Calm down. You don't have to measure up to some big Swami or GBC man and fake it. Or worse, you don't have to punch a clock for a low-wage job and eat humble pie day after day. You can stand up for your rights. Swamiji gave you a comfortable berth. Don't look for more appreciation for your service. Some ISKCON men are dedicated to maintaining this movement, and the absolute science of God forbids seeing the material world as apart from Kṛṣṇa. We see it as His material energy. It works the way a tape recorder works. We hear Swamiji's voice and it's him and not him at the same time.

Heard that the Guyanese devotees are fighting again. A mother called her son-in-law a "good-for-nothing" and refuses to recognize him. Her daughter has a different opinion. Hare Kṛṣṇa.

"Don't eat venison," he said. No, we sell books and write back-up songs for the troops. "Blow the smoke off your rifle," he said. The other guy was like that, but I don't believe it.

Lie down after this and no doubt conk out even with the lights on. I already know a dream will come rushing in from the void filled with people who want starring roles and who will live vivid lives to achieve their purposes. Who can understand? The days are changing and I am trying to change with them.

Raghunātha dāsa Gosvāmī and the *gosvāmīs* of Vṛndāvana sing that the spiritual master is the only refuge. Kṛṣṇa is the original guru. Hare Kṛṣṇa was always the essence.

8:04 A.M.

To cut the connection to the material tree, we have to surrender to the Supreme Lord. "The first qualification is that one should not be deluded by pride." (Bg. 15.5, purport) When you're always expecting honor, you cannot surrender. Also, give up controllership. I read it and note it here, but again, it's a theoretical lesson. How will I actually accomplish it? I don't even know whether or not I'm guilty of pride and proprietorship or whether I am willing to give them up. I don't know what it means to surrender. I'm already following my vows as I promised at my initiation in 1966. Is *that* surrender? Does it mean to do things you don't want to do?

As I write, devotees are ringing and ringing the brass bell at the quay. I watch this show often. Don't they *hear* the bell over there? Or maybe they are simply too busy to be running boats across the lake day and night. To continue ringing the bell takes endurance and patience. It's dark out this morning, and anyone can see the bright lights shining in my room as I sit at the desk facing the window. It's obvious I'm not going to the morning program. If I did I'd phone ahead and wait until someone came to get me in the boat; I'm no bell-ringer.

Back to the discussion about surrender. Ultimately, we say, to admit we don't know what surrender is as good as admitting that we refuse to do it. Do we want to surrender or not? If we want to surrender to Kṛṣṇa, then we must actively seek out some ISKCON authority and do what he prescribes. That's how some people see it. I just can't agree with that.

Oh, here comes the boat.

In Bg. 15.5, Kṛṣṇa mentions the eternal world, which can be attained by the detached and surrendered soul. Don't conceive of this in a simplistic, physical way. Once the surrendered soul attains that supreme planet, he never returns to the material world. "One should be captivated by this information. He should desire to transfer himself to that eternal world and extricate himself from this false reflection of reality." (Bg. 15.6, purport)

The difference between writing for myself and lecturing to devotees: for myself I admit my mood as I write—that I don't know what surrender is, and if you defined it for me, I would probably not agree with your definition. I *could* admit the same thing in a public lecture, but I'd have to give a positive solution to the problem because otherwise I may leave others in doubt. I couldn't just leave the discussion dangling like that. I'd have to add, "So we have to admit our shortcomings, but at the same time we must continue to practice Kṛṣṇa consciousness with determination. We may have to do certain things we don't like to do. We should also try to find a way in which we are *willing* to surrender. Find those persons, that service, to which we can give ourselves. Surrender doesn't have to mean raising our hands at gunpoint. Surrender has to be voluntary. In the beginning, this may mean giving up personal inclinations in order to serve the interests of the mission. It also means giving the results of our activities to Kṛṣṇa. In the meantime, keep hearing about the ideal of surrender, doing everything we can to please Kṛṣṇa without selfishness. Lord Caitanya and Śrīla Prabhupāda want us to preach. That's a big item of surrender right there. Yes, definitely we will have to give up our attachments." And so on. And I would give examples, use rhetoric, and speak as honestly as possible but with a lecturer's persona.

The one who writes for himself is quieter, less willing to accept simplistic solutions. He wants to do more than pump himself up with positive aphorisms. Whatever he is, he must learn to surrender. Honesty is part of that, either on the page or in the lecture.

We surrender when we chant Hare Kṛṣṇa, Hare Kṛṣṇa, Kṛṣṇa Kṛṣṇa, Hare Hare/ Hare Rāma, Hare Rāma, Rāma Rāma, Hare Hare—at least sixteen rounds—and wish to improve by focusing our minds. Some things just aren't possible right now, though, so we bite the bullet and do other things—distribute books, do temple service, get married or don't. Unless we surrender we cannot free ourselves from this material world. Either we surrender to Kṛṣṇa or we surrender to more misery, right?

8:55 A.M.

I'm walking on the woods path. I hear a crane or a swan honking as it flies by. The month is almost over. Whatever leaves are going to fall have already fallen. Some of them stay on the trees all winter. Many trees are still wrapped with bright green-leafed vines that will stay green all winter along with the winter mosses. The outdoors seems quiet this morning. Gītā-nāgarī is also like this in the morning.

A magpie lifting off the path just startled me! Can I think of Kṛṣṇa when I feel that wave of shock? Can I remember at least to recite His holy names? At least a few times?

What did Prabhupāda say this morning? Something about many controllers and how Kṛṣṇa is the Supreme Controller. He quoted *Brahma-saṁhitā*: *īśvaraḥ paramaḥ kṛṣṇaḥ*. I admit I'm a weak-hearted milksop creature of little faith. Great devotees have great faith. Sometimes when we feel our shortcomings, we can become arrogant about it. Rather, we need to place our case humbly and sorrowfully before Kṛṣṇa. Remember that Kṛṣṇa is kind and wants us to turn to Him. He won't condemn us. "Fie, fie upon Narottama!"

10:25 A.M.

Flakes of *tilaka*. Surreal. "Surrender unto Me." Last days of November. Having an especially good week physically—possibly six days out of seven without a headache. Arjuna dāsa rowing right now to the island.

Read more in Merton's 1961 journal. I liked it and considered carrying it to America, but the book is too large. I'll take two small paperbacks instead. Lying in bed now. Even when I don't have a headache, I rest to prevent one starting rather than remaining active beyond my actual strength. I won't take this loud-scratching pen on tour either—I have travel pens. I expect to return after the tour to find this room just as I left it. It used to be routine for me to travel; now it's a big deal. I want to come back to Ireland, but I'm sure that that won't be possible forever.

I also want to do what a *sannyāsī* ought to do, lecture, and for me, especially in the Caribbean and the Northeast U.S. where I have small congregations whom I cannot abandon. I feel the personal obligation, and I don't want to disappoint those devotees with whom I already have a relationship.

I asked to see Bhaktisiddhānta Sarasvatī Ṭhākura's essay where he says people may see him as arrogant for receiving his disciples' worship, but he is following Lord Caitanya's order. He says he cannot fail to follow that order. He almost seems to say that not only outsiders would accuse him of arrogance, but he might have to personally run the risk of actually becoming arrogant. However, he says, Lord Caitanya's order will save him. Besides, his personal consideration is not as important as the need for people to follow a bona fide guru who must be seen by them to be as good as God.

Remaining questions in my case (and other ISKCON gurus—hey, don't lump me in, but I am)—did we receive that same order, and are we qualified? I can't quote Śrīla Bhaktisiddhānta Sarasvatī Ṭhākura's speech and expect all opposition to fall silent. Every Church has its controversies and splits. How naive we were to think ISKCON would avoid that fate. But we did think we could avoid it, and Śrīla Prabhupāda didn't really make it too easy for us. He simply told us to remain faithful and to cooperate, and then he left.

PUKKA PAD SHORTIES, INSTALLMENT #6

"You're always so holy."

"What?"

"Yeah, thinking of Kṛṣṇa."

"Well, I'm close to sixty years old. I could die at any moment. I should be thinking of Kṛṣṇa and my soul, right? Even from the viewpoint of self-interest?"

"But you don't."

"No, I don't. Like today. I got a letter from a devotee that disturbed me. I read it twice. He said he had a heavy heart and didn't know if he could continue. I feel heavy-hearted too. Then I read something, an interview with a worldly man, and I forgot my heavy heart, but lost my concentration on Kṛṣṇa."

"Now I call you a Holy Joe, worrying about a thing like that."

"I just want to be real; I'm no saint."

The two men discuss these things in a backyard. As they speak, a BBT van pulls out, loaded with men on their way out to distribute books.

"Does that make you feel guilty? Envious?"

"No, I admire them. They are doing great work for Prabhupāda."

"Do you feel they are better devotees than you?"

"I'm not even a devotee at all. Aren't you from *People* magazine?"

"No, I'm your subpart."

"Sub what?"

The interviewer glances at his watch. It is time for lunch. He decides to wrap it up.

"I suppose in the future people will think of you as a Thomas Merton or an Aaron Burr. Or maybe no one will think of you at all."

"Merton wrote in his diary at a time when many of his books were being published, 'But for me, can all this have any serious meaning? . . . the irony of total destruction hangs over it, to keep me wise.'"

"Well," says the interviewer, "now that you have pegged me as an interviewer, I might as well play the part. What's your next book?"

"It's called *Every Day, Just Snooker*. It's a biography about a desert father who . . . "

Suddenly lunch arrives and Holy Joe turns to more important matters.

2:37 P.M.

I missed Śyāmānanda—I saw him getting into his boat to come to my room to take Rādhā-Govinda's photo, but I was already on my way out the door.

We are separated expansions of God, "eternal fragmental parts." We have to accept *śāstra* as Truth, spoken by God Himself. Otherwise, it has no value. It's either truth or it's gibberish. Bhūrijana Prabhu said in a lecture I heard at lunch today that the reason we don't experience the taste of Kṛṣṇa consciousness is that (1) we are ignorant of transcendental knowledge; (2) we commit *aparādhas;* and (3) we have other weaknesses of heart, such as the desire to be worshiped, etc. These things build up obstacles to taste. When I heard this, I stopped for half a moment in my wolfish eating and thought it sounded right—that's why I don't have access to the nectar.

What to do about it? He said we must serve great devotees. That sounds right too.

We are struggling in the material world with the six senses including the mind. We shouldn't, however, exaggerate our misery. Actually, by Kṛṣṇa's grace, we are doing quite well. Still, I tend to fear I'll be stranded. I fear I'm resting on laurels gained by years of vigorous service. Shouldn't we push hard all the way to the end? That's what Śrīla Prabhupāda did, risked death on the battlefield, gave up his retirement even though he wanted it.

I feel as if I have already retired. I just can't jump back into the fray. I seem to have no options because of my health. But my medical pass, that "note from the doctor"—will it prevent me from entering the spiritual world? Will I have to be reborn again because I am not dying on the battlefield? There are no easy answers for our lives and the choices we make either willingly or seemingly by force.

Qualitatively one with God; always individuals. Try to leave this world by dedicating everything to the Supreme Lord. Think of His abode, be captivated by this information, and work for Him. His mission is to bring souls back to Godhead, but we all have free will. He won't take it away from us.

Same old thing—what I write and what the *śāstras* say. Don't go crazy for novelty. New lights will come naturally. That feeling of freshness is in Kṛṣṇa, *nava-yauvana*, *pūrva-rāga*, but we must approach Him with love and surrender to His devotees in order to feel it.

GOIN' HOME

(Holding out, no sorrow (well, some), no giving into depression, and don't stay secular. It's a many-faceted world, but you want Kṛṣṇa—single-minded.)

𝄞 Hurry along, no time to waste
I'm getting sentimental.
    I can't tell you how
I'm blipping along in this
happy bubble called
    Kṛṣṇa conscious contemplation
    and along comes a presage a
    dream

will I suffer in hell? Why am I
so happy-go-lucky as if
    my number won't come up
for mugging-crashes-fires?

Is *that* how Kṛṣṇa will protect you or
    how He will test you?
Live the moment and preach
to all but yes, we each must find our way.

Listen folks
we were on the corner of
5th and Avenue B
when I heard a sound coming
out of a window.
    It was Charles going fast
getting down with
    Monk's "Sentimental."

And I told you that
        Kṛṣṇa is King the
source of all music legends
the top and bottom
        of everything including sound
ethereal or otherwise
and our own
fragmental parts.

He says
        karṣati—the soul is fragmental
but He is the healing herb
the relief from pain
and the pain itself?

This happy-go-lucky retiree
is losing his strength—He's
taking it away.

My Lord knows what He's doing
is most powerful
and it's a joke to praise
anyone in comparison to
Him.

May we meet at liberation
after I give up my crippling fears
and center on Kṛṣṇa
our worshipable
God the best
lover
and friend.
(Don't listen to *me*, it's Truth.)

REMEMBER TOGETHER

𝄞 We want to remember
a beautiful person who came
here and his followers who
try to make the world a
better place

it's confusing so
let's keep it simple

here's a song for the mission and for
the lives we spent and the ones
I heard described in *śāstra*—
nothing lost—even a little—for any
of us.

But we wanted so much *more*
    that sometimes it does seem wasted
and we cry we
    feel grief
and you know, it shouldn't be checked.

When that guy's
dog died—the guy who
walked across America,
his brave dog at his side,

I said the master was
strong. Now we're able to
hear his strong and sorrowful
song
    brought to us over roofs
into our hearts
into our temples

into our corrupt motives
while the demons hit back.
Do you remember the time . . .

I recall—
    we ate sweet rice while
the walls fell down around us,

something like that.
    Then lust called
and greed
and we saw that we were not finished with *māyā*
and our ranks were decimated—
What ever happened to . . . ?

I just want to cry
    but also to remember
    you and the mission we went
    through together.

it's sad to recall but sweet too
and as time runs down
    we wait for the Lord to call
us back.

They're already laughing
and calling us to account

for every bit of karma. We
count on our chanting
our little taste of *bhakti*
to cure us.

May the *kīrtana* never stop
even when we can't remember
the Sanskrit drift.

We are poor souls,
rescued by
Lord Caitanya's mercy
and Prabhupāda's
and we really can
smile. ||

4:05 P.M.

I heard birds squeaking and a distant truck—a *big* truck. Can I hear the water running in the lake? No, it would practically have to be silent outside for that, and even then I would have to sit outside for awhile until my ears became attuned. It's not worth trying for, especially when it is so easy to sit down and immediately hear God's names vibrated by your own tongue. Then you can be with Him from your own closest uttering. But that bird is nice. It reminds me of spring. It's a little lighter than usual, too, this afternoon, perhaps the moon rising behind the clouds. This is moving toward the darkest time of the year.

Lyrical painter dies. Who's that? Some guy I read about.

Saw a book on how to stimulate creativity and to make money from it. They said artists should travel. If they stay in one place, they will fall into a rut. That's not necessarily true. Who wants so much stimulation? *God* is the source of all, not a wider collection of sensory data. I wouldn't mind staying here and seeing all the seasons. Hare Kṛṣṇa, Hare Kṛṣṇa, Kṛṣṇa Kṛṣṇa, Hare Hare/ Hare Rāma, Hare Rāma, Rāma Rāma, Hare Hare.

5:50 P.M.

Reading Merton's journal. I'm allowed much more freedom than he had. I live in a religious movement, but still do what I want. The ISKCON GBC passes resolutions and laws, but few of them touch me directly. I think this is because of (1) my seniority; (2) I don't make trouble; (3) I have a medical reason not to take a too-active part. Also, despite the laws, ISKCON is by nature not an overly controlled organization. Only those who live in the temple come under strict control. Those who live outside can arrange for privacy and live basically on their own. This could change, and I have worried about that in the past, but no one has threatened me or the way that I have had to live. I do follow prescribed *sannyāsa-dharma* as far as possible for my health. Anyway, a *brāhmaṇa* is supposed to follow this voluntarily, not because he is pressured by the *kṣatriyas*.

November 30

12:08 A.M.

Our lives are tested at the end, whether we can remember Kṛṣṇa, and not just that last moment, but our entire lives are weighed and measured, the intention behind every action held forward and examined against truth and devotion. Gradually, as each item stands up, like a photograph developing in the lab, our new body is formed and assigned. We would like to go to Kṛṣṇa, but are unworthy or feel we are. We cannot connive our way into the spiritual world. Kṛṣṇa knows our heart better than we know it ourselves. We can *plan* to feel unworthy, knowing that humility catches Kṛṣṇa's attention, but our success is up to Him and the honesty of our humility is also measured by Him. Still, we shouldn't be anemic about our desire to go back to Godhead. Kṛṣṇa knows we're no heroes. All He expects of us is an honest and strong desire to be with Him.

We shouldn't be cold to Kṛṣṇa and the possibility of His love overwhelming our failure to serve better. I mean, we would love to go to the place beyond liberation, beyond heaven, beyond birth and death, to Kṛṣṇaloka, but we seem so unable to act for it in this world. Kṛṣṇa Himself can change that, if we want Him too.

Śrīla Prabhupāda quotes *smṛti*, " . . . when a living entity gives up this material embodiment and enters into the spiritual world, he revives his spiritual body, and in his spiritual body he can see the Supreme Personality of Godhead face to face. He can hear and speak to Him face to face, and he can understand the Supreme Personality as He is." (Bg. 15.7, purport)

Fear of God in awe and reverence, fear He'll punish us for our doubts and sins and failures, fear even that we tried to become too familiar with Him before we deserved it (*prākṛta-sahajiyā* in one form or another), fear that we have not pleased our spiritual master, so we'll be denied going back to Godhead—all these hinder out acceptance of Kṛṣṇa's love.

It is good—essential—to read the *śāstra* subjectively and to take it personally. These verses discuss transmigration. What do they mean to *me*? I'm not a Hindu and this is not a Hindu doctrine. I think inwardly about my own faith in this knowledge; I try to be submissive and earnest. I order my intellect, "Please accept it, please listen." I *want* to be convinced, but neither can I take force-feeding. I must constantly expose myself to my spiritual master's words and serve him as best I can.

And to the degree that I understand this knowledge, I should try my best to give it to others. *Everyone* is in the same boat.

PRAYER FOR WELL-BEING

𝄞 No one else but me under the
desk lamp to see how I
feel

and tell you joyful news
learned
discovered from the world
of sound.

Joyful I overflow, even though
it hurts to say it.
Hurts? Yes, because my
joy is shot at, challenged, but
I dare to share it anyway.

Dear friends, hear the earnestness
behind my offering.
Why am I trying to please
You, O Kṛṣṇa, and to sell You
to others?
I've already told my story; it's the story of
everyone in the material world.
A young man on a December eve asks
for blessings for the Irish book distributors.
Mine? I'll pray for you
and the others (beyond envy and
hatred and cowardice and dreams where
I couldn't fight yet
wanted my way).

Me, I'll try calling on God
just one alone to
gather drops of His mercy and
give them out as insight
to others.

I'll pray to my master's sweetness
to hear it in his voice and to give his strength
to others that they may see
the *vibhūtis* of people

and the sunrise, the lake,
feel peace—feel Gurudeva
always present
somehow
in all things.

Lord Caitanya, You gave
music to uplift us,
each of us walled into the cells
of our bodies
we sing with You together
and apart
studying the gentle agenda
of finding Kṛṣṇa
in the woods. ‖

4:25 A.M.

Rādhā-Govinda wear pink outfits with transparent white "shells" and peacock feather embroidery. It's trimmed heavily in gold. I am fortunate to be able to dress Them and look upon Their forms while Narottama dāsa Ṭhākura prays to worship the Yugala-kiśora. He yearns for *prema-bhakti* and prays to become the *gopīs'* maidservant and assist them in their direct service to Rādhā and Kṛṣṇa. That is what I am doing in the practice mode—placing the bracelets on Their wrists, the crowns upon Their heads, and offering Them fresh cups of water.

Śrīla Prabhupāda says Kṛṣṇa asks us for service not because He needs our work—He already has everything—but because He wants our love. By serving Him we become liberated from birth and death. To serve Kṛṣṇa brings self-satisfaction, and as we decorate Him, we feel sanctified. We can also honor palatable foods when we offer them to Rādhā-Govinda, and receive the blessings to advance on the path of spontaneous love of God.

We want to reach the stage of *sarvātmā:* giving everything to Kṛṣṇa as the *gopīs* did. Start your charity to Kṛṣṇa with whatever you can give. When a housewife said she would give ashes to the *sādhu* begging at her door, he said, "Very well, then just begin your charity!"

Prabhupāda is wearing the bristly saffron wool cap we obtained for him in Vṛndāvana. Kṛṣṇa is opulent and gorgeous. The Gosvāmīs wear the simplest dress—no crowns or bracelets, yet they are absorbed in serving the Divine Couple for Their pleasure. Nārada Muni could hardly believe when he saw Kṛṣṇa's opulence in the 16,108 palaces.

It's Sunday and I'm supposed to go over to the temple to give the lecture from *Caitanya-caritāmṛta*. I'll be reading more on *yāre dekha*. This verse is suitable for the book distributors, who are about to begin their December marathon. They can know that Kṛṣṇa is most pleased with the preacher. At the same time, we count all devotees as preachers. They are carriers of Viṣṇu.

Hare Kṛṣṇa, I'm slipping
down.

Did my sixteen rounds and will take some rest so that I'm up for class. A letter under the door overnight, probably from Manu, who just returned from a few days on the road.

No need to keep a list of those disciples who no longer care for me, or of those who have left Kṛṣṇa consciousness. Just go on yourself: Hare Kṛṣṇa, Hare Kṛṣṇa, Kṛṣṇa Kṛṣṇa, Hare Hare.

Dreamt I was with Madhu in the city and I was brushing and brushing my hair. I seemed to think it had been neglected. Finally, I went to sit in a back room. Someone approached me and wanted to ask some questions, but he had a dirty little boy with him. The boy latched on to me with a painful grip that felt like he was sucking my flesh. With great effort I pulled him off and asked the man to hold him away from me. The man did not comply. I told him I couldn't talk to him as long as the boy was behaving like that, but still the man continued to ask questions without restraining the child. Finally, I managed to disengage myself from the boy and escape. I wanted to tell Madhu not to let this man and his boy back into my room, but he wasn't there.

7:48 A.M.

Pulling on my boots. I'm going over. I'm "on." It's so dark out I can barely see, but I see the quay lights are on. I expect Arjuna dāsa will be outside, ready to row me across. I have my material prepared: stay home, don't pretend, reform your own life, find true renunciation, etc. Śrīla Bhaktisiddhānta Sarasvatī Ṭhākura used the verse *yāre dekha* to prove that the guru is under order. I also want to offer congrats to book distributors because they tell everyone they meet about Kṛṣṇa.

I want to discuss Vāsudeva the leper, who was such a great devotee. Nothing unrehearsed in my mind. The expert who wrote the book on creativity said we should experience new things and be daring. He said to read books and learn. One little chapter at the end says meditation and prayer can help too—as if the purpose of prayer is to get good ideas so we can make money, sell a book, be happy, and so on.

I'm hungry for creative ideas. At least my ideas are quickly channeled toward Kṛṣṇa. I could filch something from the book on creativity since it all belongs to Kṛṣṇa anyway. The rascals have stolen everything they have from Him.

Getting lighter bit by bit. Every five minutes I can tell the difference. One lone light provides illumination until the sun takes over.

I wrote a letter to a disciple who had some ideas about how to improve his life. I wish him well. Wrote a letter to another disciple in response to his requesting a prayer for book distributors.

A letter to myself? Okay, fellow, I know you're fragile.

Anyway, going over to speak. When I get back, Gopī-mañjarī will look at the Deities and see if she can arrange for more Vṛndāvana-style *dhotīs* and *sārīs* in addition to Their more regal outfits. I also want more peacock-feather *mukuts* and a nice bed. She will polish Them before I leave and place Them in "*samādhi.*"

I'm very serious and very afraid, but I have little perks of humor. One wonders where he or she will be at the end. We have to think of Kṛṣṇa at every step if we wish to remember Him at the end. Why don't I write a book about the deathbed? Why don't I write a book about a monk's bed? Monk's

bread.
Monks fed
up with falsity. Monks afraid
to make the real dive
at Kṛṣṇa's lotus feet. Why
afraid? Do we think
Kṛṣṇa will scare us out of our wits because He's so powerful?
Maybe. Maybe we do.

Be ready, O devotees, to face the emptiness, the desert, then the love. Even if Kṛṣṇa doesn't appear immediately, we all know He's our best friend because

the Swami said so.

10:10 A.M.

Lecture okay. Feeling separation from Govindadvīpa already, the wet, cold, bird-singing island. Light coming from the temple building early in the morning. Extra devotees here today. Sharma, the *saṅkīrtana* leader, sat right in front of me. I praised book distributors. Gopī-mañjarī came back to the house, and she and Manu entered my room. I showed them Rādhā-Govinda and felt enthused and grateful and somewhat childlike in my appreciation of these Deities. Gopī-mañjarī gave me a nice bed for Them, and I told her I'd like more Vrajalike clothes—a yellow *dhotī* for Kṛṣṇa and a blue *sārī* for Rādhā, and clothes that don't cover His feet.

Letters. One devotee back from Vṛndāvana. She said she liked Rādhā's places—Yāvaṭ, Varṣāṇā, etc., where devotees are uninhibited to chant "Rādhe, Rādhe." She hopes she's not a *prakṛta-sahajiyā*.

Busy and more social than usual this morning. Playing the role of guru, seeing disciples, talking with a spiritual daughter about what man she wants to marry. Another tells me he had a "brush" with illicit sex, but the two of them don't really want that. What am I supposed to think? Old *sannyāsa-dharma*. O little Rādhā-Govinda, so effulgent, so kind to me.

12:18 P.M.

A Godbrother was listening to a lecture by another Godbrother and found it "very powerful." I asked him to give me a copy and now I too am listening. It's about faith and quite gung-ho. Right, not wrong. I can't fight it. I respect his enthusiasm. He's a *śakti* of Prabhupāda. I feel his audience squirming.

"Be very faithful to your spiritual master," says this American Godbrother. Should he have said, "Be doubtful toward me because I am not an Indian born and raised guru?"

No, I have no objections. I just want to . . .

O Kṛṣṇa, may we all find a place in the spiritual world. Fortunately, there are many rooms in Śrīla Prabhupāda's mansion.

Shut up, Gua,
don't write this crap
or we'll pull you on the carpet a
raving madman.

2:43 P.M.

Sunshine for a change. Met three different people while walking from the house to the shed. One gave me a letter, one said, "*Haribol*," and the third was loading up his van for the next *saṅkīrtana* marathon. He said something friendly, and then I walked on. I saw other cheerful young faces with him as they loaded up. I thought of turning back and wishing them luck, but I didn't. It would have been hype. I *do* wish them luck, and I appreciate, even envy (or let's say am humbled by) their sacrifice, and I pray for them. That's more real to me than shouting out slogans and encouraging them to come out number one in the competition.

No goats today, I notice. Nothing else on the way here.

Looks like I'll have to clean up the shed before I go.

Bhagavad-gītā—thoughts to provoke Kṛṣṇa consciousness in the conditioned soul: the splendor of the sun, moon, and fire all come from Kṛṣṇa, the Supreme Personality of Godhead. That's for beginners like me. When I play the role of the spiritual master lecturing, I'll be confident and do some of my own smashing and laughing at fools, but I won't forget who I am, a very small person. I don't mean I'm really an atheist or a demon (although I suppose I could be if I misused my free will), but I'm more in need than I let on in the lecture. I depend on the first steps in Kṛṣṇa consciousness to keep me linked to Him. Yes, I'd like to see the sun and moon and feel a personal appreciation of Kṛṣṇa—something real.

The planets floating in the air are actually held in the fist of the universal form. So poetic. If only I could think in poetry for Kṛṣṇa's pleasure.

When I walk back will the men and their van be gone? Will my head be clear? I gave out more today than usual, yet it was so little. I am grateful anyway.

Kṛṣṇa is situated as sound, as air, and as the digestive fire in the belly. He is in all things.

THE SPLENDOR OF THE SUN, MOON, AND FIRE, AND GOOD MEN

1

𝄞 Jump start
it's a place
        where I go and you with me
with me
        you are in need
of a fix.

Jump
    you mean there's no
squirrel in here
        or wren
    but a way

he used to be—
    I saw the men
loading up their van/ such faces
young idealists all
soldiers of the true army

good-time *brahmacāris*
    working for guru. Who
dares touch on their morals?

I've got the left over
Royal loaf
pineapple and cream
I've got the alone wanna
bees

I've got the Lord in my
fist
    huh
I've got nothin',
realize that

rhythm and blues and
a little shelter
jump blood
    this oldster is a laugh

he longs for friends like
    this but they've got a lunch
for you
    and air for your belly.

O splendor of fire and moon
        O Brother Sun you
come from God.

She joined the Hare
Kṛṣṇas with arguments
against killing animals—
"no soul" they say

and he, DDD, became
what I thought he was a
Vaiṣṇava the one
whose hands the
master guided.

And what about Steve
and John and all those guys
        ISKCON Diaspora
no more on LSD
but moanin' perhaps

romancing for a spiritual
Dad and Supreme
to
bring us all home.

2

Now here's the walk past
graveyard, run—
you've got your bass man he'll
not fail unless the heart
itself/ fails to keep pace
with the Pacemaker.

O Kṛṣṇa in my heart
        I always knew and
prayed to You a
simple theme chord
a secret hope.

3

Splendor—fire and moon—the
people may not recognize
the best drummer
        and follow others
        lots of them—inky oceans
        blue-black scars—memories
O God   O God
this universe
gives me hope and my poems
break atheists. ‖

4:00 P.M., OUTSIDE SHED

Yellow rose as the sun sets. Clear blue—would you believe it? Headache coming, but I will push out a last poem. As always, long, unkempt grass carrying plenty of water drops. They turn silvery at this hour. Trees bare—who could draw all their etching fingers?

5:35 P.M.

Had to take an Esgic. Then suddenly Praghoṣa arrived at the door. I spoke with him about troubles in Wicklow. It was a crucial meeting—it brought me relief and brought us together. I hope, however, it doesn't offset the pain cushion I sought in the Esgic.

Kṛṣṇa is here, and Rādhā. The poems, the great rush of inspiration, come bit by bit. They come from Kṛṣṇa, these poem stories. I have to calm down now and probably take rest early.

December 1

12:10 A.M.

That speaker I heard yesterday said to his audience, "Don't harbor doubts silently, thinking, 'I have a very good doubt that no one can answer; it is better than anyone else's doubt.' Come out with the doubt and be smashed by a senior devotee. It will be good for you." Fair enough. I'm glad I heard it.

I always have to ask, however, whether the speaker himself airs his doubts and is willing to be smashed by the conclusions (often opinions) of others. And if we continue to live with certain doubts even after we have been smashed.

Some doubts simply cannot be aired. The speaker gave examples of rotten doubts—that the Brahman is ultimately more important than the form of God, or that the whole Vedic presentation may simply be a myth. Sure, if you come out with such doubts, they will be smashed, and actually, they're *easy* to smash. My only objection to what he said, really, is to the concept that doubts must always be aired and must always be smashed. If we are always treated harshly or heavily, with boots instead of kindness, we may find ourselves less inclined to trust. Sometimes it's better to bring out doubts with a close friend rather than with someone who will smash us. Confidential talks between friends can be for that. Friends may be more inclined to admit their own doubts and to share how they deal with them. When we are treated by a supercilious mentor who is above doubt and who pounces on ours like an all-powerful cat chasing a helpless mouse, it scares the mouse, but perhaps not for good. Perhaps it chases the mouse back into our hearts where it hides even deeper. I'm not sure doubt is always eradicated by this method.

I am realizing more and more that if I get pain on a particular day, I'll live with it. Pain has become a natural part of my life. Not only for me, but for everyone, whether we all realize it or not.

In his purports in the *Bhagavad-gītā*, Śrīla Prabhupāda informs us that God comes to us in many ways. It's more of what we heard in the seventh and tenth chapters—ways in which He can be perceived even by beginners. He is present in the moon, the sun, fire, gravity, and as digestion, *prāṇa*, and *apāna*. Then there is the climactic verse, *sarvasya cāhaṁ hṛdi sanniviṣṭo:* "I am seated in everyone's heart, and from Me come remembrance, knowledge and forgetfulness. By all the *Vedas*, I am to be known. Indeed, I am the compiler of *Vedānta*, and I am the knower of the *Vedas*." (Bg. 15.15) In all these ways. Please meditate on Him now that you have this information. But if you can't, don't worry, I won't smash you. Simply lift up your doubts and put them aside. You don't need them anymore. We have to be willing to do at least that—this is Kṛṣṇa's advice to Arjuna, "Therefore the doubts which have arisen in your heart out of ignorance should be slashed by the weapon of knowledge. Armed with yoga . . . stand and fight." (Bg. 4.42) Get rid of them.

Yes, to admit that even the lecturer, the guru, has doubts. I remember one devotee telling me that he never, never had doubts and that I should never, never have them either. I found his words reassuring. But since doubts or lack of taste or even *aparādhas* persist, we can only become more and more dependent on the one who can remove them, the surgeon-guru. O Prabhupāda, I trust you.

We can also ask friends to pick them off our hide like a monkey picking lice from a mate. Or we can blast them into the ether through sound—self-expression, not for others' nourishment but as a cry of pain that becomes a dissipated demon.

HELP YOURSELF—SURRENDER IN YOUR WAY

𝄞 What's that about love?
Oh, it's just that we all feel
some sultry stuff, we don't
    sometimes know what to do with it.

You mean on radio you hear a soupy, too-much-complaining saxophone?

No, well,
yes, that too, the
stuff--when the people who are meant to help us don't reach out.
There's no remedy for anything
but pure Kṛṣṇa conscious sound, I know,
but we want to feel love.

I sing and do my art
    with some intention
and can't be helped by you
or another anyway
I had to go to my one and only

And say please allow me
        and allow *Him* to have power over me.

This process is not an arbitrary one
but He must really command and
we must really trust

touched by his wisdom and
overcome.

O Kṛṣṇa give me faith
and wisdom and tenderness and
toughness

and the wisdom to ride with the punches
to stand up and teach
in a way I would like to be taught

a sultry love mood and
grateful
for Your touch, me
a loving integer.
        O my Lord
         Govinda.

4:28 A.M.

Write while you can, while you don't have much pain. Rādhā and Kṛṣṇa wear light green again today, this time with gold trim and dark green crowns. Eventually I will gather more outfits and turbans for Them. I also want more flutes, more peacock feathers, more devotion, more thinking of Them. I plan to carry photos of Them when I travel, so I have asked two different devotees to take pictures. I want to get as many good photos as possible. Then I can put different pictures in the frames, and that will become the worshipable Deity to whom I offer the food.

O Lord of the universe, O soul of the universe, kindly cut my attachment to the Vṛṣṇis and the Pāṇḍavas, Queen Kuntī prayed. I pray that my attachments to the body and mind may be cut and that I'll be free to love the Lord. Let everything else be taken from me.

I write these words, but I know that to some extent, they are poetic ideals and I haven't yet made that request with my whole heart. My prayer is more compromised: "O Lord, may I worship You without too much effort or pain, without being jeered at by nondevotees, without much physical suffering or austerity . . . and may I go back to Godhead after this life?" That's really the way I pray. I have to learn to do better. O Lord of the universe, as the Ganges flows down to the sea unobstructed, so let my love flow to You. Again Queen Kuntī.

Hare Kṛṣṇa.

There is no yogurt this morning. My breakfast will consist of a pear, an apple, and two bananas. I could put a little jam on the plate if I desired. Simple, but enough to fill the belly. Hare Kṛṣṇa

Hare Kṛṣṇa.

I was worried I wouldn't be able to chant fully—I thought the pain was coming—but I squeaked through okay. Now I am sailing along relatively free. Madhu will be back today, then tomorrow is our last full day here. Hare Kṛṣṇa, Hare Kṛṣṇa. I want to pack my suitcases so that the customs people don't know my inner intent.

Hare Kṛṣṇa mantra, both ancient and modern. It is the mantra for bringing control and higher ethics and is truly the way to attain love of God—the way and the goal.

"Now I will have to tell your mother that you dribbled your breakfast down your bib and spit out your food. Mother will tell Father when he comes home, and he will beat you." I was afraid of that when I read the baby book my parents gave me when I was a toddler. The drawings showed a baby in a high chair spitting out his food—that was his offense—and the words said he would be reported to his father. I don't think the father beat him in the book, but it scared me nonetheless. Hare Kṛṣṇa. I couldn't figure it out, but I did learn that life was complicated.

Rādhā and Kṛṣṇa are going to market. Rādhā and Kṛṣṇa are in divine play. Rādhā and Kṛṣṇa have nothing to do. If God *has* to do something, then what kind of God can He be? He is Nanda-suta or Nanda-tanuja, the son of Nanda. God has no mother and father, but when He comes to the world He accepts parents.

"Why did you print my letter?"

"I don't go to the temple," she said, "but I chant Hare Kṛṣṇa anyway."

He said, "I am feeling low. I have to collect all this money. I don't think other devotees are forced to work like I am. Some of them get to go to Vṛndāvana."

Kṛṣṇa is the source of the *Vedas* and He is the *Vedas* personified. He is giving us the sun, yet ungrateful men do not thank Him even for a glass of water, although we would thank an ordinary person. Kṛṣṇa is both close and far away.

5:15 A.M.

The purpose of the *Vedas* is to understand Kṛṣṇa.

Faith: It seems an over-simplification to say, "Accept the *Vedas*." You can "accept" them (not be rebellious toward *śāstra*) since you have vowed to do that (fourth offense in chanting). Take this statement: "The Supreme Lord is situated as Paramātmā in everyone's heart, and it is from Him that all activities are initiated." (Bg. 15.15, purport) Do you believe it?

"Yes," you say, but what does such a "yes" actually mean? Can you explain the essence of the purport?

"Yes," you say, "I can explain it." And you proceed to give an intellectual description of the purport's contents. But have you experienced that essence? Have you proved to yourself that Paramātmā is present in the heart and that all activities are initiated by Him?

"Yes," you say, and I'm glad. This is not a doubt session, but an examination of faith.

We can also look at it the other way around. We could ask why I am interrogating you about your faith. Faith cannot always be inspected by reason. Śrīla Prabhupāda states again and again that a devotee simply accepts the authority of the *Vedas*. "Regarding those things that are beyond the mind to comprehend, it is useless to argue," Prabhupāda said. Or, *tarko 'pratiṣṭhaḥ śrutayo vibhinnā* . . . Neither the use of logic nor the study of the *Vedas* can give us the Absolute Truth. The Absolute Truth is hidden in the hearts of realized saints and sages. *Mahājano yena gataḥ sa panthāḥ:* follow them and find it.

The *Vedas* state that all *jīvas* in the material world are fallible and undergo six changes. "According to the statement of the Supreme Personality of Godhead, Lord Kṛṣṇa, there are two classes of living entities. The *Vedas* give evidence of this, so there is no doubt about it." (Bg. 15.16, purport) Before 1966 I didn't accept the *Vedas*. Most people in the world don't accept them now. It doesn't matter. This is a personal philosophy. I don't really need to play around with intellectual challenges. I would rather look up and see the pink smudges coming through the clouds. The sky is a beautiful light blue behind the layers of thick fleece. The lake water is two shades of green. Why don't I take a walk? Let those other thoughts go up the chimney.

8:05 A.M.

Colder today. Good for an arm-swinging walk while I chant. I'm glad I have this coat. Know who gave it to me?

Thought of Vancouver. One thought led to another, and not all of them were pleasant. The thoughts become roadblocks to turn me in one direction or another.

Leaves still falling. The collie walked with me for a while, then disappeared. I like his detachment. I gave him a pat on the head.

12:12 P.M.

Madhu is back. He had a heavy weekend, meeting with his three daughters and his son. What can it be like, plunging back into that? On the return trip he met a woman from Chile and a man from Mexico and preached to both of them. He also went busking in London Friday night with his fiddler. He said the people he met were mean, the Londoners. Still, he's game for adventure.

3:05 P.M.

Clean up paint jars, etc., in shed, and take most of them back into the house. Even when we come back at the end of January, we will not spend much time here. We'll move soon south to Ireland. O Kṛṣṇa, I would like to dip regularly into *Bhagavad-gītā* while I'm away. Sunshine glinting in this window a last time.

Śrīla Prabhupāda says Kṛṣṇa feels the pain of separation from us more than we feel the pain of separation from Him. Kṛṣṇa *wants* to be with us.

The Supreme Person is above the fallible and infallible souls. His extended Viṣṇu form is Paramātmā in the heart. He resides in the spiritual planets. Please go on hearing if you wish to join Him. If you must doubt, then express it and struggle with it honestly. Pray and yearn for the clearing of doubt. Prayers are always answered.

I want to read in faith and let the tears of contrition come—tears because I could not attain pure Kṛṣṇa consciousness. In the meantime, let me always sacrifice my life to attain the goal. All glories to the Lord of the universe who, in His original form, plays with the cows and *gopīs* in Vṛndāvana.

"Whoever knows Me as the Supreme Personality of Godhead, without doubting, is the knower of everything. He therefore engages himself in full devotional service to Me, O son of Bharata." (Bg. 15.19) Speculation and doubt are a waste of time because even after many years, those who indulge in it will fail to understand that Kṛṣṇa is the Supreme Personality of Godhead. So states the *smṛti. Ayi nanda.*

Now my mind like Madhu's has shifted almost entirely to the task of packing and then departing. Within I feel the fear that turns me toward silent chanting. I let go, but not of Kṛṣṇa. Nothing else counts. I go through the motions of having personal relationships, but my mind is more and more turned toward the spiritual seeking. I want—I *want*—I bypass material desires to find the core: Kṛṣṇa consciousness according to my own capacity, something I cannot fully express except for in one sincere utterance of the Hare Kṛṣṇa mantra and a submissive hearing of devotional literature.

The windows are fogging up, so I had better turn off the heat. It's already getting dark, but I still have time for a poem at least.

What about these half-finished drawings? Should I just draw a hasty face out of the colorful chaos? Attach a holy word fragment? A *tilaka* stamp?

Yes, if I must. What else am I *looking* for? Express train to Kṛṣṇa, express to my heart.

Drew a man with sunglasses, a raven, a blue heron, my skinny neck (do I still think I'm a young man? No delusions, please.)

Now, a poem. To clear away the fog.

CRYING OUT LOUD

𝄞 Overcome the inner noise
The place is my head—a
noisy venue
where we used to do
where I used to be exploited
where I still dream
confused.

Now I can play a tune on a kazoo
or wooden recorder

I have a soul, a brand new
bag-a-roo

silent night/ silent boy—I
was alone all weekend and
can account for it
in pages
written
each one.

I want to *now*
be a devotee and
a real person to
bow down
put myself out
pull myself free
of sense grat—although
I can't yet claim perfect success.

My master wants it and
    I want to reach
him. Don't hold me back

with light chatter. I'm on an inner road
and already can't find my way
the subterranean heart/
is sure hard
to find.

Squeeze, don't hurt, and
go to Kṛṣṇa. My master said
when he took my money and
my mango I looked dirty,

crazy
and I was.
But he remembers me,
I know.
    O Kṛṣṇa, Kṛṣṇa, Kṛṣṇa,
    Lord of the *gopīs*
I tried my best in this
my poem. ‖

4:07 P.M.

This might be the last time I'll be in this shed. My bag is chock full of things I'm carrying back. If I have a clear head I'll come out one more time tomorrow. More songs from me, more music. I just wrote about how at the end I ought to kick off my baggage. I'm worried that I won't be able to renounce the paraphernalia and genres and literary expressions I've been using and accumulating. Think of Bhaktivinoda Ṭhākura shutting the door, donning a *bābājī's* white, and spending his last weeks completely internal. I don't have that kind of inner life, and I don't know if I will get the same warning. I know what it's like when the head closes me down. I'm sure Kṛṣṇa will take me in one way or another. He's much more than a judge; He has already given me so much mercy. So much pain in this body—and then there's the mental pain and the world's pain. But as Prabhupāda says about great souls, they transcend suffering. They're not *of* this world (where all the pain is).

Of this world—green-grass Ireland, gray-blue sky, like Śyāmasundara. Keep walking and let blood flow and pound for Kṛṣṇa. Hare Kṛṣṇa, Hare Kṛṣṇa, Kṛṣṇa Kṛṣṇa, Hare Hare.

December 2

5:45 A.M.

After an exceptionally light week last week—six days pain free—this present week has begun just the opposite. Last night I had sharp pain all night and it's still here.

Dreamt a company reissued a jazz album that had come out in the '60s. There was then a live performance of the same music done as a Hare Kṛṣṇa benefit. My memories were stirred and I was excited to tell the devotees what had happened—how whenever the musicians would come out, we would beat our drums fast and it would turn into a *kīrtana*.

2:26 P.M.

Long hard day for me. Wanted to do things but couldn't because of the pain. It's like an ice cube behind my eye, or something prodding at a sensitive area. I have been told that blood is squeezing through a too-tight artery, but why should it hurt so much? Because I identify with the body?

The day used up. M. and I are entirely into the upcoming travel. All I can think about are the various details of our move—tomorrow to Dublin and then Friday to New York. Thank you, Lord, for these past two months. You have blessed them, I know. And I know this pain is somehow part of a plan to release me from birth and death.

I know nothing of my actual position, whether I stand a chance of going back to Godhead or have millions of lifetimes. But since the qualification is single-minded devotion to Kṛṣṇa, how can I claim *that*? I do wish to be brought up to that position. You know how, dear Lord.

THE SEMI-INVALID ASKS FOR A BREAK

(I'm afraid of heavy emotions, you know. What can I say?)

𝄞 Music is a trip, of course, and we don't
have to be afraid if we have our own
souls
are our own gurus—take ourselves
to surrender
at Prabhupāda's feet. We *don't* have to
be afraid
but
this world is scary
despite that solace.

The sunshine is out on this
my last day. I had better find Lord Kṛṣṇa
in all I do.

No other way, friend, but these
music notes and
hoping my secret file

will allow
        God consciousness to filter through
every inch of what I do.
        You have to get into the car—you
don't know if it will make it or not—
        then a plane—even more dangerous.

Lord, that prayer—Hare Kṛṣṇa in chant—
is all I have within me I
don't know anything
else.

Scared, the inner man
hides, bluffs from the outside,
plays "guru retired,"
expects care in return
for wisdom lectures.
He behaves, they say, and they hope
he is taking them somewhere
to Prabhupāda
at least.
He's respectable enough.

But I can't do it, wind down, lie
in bed, a pain in that place behind
the eye. I can't do all the things
I want or
have the things
others want. Even my mind
I can't keep under control.

        "Go down, go down, why
don't you go down?" I coax the pain
or blood—whatever it is, the cause—but
        it has it's own life
and will leave only when
the medicine chases it.

I'm half sick with pain—no strength—
but I'll tell you this:
when Kṛṣṇa says, I will go
down.
So give this semi-invalid
with the jazzy soul
a break.

3:25 P.M.

Last time in shed for sure. The door was swollen and hard to push shut. It has gotten quite cold, although this last day is bright with sunshine. Let me get through packing and my remaining aches. O Kṛṣṇa, where are You? I ask Your forgiveness. You have given me my penance.

We all love the strong faith of a yea-sayer. O Kṛṣṇa. I am a blues man and don't want to betray what You have given me. Please forgive my complaining, but I seemed to need to get it out. I know love will find its way into my heart by Your grace.

Walking up the green path, I see the collie at the top of the hill. He's sure going nowhere tomorrow, neither to Dublin and certainly not to New York in *this* lifetime. He can't even dream of it. The birds, of course, can fly, but Madhu said there'll come a time when I won't be traveling at all. I'm not sure when that will be.

4:55 P.M.

So dark. Water and trees, with bony fingers. The earth green.

The Lord Reigneth

Every Day, Just Write

Volume 17

December 3–22, 1997

Satsvarūpa dāsa Goswami

GN Press, Inc.

December 3, 1997

12:08 A.M.

"Besides these two, there is the greatest living personality, the Supreme Soul, the imperishable Lord Himself, who has entered the three worlds and is maintaining them." (Bg. 15.17)

"Oh yeah?" the skeptic scoffs. "You expect me to believe that?"

I expect you to sit in the back seat of the car during the drive to Dublin. That's all. Four of us are going. Ask the front seat passenger, Śyāmānanda, to keep the driver, Arjuna, awake while I fall asleep in the back seat. We expect to make good time, but you never know. As for disbelief in God—you, whoever you are who said that, "Oh yeah?," why don't you put your intelligence to better use?

O Kṛṣṇa, may we always hear your words and insist upon their truth with faith and intelligence.

I have discovered over the last few years—and this is not a terrible thing—that my work in this life is not to gather extensive knowledge of śāstric details but to learn and preach faith. We should pray to Kṛṣṇa to reveal Himself to us. We should pray to Prabhupāda to reveal himself to us in his books. We should face the challenge of doubt and live with whatever unresolved problems exist in us, but at every moment we should approach Kṛṣṇa with whatever faith we have and surrender. "Whoever knows Me as the Supreme Personality of Godhead, without doubting, is the knower of everything, and therefore engages himself in full devotional service to Me, O son of Bharata." (Bg. 15.19) Prabhupāda: "But if anyone, after speculating for hundreds of thousands of lives, does not come to the point that Kṛṣṇa is the Supreme Personality of Godhead and that one has to surrender there, all his speculation for so many years and lives is a useless waste of time."

GOD AND THE RIVER

𝄞 There's a way we all know—
hey, don't tell. Be alone and
listen. Woodshed.

If you are alive among people in
crowded houses, be secret
live inner, private, write and send the message
        this way.

Old man river keeps rolling past
the tragedy of wasted lives, and
        he don't do nothin' about it.
He jes' keeps rolling along.
        Indifferent nature of the mighty
        waterways
like Time itself
simply witnessing
speaking not.

O Lord in the heart You
are not quite indifferent or why
would you sit in each one of us?

They say we shouldn't protest
man's inhumanity to man, but I
protest, I speak by being a devotee
of Kṛṣṇa and preaching among the ignorant
starting with myself.

O Kṛṣṇa, I know nothing, but please
give me the right
to know You.
I'm tired of these doubts and want
blessed space—peace, to be
one-pointed
centered on You
in all I do
despite pains and limits
the body no good
and finally dead. ‖

DOWN BY THE RIVERSIDE

𝄞 Let's go down to the river
and sing religious—see
God in all things
in the company of His sincere
devotees.

I pray to be allowed
another day to be His like that
to be true in the world of false—
that's His world too, I know and Lord,
I don't mock it as Nothing.

I pray to know that other world that
sanātana, the millions of them
and I wish to go there
when I kick off all that clings to me
here. O Kṛṣṇa, will You help?

Down by the river we'll
hold *kīrtana*, honor *prasādam*
the Indian way—in Slovenia,
Nārada's transcendental way in Ohio
feel the triumph.

Down by the river of the
self I'll cry and play my horn
and do the dance
I've known for years
learned by His protection
His love, my dance of
gratitude.
Please take me home.

9:10 A.M.

You don't know what to write? I'm no Merton oppressed, cornered in a monastery and vowed to follow an abbot who doesn't understand me. I am removed from all that. Or am I?

I follow the GBC's resolutions and viewpoints; I'm part of a system that has made me a guru. I must live up to that. I follow my spiritual master as absolutely as possible by conscience and social custom. No other force is necessary to keep me in line. If I step out of line, it will be obvious.

In a more private sense, I am freer. I could say I conform outwardly while maintaining a private life, although I publish from my private life. What would I do if I had no one to answer to? Absurd. If I had no one to answer to, I would be God.

Okay, what if you had no *earthly* person to answer to? Everything could be measured by you and your responses to

God. Also absurd. Too much speculation. We are all followers in any case.

As I write this, M. is at the American Embassy in Dublin. We left Inis Rath at 4 A.M.; twenty minutes later he said he forgot his medical papers and we had to go back. Somehow we remained cool (*cold*, in the car), and I didn't complain once. Arjuna and Śyāmānanda were particularly saintly—no complaints. When we returned to the house and M. went inside, I tried warming my feet and said to Arjuna, "The conditioned souls make mistakes" (referring to M.'s forgetting). Arjuna replied, "Yes, I make so many myself."

When we were again underway, I started a conversation to deflect my silent resentment for the delay. The mental disturbance was silly, I know, and the conversation was interesting—we spoke of *Bhagavad-gītā*, of Inis Rath, even of my attitude toward my health. We arrived forty minutes late. So what?

It's no big deal whether or not M. gets his green card. He has no intention of residing in the U.S., but he wants to be able to come and go as we do every year in peace. His applying for residence almost seems a provision for the future—in case I ever decide to stay in America.

LOOKING OUT A FROST-MELTING WINDOW

(In Dublin at a desk, facing a frost-melting window . . . a busy town instead of the quiet lake)

𝄞 An angry man is nevertheless an artist
I don't know what you mean.

Well it's like this—everyone has to go
to work.
Except me.

Signboards—a guy who could kill
you, a dissolute young beauty—a
woman. They flash by so
fast I can't see, and don't try to see
anyway, from the back seat.

Millions of offices and schools and
people on the streets, dreamers and
hard workers, those who curse and
the priests who bless, people on the dole—
plenty of them—and even more
in the pubs even this early.

O priest and your congregation,
Are you an angel of mercy? Is your heart
sacred? Yes, I
sit apart.

I am an ancient one, a rune, an act
of digestion, a pancake *muni* and
critic of lectures, a shorthand clerk
short-order cook-poet.

Wry master, posing
novelist, but shivering
in my boots.
What I do is
matter-of-fact.

It's cold and I am definitely in
this body. Hey Hari Hare
Kṛṣṇa. No lion here just
a toothless hyena a
baby polecat, both
skinny and fat like the actor
poorly cast
who
played Gaurakiśora dāsa Bābājī
in the film.

Am I self-centered? It's because
I can't see out the window and
I know no one else.

Except in dreams, and there
I'm not safe, ever, but running,
praying that they don't become
flesh and blood reality.
Alfred E. Neuman, Prufrock,
Milquetoast, Mr. Magoo
Mr. Peepers, an angry
Archie Shepp, James Dean,
Sonny Rollins, Tommy Oakland, me
treading on snow with my own
four hundred in the bank
circa 1964. Dreams. Now in
solitary confinement.
(At least they bring lunch.)

O readers who face bitter trials,
any heavy storm could knock
out the lines.
Pray to God just
pray to God.

I mean it.
And that's it from this
    wounded lion, from
    the influence of my soul
    the child's cry as
frost clears and I see
a row of houses. ‖

10:55 A.M.

"This is the most confidential part of the Vedic scriptures, O sinless one, and it is disclosed now by Me. Whoever understands this will become wise, and his endeavors will know perfection." (Bg. 15.20) The knowledge referred to here is that Śrī Kṛṣṇa is the Supreme Personality of Godhead. Do I call the inner world inner knowledge? It's transcendental. It's in the *śāstra* and I accept it.

11:00 A.M., but no Prabhupāda *pūjā*. I left him in "*samādhi*" in that cold, dark room at Manu's house locked up. I dressed him warmly first, of course. I'll continue to offer food to him wherever I am. Same with Rādhā-Govinda. Think of Them; the photos will help. Hare Kṛṣṇa.

"Devotional service to the Lord and the Lord Himself are one and the same because they are spiritual; devotional service takes place within the internal energy of the Supreme Lord." (Bg. 15.20, purport) Did I used to be able to feel statements like that better than now? Merton says, regarding his compilation of the Desert Fathers' sayings, "It would be futile to skip through these pages and lightly take note of the fact that Fathers said this and this. What good will it do us to know merely that such things were once *said*? The important thing is that they were lived. That they flow from an experience of the deeper levels of life."

I want to live what I read too, with hope and faith. Maybe I once had a more naive faith in what "the Swami said," to the degree that I either misunderstood him or misunderstood myself. And my faith was extremely simple in the beginning. When I would read, edited by the early editors of *Bhagavad-gītā*, that there was a planet of trees *(pitṛs)*, I thought, "Why not? It's *all* inconceivable, right?" I believed such things on the understanding that Kṛṣṇa consciousness was way beyond my experience. If any doubted, I was prepared to smash them. It seemed so much easier that way than what I feel now.

3:02 P.M.

Śrīla Prabhupāda writes that once you come to devotional service, you automatically arrive at the stage of sinlessness. We are ushered into such purity by following the four rules.

But there are other sins. For example, isn't it a sin not to attain love of God? To remain attached to self and body?

These are sins of omission. How does Kṛṣṇa count it all up? What about weakness of heart? Prabhupāda defined weakness of heart as coming under the influence of *māyā's* throwing and covering potencies. Just another form of material attachment. O spirit soul, rise above it all and become transcendental to the modes.

Chilly in this room despite the heater, and chilly in my heart too, despite the fact that I spent the afternoon reading. There was so much noise in the house—the children in the bathroom calling, "Daddy!" Cheerful, they were, and Madhu cheerful too, playing his melodeon and talking on the telephone. He is to pick up his green card at 4. Now it's quiet—everyone seems to have gone. Chant and hear and keep alive.

SWING LOW

(Alone at last, I hear a train horn, but otherwise a lonely spiritual in my head and blood. Remember "Swing Low, Sweet Chariot"?)

𝄞 Swing low, sweet chariot.
A simple rescue at the end?
Sweet Jesus—I don't know.
All I know is that I have been taught
to cling to the mother like a baby
monkey.

But seriously. You know, you gotta work in
this life and be a man, accept what comes.
You gotta cry to God almighty
God sweet Kṛṣṇa
        the central secret of existence
no matter what the material
world deals up.

It'll be Hare Kṛṣṇa through an
empty room an

empty heart
chanting mantras and not knowing
where I lost
myself—*somewhere*—oh,
old man
you gotta laugh.

I looked over yonder and
what did I see? Not much—
just the sun so bright I couldn't
look again
going down over Dublin's row
houses and
coming for to carry me home.
I am grateful no matter what
form that chariot that
remembrance
appears.

LISTENING ALONE

𝄞 I'm on my way wild Irish
rose, I'm taking you to where I'll go
across the world to listen in

roaming rooms everywhere
saying God God
quiet
God
I didn't have to decide anything it
was all decided for me.

O Kṛṣṇa, I'm not courageous
but if I could know why you told how
the *gopīs*, cows
everyone

Your flute—
Kṛṣṇa's flute—*I* didn't hear
anything.

O Prabhupāda, I typed your
Kṛṣṇa book with my own hands
and I came alive.

When Kṛṣṇa plays His flute
the calves stopped sucking,
the *gopīs* and demigods' wives
felt conjugal attraction
and I listen to *that*
    oh my.

PUKKA PAD SHORTY, ACTIVE IMAGINATION, EPISODE 1

"Kṛṣṇa is God, you see? It says so in the preface to the *Kṛṣṇa* book."

"But I don't believe that," said Henry Grimes.

Well Sats did, and he was joined by a Godbrother and a spiritual son who wanted to believe too, all believers in the Vedic *śāstras.*

Śyāmānanda's uncle is a Catholic priest. I met him on Inis Rath two years ago at the open house they held. He and a friend walked through the wooded path and saw the unusual species a previous owner had worked hard to gather, a dog full of teeth barking outside.

Are you getting sleepy yet?

I hear a factory whistle, or is it a train. It's twenty minutes to 5:00.

You were saying?

Kṛṣṇa is the Godhead because He is, and no one could equal Him. Atheists don't accept. I beg for mercy.

Police siren. We're a long way from the ambiance of Geaglum. Oh, 'twas nice there. I'm letting it reach me here.

The perennial question: Am I worse off than ever before? Or is this normal? Still honest. What little I can embrace of my spiritual life is sweet, real. Kṛṣṇa is the Supreme Person, beyond the fallible and the infallible, and this is the most confidential part of all Vedic literature, and I already know it. Imagine that.

Adolf Eichmann admitted belief in God just before he was hanged. Did he lie?

O *Kṛṣṇa* book, I put you down and pick you up again. Your characters don't sit in stiff, fold-up chairs to wait for someone to come back to the house. Your characters are active, imaginative servants, happy.

Six fairies, two poor boys—get Wisdom of the Heart (*sophia*). Kṛṣṇa consciousness was around long before Constantinople.

Kids out playing in this housing development until the last light. Their voices sound Irish. It gets dark early. The same dog yapping everywhere I go—Bombay, Geaglum, Second Avenue during the Swami's lectures. We are a United Nations of barking dogs.

5:45 P.M.

I have been noting down whenever I read Śrīla Prabhupāda stating superlatives about Kṛṣṇa as the Supreme Personality of Godhead. And sometimes I (or my subpersons) have been voicing doubts. I don't seem to have such fully faithful, single-minded love of Kṛṣṇa. I seem to need to wrestle with God, or at least with my mind *about* God. I guess that's all right. I don't want anything else in life. I admit I lack desire (*laulyam*) to love Kṛṣṇa, but I keep asking myself (and Kṛṣṇa) why this is so—why I can't enter the loving network, why that loving network can't enter me.

I think constantly about how I fall short. I talk constantly about my lack of Kṛṣṇa consciousness. As soon as I get started, the words just keep coming: then, "Kṛṣṇa Kṛṣṇa"—love of Kṛṣṇa.

Reading the preface of *Kṛṣṇa* book, I find so many sentences upon which to ruminate, each pregnant with meaning:

"Since Kṛṣṇa is all-attractive, one should know that all his desires should be focused on Kṛṣṇa."

"The art of focusing one's attention on the Supreme and giving one's love to Him is called Kṛṣṇa consciousness."

"But the real fact is that people can be happy only by loving Kṛṣṇa."

"One can love Kṛṣṇa as the Supreme unknown, . . . "

"Whatever percentage of Kṛṣṇa consciousness we can perform will become an eternal asset to our life, for it is imperishable in all circumstances."

Do these statements sound dogmatic to me? Yes, sometimes. I feel frustrated that they're not real enough to me, even though I do accept them theoretically. So many possible responses. I know eventually my resistance will be worn down. " . . . and ultimately, by reading this one book, *Kṛṣṇa*, love of Godhead will fructify."

6:05 P.M.

I was flicking ink from the pen to the page to get an "artistic" effect. A small drop stained my new sweatshirt. "Oh!" I exclaimed, and hurried to remove it with soap and water. I can still see a trace of a stain. Ink also on my forefinger. Might as well live with it. Did I want to present a stain-free image to the people I meet on my travels? "Look at that neat Hare Kṛṣṇa man." As if anyone would notice. It's my emblem as an ink splasher, and that's nothing to be ashamed of. Even if I die ink-stained, Kṛṣṇa will accept me if I used it in His service.

This is the travel book. It's not a neat novel starting off with drama and a fast pace. Not that kind of book at all. I could write a hundred pages about just sitting in Dublin for two days.

December 4

12:10 A.M.

The effect of the dream I had last night was strong. It was the first time I remember my devotee identity in a dream being so strong. I felt that I was being given a clear indication of what I should do with my remaining years. In the dream, demons were being reborn and no one could be saved from them. In one scene, they turned on me and I ran away. I fell exhausted and stripped of strength, but my last remaining power was that I could choose not to be part of it. I began to chant with my breath: Hare Kṛṣṇa, Hare Kṛṣṇa, Kṛṣṇa Kṛṣṇa, Hare Hare/ Hare Rāma, Hare Rāma, Rāma Rāma, Hare Hare.

When I was dreaming, I saw my life as not concentrated or potent compared to what it could be. Of course, I am aware of my lack of focus, and I lament that often. I seem to have no choice right now. But the dream offered a possible breakthrough. I *can* change my life and make it more concentrated by chanting as I did in the dream—on the exhalation and inhalation of each breath. My writing is not going to help people as much as I can help them if I was more Kṛṣṇa conscious—and the dream showed me how to attain that by constant chanting—chanting to save my life. Such chanting can save me, and it can save others.

This reminds me of what I read in Merton's journal, where he repeatedly thought his writing might be a distraction from his attaining deep contemplation and disappearance of the self into God's love.

Thinking practically, it occurred to me that not only would it be good for me to take on more than sixteen rounds, but I could speak from *Nāmāmṛta* while in the Caribbean. Perhaps I should give up my writing and concentrate only on chanting. It's not that I got a strong feeling that I *should* give up my writing, but it was an undeniable fact (in the dream) that only when I chanted did I discover the most important deterrent to the reality of the demons. By chanting, I escaped them and escaped annihilation. Chanting has that power, and the dream hinted to me how to break through the impasse where I have no taste or real experience of Kṛṣṇa consciousness.

I don't usually like to increase my *japa* quota because it puts more pressure on my day, and thus becomes another thing that could cause headaches. That's why I thought of possibly considering reducing my writing, because *that* is so time-consuming and requires so much energy. The little energy I have left after headaches and near-headaches could be used to chant and read prayerfully.

Actually, there is no need for me to stop writing, but I should use it more to help myself in spiritual life. Don't write for popularity or think the published books will bring immortality. I have already written so much. Why not try now to experience chanting?

3:35 A.M.

Chanted sixteen rounds, but felt no sign of that urgency like in the dream or during my reflections on it. I think I will chant extra rounds today. I would like to honor the mood of the dream message.

NOBODY KNOWS

𝄞 Nobody knows the troubles I've seen
just because I'm one and you each are too.
That's just the way it is.
Well, brother, I don't mean to say
I've had it so hard—my yoke as heavy as
a pure devotee's
but I have my own pathos—a personal
threshold of pain and
sorrow
that no one else
can feel.
    Although the doctor or
shrink or priest or Hare Kṛṣṇa confessor assures us
    that we just got a little hepatitis, lad,
    a little karma in
your row to hoe,
that we don't need to bother about it
and don't forget
to pay at the desk,
we frown, wear baggy pants
a *sannyāsī* with a silly grin,
wanting breakfast on time.
Tragedy. ‖

PUKKA PAD SHORTY, ACTIVE IMAGINATION, EPISODE 2

Sitting by a cold window, feeling the outdoor freeze.

"Turn up the heat, Henry!" he called to his roommate, tousle-haired Henry Grimes, who was still in bed.

"Can I wash my pants and have them dry by tomorrow?"

After serious deliberation, the secretary said, "No promises."

To talk of many things—shoes and ships and
sealing wax
of cabbages
and kings.

It sure is cold. I wouldn't want to be out there, homeless.

Ah, but do you care for others? To love another you have to become that person to some degree. A Christian writer said that.

We Hare Kṛṣṇas love others by selling books.

Love is for Kṛṣṇa. "Pick a girl," Prabhupāda said, pointing out his window to the street below, but love is for Kṛṣṇa.

He's outliving Chet Baker. Don't know about Lieutenant Commander Richardson.

No, no, this
has to be made
clearer.

Oh, boy, we're each so different, especially in our opinions, but the captain insists we chant our rounds, all except for Junior, since he's only three years old. Bob-Nārāyaṇa was ordered to give Junior his bath and not to make the water too cold or too hot.

As usual, the captain has his way, at least externally, but there sure is a lot of grumbling around here and people living in secret worlds, doing subversive things that affect the whole family.

I'm just reporting in. As you know, everyone talks about dreams that end with us chanting Hare Kṛṣṇa on *prāṇa.*

"Oh, that'll be the day," Henry joked, singing in imitation of Buddy Holly, "Yeah, that'll be the day that I die!"

We're a loving family after all.

5:33 A.M.

I appreciate that you are grasping for faith. It is both good and bad when you read words like "Garbodakaśāyī Viṣṇu" and you ask if they're true, whether there really is such a form as Mahā-Viṣṇu from whom all the universes come. It's good you want to verify it in yourself, actually feel the truth of it, and not accept it merely in a conventional way as if it's "our religion." It's not good, however, that you still entertain doubt that the Viṣṇus, the creation, and the spiritual world are possibly mythical. You have no choice but to read and grasp for *śraddhā.* Giving up is not an option.

I appropriated two books I found here: a handy but decently printed edition of *Bhagavad-gītā As It Is* and the first volume of *Kṛṣṇa* book. I have already put transparent plastic covers on them. I will read them all the way to the Caribbean. Nothing left to do before we go but to rearrange our packing items, sleep, eat, meet with one devotee, and then another.

11:08 A.M.

I answered a batch of Vyāsa-pūjā letters from Wicklow. Now I'm too scattered to do anything concentrated, including reading.

This morning after my dream, I thought I could stop writing and give my time to chanting and reading. Now I realize that for me to do that would be the same as becoming a *bābājī.* Writing is my main preaching. A devotee wrote me a letter stating that my personal example is more important than the books I write. That may be true. The comment reminds me of the Japanese poet-priest Gensei, who called morality the root trunk of the tree, and writing-literature the branches and fruit. If I weren't a practicing disciple and aspiring Kṛṣṇaite, my writing would be in vain, even if I could be very honest. I know I sometimes write like a jack-in-the-box suddenly springing out with, "Hare Kṛṣṇa! I want to follow my master! Everybody be a devotee!" That's better than being on my own in the unknown, I suppose. There is enough unknown even for one who tries to follow the *śāstra.* For example, one doesn't know if he is doing right, doesn't know where he's going in his next life, and his worshipable Lord remains Unknown, never fully knowable.

THOUGHTS COMING TOGETHER BEFORE LUNCH

1

𝄞 Things and people are favorable but
the astrologer says
if you go South it'll be a disaster,
There'll be no
mint tea.

Go east instead
to that secret place
where Kṛṣṇa is
the treasure
buried. Don't look
to the north, unless you're going
to see Rādhā-Govinda alone in Their alcove
in a house near a lake strait.

My voice is hoarse and
the kids in this house have chicken pox.
I once yearned to be free
of Navy life to
drink liquor
to be
sentimental.

2

A devotee's life is busy but
they call us a cult. We don't care.
They have nothing like what
the Swami gave
in his own sweet voice. A contributor-
poet said she sent three

poems but they printed only
two and
was disturbed.
But you know, two out of three ain't bad.
Keep your wig on.

O my Kṛṣṇa my
Rādhā—I want out
screamed the man and
I took it well; I knew just what he meant
and tried to remember
it myself.

3

Honest—surrender is a thorny path
especially for those
who seek ease, love, nourishment
but selfishly
like when she told me something important
that a guru should hear
I didn't hear it. Later she was more
polite, as if I cared—so
selfish,
non-lover.

It's unusual that this lion
roars from his bush.
Doc, I'm moved when I hear *your* anger
your hurt. I know
you are running out of time
and I can only limp along
in this bad neighborhood
no money
a naked sixty years old
aware
in my dreams.

4

All right, be calm
you too, and speak what
Kṛṣṇa says—the
qualification of a speaker
really. He's just got to say
what it says in the books,
has to have the guts for that.
        As for *feeling* the truth . . .

What hurts is when he
doesn't believe or is bored
out of joint and
passes that on
to us—but worse
is the blind autocrat the
dictator who rams it down
our throat.

Sweet Kṛṣṇa speaking
I am no longer afraid
to hear You. ||

Dreamt I was back in the Navy PIO office. As things developed, the office was crowded with workers, but I had no engagement at all. I was bluffing, picking up papers and cleaning, talking to people. I didn't even know who my supervisor was. I thought of telling someone I had nothing to do, but I didn't want him to give me *too* much. It was insane the way I was just there, feeling sorry for myself that I had no engagement, and being stuck back in the Navy against my will. I kept wondering if I should confess my lack of engagement, or wait until they discovered it and discharged me themselves.

4:24 P.M.

All the Viṣṇus appear within the body of original Kṛṣṇa when He appears. I would love to accept such statements the way the cobbler who spoke with Nārada did. He had faith that everything was possible for God, and he saw, even in the simple example of the oak tree appearing from an acorn, how God can do the inconceivable. Why not? Why *can't* all the Viṣṇus be within Kṛṣṇa? It's not a matter of Kṛṣṇa following material physical laws. *Get that prejudice out of your head.* Kṛṣṇa has been kind to me in this life because I know almost nothing about actual physics. I wouldn't know a quark from a black hole. I only know that the Viṣṇus come when Kṛṣṇa appears because that's what Prabhupāda says in his introduction to *Kṛṣṇa* book.

When Kṛṣṇa kills demons in Vṛndāvana, it is not original Kṛṣṇa who does that work—original Kṛṣṇa doesn't work—but Vāsudeva Kṛṣṇa, an expansion of the original Kṛṣṇa. Vāsudeva Kṛṣṇa also speaks on the battlefield of Kurukṣetra and performs other activities outside of Vṛndāvana. "Kṛṣṇa actually appears in order to demonstrate His Vṛndāvana pastimes and to attract the fortunate conditions souls and invite them back home, back to Godhead." *(Kṛṣṇa*, Introduction, p. 3)

Peter Pan flew in the sky with Wendy and the kids (in their pajamas), but that's make-believe. Are U.S. and Russian spacecraft real? I don't actually know. What about the *Bhagavad-gītā* description that "there is another unmanifest nature, which is eternal and is transcendental to this manifested and unmanifested matter"? Do we listen to Kṛṣṇa or to such pundits as Carl Sagan and Stephen Hawking? *They* think there is nothing out there but star dust. O faith, please come to me.

I got a big stain on my beadbag. It's because this room is so small that I don't know where to put stuff. I put my beadbag on the writing desk next to the pens. A Pilot V7 pen was open and a blue circle of ink soaked into the cloth. I discovered it only when I noticed the blue stain on my *dhotī*, which had soaked in from my beadbag. My beads were also stained blue.

I took time to wash off my beads with soap and water, but the other stains are permanent.

AN EARLY EVENING PRAYER

(A romantic mood . . . for a person about to travel, he knows not what will happen. He has to put his trust in airlines, but it really means he trusts God within. If one could only love.)

𝄞 Inner way with guru
is scary sometimes
but I'm never the controller,
only a weeper a whimper
can't even reach up to
hold his hand.

But no blues—I won't allow it—this
universe is meant to be happy.

As they look at me, either smiling or
frowning, I tell them
that every Sanskrit word bears
meaning is
truth
and we must believe—
and here's why (briefly)—
what Swamiji
says.

They want to know how that tallies
with what they feel. Is that not
required? O dark night
when dreams come and
I am helpless, and bright day,
those doubts—I'm more aware
that I have to fight
those bastards.

This is the way for a heart
to beat one more of countless
times.

I pray for attention and surrender to
Kṛṣṇa's sweet will, sweet names
the Rādhā-Kṛṣṇa festival
on a faraway star
that comes so close when
I fold my hands and
pray to
nāma heaven. ‖

PUKKA PAD SHORTY, EPISODE 3, AN INNER INTERVIEW

"Do you want to go over last night's dream again?"

Not really. The main point was the strong aftermath, the feeling that I really could change my life, that I really could concentrate my breath and chant with the awareness that it really is the only thing that can save me. Could I do it for a whole lifetime? After all, I'm an aspiring devotee, a servant of Kṛṣṇa. I remembered the chanting only when I ran for my life. And now?

When I awoke, I went about my business, not sure if I had been changed deeply. The single-minded resolution seemed unrealistic. There was no need to renounce everything else, I told myself.

That's the letdown—such a stark revelation, an answer to my prayers and strivings, and actually, I rejected its import.

But I did gain *something*. Today I feel more aware that I am struggling with every sentence when I read. I'm not glossing over doubts and pretending I'm attracted. I'm facing it and learning to be real.

It all seems so slow. The dream promised heightened awareness of a devotee's bare reality. How much longer do I have to live? In the meantime, big plans for a man who doesn't know when he will die. Wee Willy Wilkins will write on until he dies. He'll tell them to give his boots to someone who can use them.

Art produced, future reduced, his birthday on the way.

December 5

1:00 A.M.

In a dream I was living next to the Philadelphia temple, but it was a combination of being in the Navy and being a temple devotee. On my way to the temple one morning, I purchased an inexpensive, manual, portable typewriter. Then I worried how I would defend the purchase when I entered the ship-temple. The dream was permeated by legalities and bureaucracy.

1:10 A.M.

Started reading Bg. 18.53. I'll take that book with me on the plane. Kṛṣṇa is describing the good qualities of a tranṣcendentalist, including that he lives in a secluded place. He doesn't become angry when his senses aren't satisfied. Then

18.54 describes how he's above the material modes and eligible for devotional service. As I read, I remembered Śivarāma Swami's explanation of this verse—that it does not apply to "us." We are still under the modes. In one sense, we are not performing pure devotional service. He made a good argument. Śrīla Prabhupāda sometimes was generous in how he allowed us to think we were performing pure devotional service, although he also said that *bhakti* comes after liberation.

My mind then drifted off to a book by an English priest a devotee gave me unsolicited. It's called *Honest To God*, and supposedly contains painful admissions by an insider as to how Christianity has failed. Should I carry it with me? Another burden? Look at it when I return? Why not just stay with what Kṛṣṇa says? He is *para-tattva*. Be true to Him and you'll be honest to God. I want to find a *Bhagavad-gītā* verse to comfort me, just as Gandhi said the verses comforted him: "Those who meditate on the *Gītā* will derive fresh joy and new meanings from it every day." It is not an ordinary book by an ordinary *jīva*, but it is divine revelation and divinely spoken.

I write for myself. As one draws comfort from the *Gītā* in times of doubt, disappointment, and sorrow, I draw solace from my personal expressions. My ability to express how I feel is a gift Kṛṣṇa has given me. I want to use it to reciprocate with Him. I can't write scripture; I am too imperfect. I can't see past, present, and future unless I see *through* the scripture, and I can't even always do that. If I had complete faith and realization of scripture, my vision could be one with the scripture, one with God.

Honest to God, honest to self. When we practice self-examination, we dig a little and try to remain true to what the body and mind say. Eventually, self-examination has to be given up in order to give ourselves fully to Kṛṣṇa for the answers. I don't like to turn entirely away from doubts or to pretend I don't have any. Neither do I want to reject the Vedic direction in the name of self-examination and the discovery of doubts. I make the deliberate choice to admit where I'm at in my gut and with my wavering mind and to refer myself for direction to the absolute source.

Turning to *japa*, I have to whisper. Better to get sixteen done now rather than trying to chant in the crowded *saṅga* of the Aer Lingus economy section. When I'm there, I will try to chant within. "Thank you very much. May Kṛṣṇa save you from calamities. You are very pure."

SWING LOW (TAKE TWO)

(Don't want our chariot to swing *too* low over the Atlantic, but when it's time to go, it's time to go—as Kṛṣṇa likes. May I hold onto His names on the sweet chariot ride.)

𝄞 Swinging sweet Lord
I pray—a fool I be—
that You come and a-carry me home.
You've sent Your trumpet calls, You've sent
Your messengers, sometimes
Your kick to
wake us up—like Indra, when he
became a pig.

December cold but I look yonder and see
with eyes not anointed with love
Your kindness still visible
in all You've given
especially the guidance of my
spiritual master.

O sweet Lord, You have already done it
as You told Arjuna
before he fought.

Your name is the carrier
of souls like me—may I one day

become a ripe harvest
of words and thoughts
and prayerful days spent watching
the sun rise over another dirty town
while chest and head and blood
flow on, confusion and congestion
      temper the yearning spirit
my Lord. ‖

5:54 A.M.

Clock hands move slowly, but around and around they go. The plane will leave on time, they say. Cramped room—too warm. All bags packed except for last items I'm using. Listened to Śrīla Prabhupāda while I ate breakfast. Offered the porridge, apple, and hot milk to his picture on the cover of *Science of Self-Realization.*

PUKKA PAD SHORTY, EPISODE 4, AN IMAGINARY TOUR

Oh, I imagined we went from New York to the Caribbean and back and it was all lovely and I didn't get much older (in fact or in imagination). Rather, I became physically stronger and had a permanent breakthrough to attraction—even addiction—to chanting the holy names.

But it's not true, is it?

No, it's
not so
easy.

Then what's the point of activating your imagination like that? Why get all worked up for an illusion?

Hmm. I *did* write an essay, "Follow Your Dream," where I advised devotees to pursue their personal vision to do something wonderful for Kṛṣṇa. Some dreams, however, are fulfilled over time and not immediately. The real point is that we shouldn't give up on them.

My short-term goal right now is to get through this tour with as little wear and tear as possible, few delays, no problems, no disasters—not even any worries. Hey, that means I have to go Vaikuṇṭha. See? It's all connected.

The truth is, this isn't Vaikuṇṭha, and here I have to endure minute-by-minute weakening and pain that even Esgic cannot allay.

Did you know that Bhaktin Sile wants to go back to acting on stage and Śyāmānanda wants to dance? Madhu is already swinging with his melodeon and bouzouki, singing Irish traditional music, and Rādhānātha is building a glass-blowing studio. Manu and others are discovering their voices in writing. Hare Kṛṣṇa dāsī is in *samādhi* in her backyard garden. Her husband is in his heaven when he's preaching.

So follow *your* dream. Even if there are no free tickets or flying carpets to carry you over the world's many bumps ("the shocks that flesh is heir to").

Imagine . . . we
all make it to pure devotional service.
We learn to encourage each other.
At least we die trying.

It's not a matter of imagining, but śāstric truth: we really are eternal spirit souls. Realization is possible when Kṛṣṇa desires. Until then, keep pushing on in faith.

So spoke Hari-kīrtana dāsānudāsa just before leaving for the Dublin airport for the first leg of his journey.

9:45 A.M.

We had to drive through rush-hour traffic to get to the airport on time. Bhaktin Sile was in such a hurry that she didn't give way to an ambulance. Now we are here, filling out U.S. customs forms. Country of residence? Ireland—a house where Hare Kṛṣṇa devotees live in Dublin.

Irish Diaspora—a photo display at the airport: forty-two million Americans claim Irish descent; since 1841, half of the people born in Ireland have emigrated; this is unique for any European country. They have been driven out by famines. Most who have emigrated have been Catholic; all have been poor. My mother's family was among them.

Now I'm an "Indian"? No, not Indian, but a follower of the *Vedas.* I'm a "cultist" cut off from all nations while maintaining citizenship in all of them. We devotees are both exiles and givers, and even though we live far from the world's troubled heart, we live close to the troubled heart of ISKCON.

I'm writing this in the empty U.S. Immigration pre-inspection hall. No workers here yet—not even any travelers. Just me and Madhu and the Christmas tree. A nearby sign reads, "Refresh the Christmas spirit—drink Coca-Cola."

Diaspora. My hands are cold. I can't always stay in the room at Manu's house. O body, just relax.

M. has just gone off for another green card interview. Maybe he'll actually get the prized card. It doesn't seem to mean much. He could travel to America without it. It doesn't give him a "back to Godhead" passport. What if I could get the equivalent in Ireland, permanent residence? Yes, I'd be glad for it. I'd settle into that house in Wicklow. But it too would not guarantee my going back to the spiritual world. Would my karma drive me somewhere else eventually? O Kṛṣṇa.

11:50 A.M.

Onboard Aer Lingus flight 105. Madhu was told they'd mail the green card to him in Baltimore. Noticing his return ticket to Ireland, the man told him he must live in the U.S.A.—that's what the green card is for. He said they might want to see him, and if he's not living in the U.S.A., they'll revoke the green card.

I told M. it would be whimsical of me to consider living in America just because he has a green card. The situation in Ireland is too good. But I admit I have started putting out feelers to see if I would even want to stay in America. It's not imperative that I return to Ireland immediately after completing this tour.

But Rādhā-Govinda. And Śrīla Prabhupāda. They are waiting in *samādhi* for me to return. It wouldn't seem right for me to stay indefinitely in the U.S.A. while they sit in a room in North Ireland.

2:09 P.M. IRISH TIME

Distracted.

"Would you like chicken or beef?"

"Nothing, thank you."

Can't read *Bhagavad-gītā* through the mealtime. Can't sit back comfortably either. So much noise on this flight, and closeness of bodies and movie screens, sound leaking from Madhu's earphones—Irish music. I put in an earplug, and it doesn't feel good. Vise pressure in head, but it hasn't moved behind the right eye yet. Sorry about all this.

Beef or chicken? Again? I already said no, thanks. Chicken—think of it. They cut its head off so someone could eat it. And beef, a cow.

I just read the introduction to *The Wisdom of Teresa of Avila*. I would like to have such a vocation—I mean, to feel God in me giving me the strength to trust Him fully. Teresa had miraculous favors from God. The fruit of her prayer was her ability to found Carmelite convents and write books. Could my books be a fruit of devotional service? Could they be useful to Kṛṣṇa? I hope so. I don't want to write only for myself.

Images on the "sky screen"—movie, men, and beautiful girls, pop music stars . . . O Kṛṣṇa. Teresa of Avila and Satsvarūpa dāsa from the Lower East Side.

We passed through U.S. Immigration in Ireland, so we won't have to go through it again on this side. Both M. and I will get our luggage and go straight to customs. Sounds easy enough. On the other side we should meet Rasarāja dāsa.

Teresa gave up the world. She says a religious person should maintain his or her humanness and not be uptight. She said he or she should see God in all things and in all people and should carry out His mission.

The "sky screen" flaunts the world's glamor. They do a spot about a young movie director making a film. Beautiful women play the parts in movies—and this one too, a movie about a movie ("All we see or seem/ is but a dream within a dream"). They make it very difficult to avoid seeing the movie while flying.

Bhagavad-gītā—read and meditate on Kṛṣṇa's promise that we can pass over all difficulties and, despite everything, go to Him.

Changed my watch to New York time: 9:55 A.M.

11:50 A.M. NEW YORK TIME

Tight pressure on top of head. I took an Esgic and hope it will prevent the pain from going further. They showed a silly Walt Disney movie, *George of the Jungle.* The usual good guys and bad guys—corny stuff along the lines of Tarzan, suitable for children and retarded adults. Family fare.

Soon we will be over Canada. Three and a half more hours to New York. Maine is mainly a state of mind. Oh, to return to my quiet house in Wicklow or to Manu's room. Beloved solitude—it's real and I like it. I'm grateful for it. I could live there for the rest of my life, but what does Kṛṣṇa want?

I feel I can't lecture well now. I mean, I'll do my bit, but I'm going deeper within myself, and too much is churning. Lecturing seems boring to me right now, and therefore my lectures are probably not so interesting to my audiences either. I can only repeat the same examples. I can't put my whole heart into it because my heart is taken up with other things.

But life is for sacrifice. O Kṛṣṇa, what do You want of me?

During this plane trip I have been doing nothing but sitting in space. I keep the *Bhagavad-gītā* on the food tray and hold my beads, but I'm not really chanting on them. I tried closing my eyes to say mantras or even just to feel them and that was nice.

The beautiful girl will probably leave the beautiful Tarzan in the jungle, right? She can't live there and he can't leave. A perverted reflection of Rādhā and Kṛṣṇa in Vṛndāvana. *Very* perverted.

Kṛṣṇa, thank You for everything.

1:00 P.M.

My head is not as bad, but I still feel the vise. I'm chanting, but it's difficult to concentrate because of the environment. After *George of the Jungle*, they showed a film called *Show Me New York*, with footage of restaurants and the sites and none of the actual misery of New York City. Then a film by Aer Lingus showing what will happen as we go through JFK. Then some kind of New York City love story. Kept on chanting. I held in my mind the ingredients of the *Bhagavad-gītā* verse, *bhaktyā mām abhijānāti:* Only by devotional service can Kṛṣṇa be known as the Supreme Personality of Godhead, and when you are in full consciousness of Him you can enter into the kingdom of God.

1:26 P.M.

Stupid movies—they're endless. Now one called *Taxi*. I wish I could stop glancing up at them, even for a few moments, but the screen is positioned in such a way that they're unavoidable. This one has more of the savagery of life, the anger and violence and lust. It goes around and around—this must be America. I'm sure I'll see these images flashing in my mind tonight when I try to sleep. Polluted mind.

"We have started our initial descent to JFK . . . Cape Cod is on your left." Weather. Twenty-five minutes early. Thirty minutes to arrival. Hare Kṛṣṇa. Guy in white turtleneck sweater and dark blazer drinking a stein of beer in a restaurant—in *Taxi*—posing, living, pretending to be real. Get me out of here.

December 6

2:00 A.M.

Rasarāja's baby boy, Rasa-pārāyaṇa, is cute. Oh me, oh my. To be in Jackson Heights at last and sorting out the mail. I'm too tired to answer it right now. Jet lag.

SOMETHING SWEET, SOMETHING TENDER

𝄞 A man in my mind said
something sweet and
tender
should be offered
to God.

"Oh, why do you always talk of
Bhagavān?"
I said I'm a
Prabhupāda man, didn't I?

He said, "You are, true enough,
but I'm sad to see you in New York
City. You'll regret it—that East
Side River, the old roads, the Greenpoint blacks.

A young woman conducted traffic
in a yellow raincoat—told the
kids when they could cross safely and
waved down cars—did they stop because of her
frail gesture?
Another person I don't envy.

Tender doesn't mean
soupy or
soapy like on
Dr. Bronner's soap bottles.
That's just the body meaning.
Lord, a tender soul came down with
hepatitis, then gangrene, then cancer, and
he actually died—he was only
fifty-three years old. Did you know
him? He's gone now. He
went to Vṛndāvana and left from there.

I said, "Take me to Krishna-Balaram
Mandir at my end." Something
sweet and tender even in death there.

This eight-week-old baby
sleeping peacefully in bed, he
sighed and heaved a little, took

one breath after another while
Madhu played his melodeon.
May this child not have a sister who
beats him up or a father
who abuses him. Life is too
tough on us here in this world.
Today is my birthday and
I'm feeling tender. ‖

DAYTIME IN JACKSON HEIGHTS

1

𝄞 Here we are in New York
and at least
there's no subway in this
room or under it.

But Mickey Mouse and Donald
were taking photos in
the "sky screen" theater
yesterday.
I won't be going
to all those restaurants
they showed.

Shaven-headed girl writes
that she's happy in the temple, she
wants me to initiate her but I should know
that on some days
the cookies burn.

Madhu's going busking at the 42nd Street subway!
With his melodeon! He's
got guts—"You mad bastard!" someone yells.
"Hare Kṛṣṇa!"

And I'm not able to open the window
my pinafore stuck with safety pins and
I see the baby smile
through no TV
no football no eggs.

2

"How can we be blissful but
not lovey-dovey?" Another
letter.
Having come to this
miserable and temporary
office
        don't get
robbed.

There's no way Kṛṣṇa can
be attained but by a
direct attack
direct action
        a military assault
of love
        in *vaidhi* steps.

The New York night has a thousand
eyes, I hear.
        "I's Nancy," said
the ugliest girl of three sisters.
My mom was
        pretty, but now
she's dead.
Not me.
No skeleton can dance.

3

Alone monk alone
joy
        stick with Kṛṣṇa
it's just funny
old music with a sad wind-up
toy
best
quality.

The night sees a gold
cat die against golder
leaves in
        Jack's Heights—a fenced-in
yard and no flower pot on
the sill.

Epiphany moment: a black guy
wearing a beret hiring a Skycap to
carry his electric guitar—his dyed blond
girl with dark glasses—
        I saw that
yesterday. ‖

12:04 P.M.

I decided not to carry my fountain pens to the Caribbean. It'll save space. I'll miss the friendly scratching.

Grip your teeth. Your faded old face. Your hairy chest has long white hairs mixed in with the darker ones. You make deadly punches toward your mirror image. Try on the turtleneck jersey—see if it fits. I'm ready for winter at Gītā-nāgarī, after the tropical Caribbean.

Heavens, the aspect I want is to be loving, caring, empowered, healing—purge the line of all those worn-out words. Inspect, art, showcase, downline, crabapple, Henry, fool, peppermint, word play.

Bhagavad-gītā for children, *Our Most Dear Friend*—yeah, that's the essence of it even more (for me) than, "Surrender to Me." Kṛṣṇa is our friend; He spoke to Arjuna because Arjuna was *His* dearmost friend.

The one who is perfect in all disciplines, including detachment, is very, very dear to the Lord. The book distributor and other types of proactive preachers are very, very dear—the most dear—servants. What about those who are fallen, the enjoyers, those who wink at oppression, and the oppressed? What about the sufferers, the social workers, the body's caretakers, and the backyard cats? All are dear to Him, although they don't know it. Our job is to awaken ourselves and such other souls to the awareness that Kṛṣṇa is our best friend.

Oh me, oh my.

I had better read more scripture. Although today I need to finish the mail. O Kṛṣṇa, the shoes fit, and the new long underwear too, both top and bottoms. The label shows a guy who looks like Robert Kennedy out hiking—and an attractive woman with a knapsack walking with him. Stylish clothes, chic-y—even the underwear.

"ISKCON ripped me off."

"Can I help you in any way? Please tell me how."

"You can give me *mahā-prasādam.*"

"Anything else?"

"No, just keep doing what you are doing."

"I was glad to see you cut loose."

"Kṛṣṇa consciousness has made me miserable" (from someone with a one-sided view of things).

"I'm working on the Vedic planetarium."

"Shoot him down."

"Lady Diana and Mother Teresa met briefly with ISKCON devotees. Therefore we should pray for them."

"Who is this? Is it Philip Sydney or Sir Walter (kill-the-Irish) Raleigh?"

"Who is this Stefan? We will meet, I will be hired, and I am a beggar."

"If in my house I put the bed in the wrong way or the door hinged in the wrong direction, I will have legal problems and lose supporters."

Friends, calm down. Let us pray. Then let us be ourselves constructively—like that school-crossing lady. Let's really be devotees and can the trash.

4:55 P.M.

A good day for recovery, meeting, receiving gifts, but not for reading or writing. More reason to go back to the "old sod." I'm at a stage where I can write-harvest from my lifetime of Kṛṣṇa conscious practices, and I want to go for it.

They throw out the master's papers—heave-ho the archives. It all ends anyway. We chatted together, sitting on the floor, me and my old buddy, Baladeva.

December 7

1:05 A.M.

I tend to develop the mentality that I can't read *śāstra* unless I'm in a special state of mind. Rather, I should know that even when distracted I need to hear from Kṛṣṇa. Distraction means I am "out of station." When I'm traveling I have more of a tendency to medicate my headache pain at an early stage because people expect something of me. Right now I'm in someone's house. Soon I'll have to catch another plane and meet a new set of expectations. Anyway, I'm up, so let me read.

"Though engaged in all kinds of activities, My pure devotee, under My protection, reaches the eternal and imperishable abode by My grace." (Bg. 18.56)

If the devotee is *mad-vyapāśraya,* under the Supreme Lord's protection, he is free of material contamination. This means he's engaged twenty-four hours a day in activities under the direction of the Supreme Lord or His representative. To that devotee the Lord is "very, very kind." In spite of all difficulty, "he is eventually placed in the transcendental abode, or Kṛṣṇaloka."

That's it: twenty-four hours a day, no rest. Don't be a part-time devotee. Devotional service requires that we give our entire selves while begging Kṛṣṇa to accept us. Giving our whole selves includes our warts, not just our official presentation of who we wish we were. On the other hand, we don't want to give Kṛṣṇa less than the best. We can trust He will accept us if we make a sincere move in His direction. We can accept our smallness among the other devotees. We don't have to compete with anyone. We are simply one small servant of the servant of the servant.

A devotee doesn't act as master but as servant. He has no individual independence. Such phrases always sound terrible to me, but I balance them with other statements, such as how individual initiative is never lost. What it means in the deeper sense is that a devotee acts always according to Kṛṣṇa's will because he has become one in interest with the Lord *(tad-ātmikā)*. We can't do something whimsically and offer the results to the Supreme Lord. In ISKCON, using this purport, we would sometimes enforce narrow definitions of "whimsical" and "independent". Our judgment as temple president or ISKCON authority was itself sometimes whimsical or independent of Śrīla Prabhupāda's deepest compassionate teachings. Spiritual life is a razor's edge. We have to think things over carefully to understand them properly.

EARLY-MORNING ROOM

𝄞 There's no way to step into it
stars twinkling
there's no way I can conceive.
I'm looking for Kṛṣṇa
in many places—crips

and licks and
all
an exciting
prospect.

But your dear-friend-most
is Kṛṣṇa pointing to His heart
wearing garland and *dhotī*
His form cannot be contained
and I can only recite
the truth.

They bought me boots and I will soon
go to Trinidad on Guyanese
Election Day—I hope there'll be
no trouble.
But I can't expect smooth sailing.
Just see what Prema went through
to deliver her child. She
relaxed when she heard
her prayer had reached me.

Life or death it doesn't matter
as long as my guru knows me
and I find a wild way out
now that I have agreed
to sit on the floor
and tell where
it hurts.

In NYC style, someone asked
me to tell him how
our religion fixed my hurts
and I used to drink
only orange juice from *bodegas*
taking pills for energy—no love

no food no
trusted friend
not even any
sex
no
        fun.
And now.

Now it's getting late
indeed but I
am merry, prepared to
go home
        and on the way
to beg God to please protect us even
at the hour of death
and beyond—our
remembrance of
Him. ‖

5:24 A.M.

Kṛṣṇa says despite difficulties the devotee will come to Him. But how soon? One answer: How bad do you want to go back to Him? And: How hard will you work for it? *Are you convinced?* That was Śrīla Prabhupāda's challenge to us at a 1972 GBC meeting. Are you convinced that Lord Kṛṣṇa is the Supreme Personality of Godhead? Lord Brahmā saw Kṛṣṇa standing like a small village boy holding fruit and yogurt in His left hand and carrying His flute in His belt—yet Lord Brahmā had just witnessed Lord Kṛṣṇa's mystic potency as all gods and entities emanated from His original form.

You are not *ready* to go back to Godhead? You have something left to do here? Don't you know the whole world is void without Govinda?

Govinda is everywhere. "For one who sees Me everywhere and sees everything in Me, to Him I'm never lost and he is never lost to Me."

Kṛṣṇa, Kṛṣṇa, Kṛṣṇa.

9:51 A.M.

Pause before going forward once in a while. It's Sunday morning. He told me he was suffering and asked why. We discussed going with the flow of it and what that meant—no longer resisting or wishing for something else, no longer trying to control our lives. It *is* happening, so pray to Kṛṣṇa for protection. We suffer and can learn a lot. While telling this, I hope I haven't trivialized it.

Glanced at Coltrane's biography today. He was quiet, yet friendly, searching to make his best creative music. The biographer writes from the viewpoint of a black person in a white society.

10:55 A.M.

Too cold (thirty degrees) to open the window for fresh air. Too crowded in the city to take a walk. Besides, we wear *dhotīs* and we'll get cold. I'll stay indoors. It will be different in Trinidad.

We can't only play it safe in spiritual life. That is not setting a good enough example. We have to be prepared to be actual people, to take that risk. Not to live a concept of ourselves, whether it's a self-created concept or a concept imposed upon us. Live as a person, with some restraint and some release, living with risk, but exercising caution. That's how we mold our lives into servants of Kṛṣṇa, not by cardboard service.

DON'T PUT DOWN THIS MUSIC

(Hurry get it in)
𝄞 Simple he was
a lyrical and consummate player
a lyric a
flower
a distracted man in a shirt
listening when words
collide.

Alpine tree ain't direct in
bird pad
oh, it's pumpkin
Inis Free
despair.

A man from comfrey to
interrupt the genius
        and Coleridge
an integer, a non-scientist
me
a *burfi*-maker
a thin lad from
Shopshire
        I can't spell with
ink on my fingers
but I know Kṛṣṇa consciousness is a joyfest
on the River Swanee
transcendental to any other
and I can't reach out
        and carry us above.

Don't put down white men
black
        yellow
this dissonance
is body
skin disease.

My words are yours.
on the sonorous ridge.
Be real. ‖

2:50 P.M.

Packing. Daylight through Venetian blinds. Hum of traffic. People live this way, obliged to one another, all the time.

Heard on tape Bhūrijana Prabhu speaking from the *Sandarbha* about the *Bhāgavatam's* "emperor" verse, *ete cāṁśa* . . . Then I put on my sweatshirt.

A typewriter will meet us in Trinidad, and I've decided to take my fountain pen after all. As if I have something important to say.

Actually, I do have something important to say: God is the source of all. And I am obligated to say it, not only to reciprocate with Kṛṣṇa, but to give something to those who have washed my clothes, prepared my lunch, paid for the house where I'm taking shelter, and who will drive me to the airport tomorrow. I owe something in return. Give Kṛṣṇa.

4:58 P.M.

People approach the Absolute Truth in many ways, usually through one form of speculation or another, until they find the spiritual master. Even then, their research into the nature of the Absolute Truth may be different from another's research. In the end, we are all dependent on God to reveal Himself. And even then, not everyone will understand the form such individual revelation takes. Whenever I read of other paths, I am left with the impression that the Vedic path is the most solid and scientific. In Coltrane's biography I saw a section about Sun Ra, another jazz musician, and his relationship with the Universe. What can he actually know without a bona fide guru? Yet he has written music for his God. Still, it's not quite *bhakti.* If we are going to give up the path of materialism and seek out God, best to find a guru who will teach the essentials of *bhakti* to Govinda. Best to learn to chant the holy name and to learn how to offer our service through whatever we do in life.

It's a shame that our institution (and its offshoots) becomes so distracted by lesser issues. It's also a shame the larger society rejects Kṛṣṇa consciousness. But such obstacles need not stop a sincere person from contacting Kṛṣṇa and engaging in devotional service.

"There is no need of strenuous effort to free oneself from sinful reactions. One should unhesitatingly accept Kṛṣṇa as the supreme savior of all living entities. With faith and love, one should surrender unto Him." (Bg. 18.66, purport)

December 8

12:12 A.M.

In a dream I was walking with a long staff made of iron encased in wood. It was my weapon. I was always afraid—there were many tough young guys out. One person stopped me and asked to look at the rod. I didn't want to surrender it, so he had to look at it without me loosening my grip upon it. I told him I had just walked from Florida. He decided to let me go. A little further along a policeman grabbed me by the skin above and between my eyes and forced me to follow him, no questions asked. Eventually, he opened the door to his truck and wanted to throw me in. I was helpless. I wanted to demand, "What are the charges? Why are you doing this to me?" but the dream ended.

When I awoke, I thought of how the modes of nature can pull us along. We do something and reach a certain point in our lives, then the "cop" comes in. At that time we can't speak nicely to him because we have already fallen into karmic reaction. The cop will just pull us cruelly and we have no choice but to follow.

12:25 A.M.

After that dream I felt like drifting into a more simple life with more attention given to *śāstra* and prayer during the day.

RAMBLIN'

𝄞 Yes, I know you
remember you
    you who
have no malice
and for whom
I feel no malice
let's have peace.
We may have warred
we may have wronged
me and you
but I know Kṛṣṇa for
example.
    I know Kṛṣṇa and you
remind me
    rambling is
permissible it
can be
helpful
especially in dreams.
You got beat up
once by mean dudes and
you went to cops who
said, "Get out of town by tonight
or we'll kill you."

I wandered, he caused
trouble for others
but forgive us, God, we will
tell the truth and
beauty of it despite
our woes.

I go to primitive lands at risk of pain
    to deliver Kṛṣṇa consciousness
although I sometimes doubt
the reality of it all—the travel
my place
    what I know and
what I feel
the way
but for old-times sake and because of gray-
haired, paunches and eyes lined
my dear disciples and dear
me with upper and
lower bridges still
    chomping
I go.

The language of Kṛṣṇa consciousness is
so nice, isn't it?
    To be in synch, to rise, to be there
to advocate the Swami in
'66
in
'96
and say he taught us how
to smile—only Kṛṣṇa/ no
Māyāvādīs
and fight your
rasslin' mind. ‖

6:45 A.M.

So far so good. Heavy traffic jam at JFK and a long line at the BIWA counter, but they moved us along. Madhu, Bhakta Kevin, and I flying together. Rasarāja brought breakfast—muffins with butter and jam, a banana, milk sweets, and hot tea. There was no place to sit, so we sat on the floor. Small, gentle talk. Madhu's hand luggage was ten pounds overweight, but when he showed them he was carrying "a melodeon, a delicate instrument," the woman let him take it.

Hare Kṛṣṇa. Sixteen done, but more to go today. On the plane I plan to look at *The Beginning*, a book about Śrīla Prabhupāda in New York City 1966. I hope to lecture on it when I get there.

Milling, pushing, blocking—the passengers don't cooperate with the boarding agent. He says sarcastically, "It looks like we'll be here all day." Almost everyone flying is black or of India descent. No change in behavior after the sarcastic comment and the agent repeats it. Another agent joins him and makes a similar announcement. "All right, you guys, get back against the wall or this plane isn't going to leave." Bit by bit it happens. First-class and children, then those with seats rows 30 and higher, then 20 and higher. Our seat is row 6, so we stand back and cool it. If I look at what's happening I get agitated, but not too much. The people are relaxed, casually dressed for winter in NYC, but en route to Trinidad.

10:40 A.M. TRINIDAD TIME

I feel somewhat empty of identity or purpose, like a piece of luggage, when I travel. Don't know what I'll speak exactly when I get there. I know that I will do better once I arrive.

Carib beat. O disciples, Kṛṣṇa consciousness is very important, and we have a relationship. I don't feel I'm special, yet I feel pressure, as if the purpose of my visit is to establish my specialness, or that it is based on that specialness: people think that just by seeing and hearing from me, they are supposed to benefit. But I'm not special; the śāstric message is special. Rather than pressure, let's share the inspiration to share that message and to grow with it.

Odor of baked chicken coming down the aisle. I'll avoid looking at it. For every chicken killed and eaten—who listens to the music of these chicken-eaters?

Yes, that's the point—my purpose. I count on the devotees in Trinidad to like me, to be polite, to be willing to hear from me. Otherwise, why would I go to all this trouble? I'll also expect that when I'm seated on the *vyāsāsana*, I will be able to deliver something. I'm not special, but I hope to carry a fresh voice of inspiration to them. Let us share the Vedic truth. *Śṛṇvatāṁ sva-kathāḥ kṛṣṇaḥ*. As we attempt to speak and hear *Bhagavad-gītā* and *Śrīmad-Bhāgavatam*, it will happen. Don't worry about anything else.

I think I went to the Caribbean for the first time in 1980. Is there room in my passport for their stamp? If not, I'll have to get a new passport when I get back to Ireland. Oh, that quiet routine. Well, this is good too.

Board flight: three hours and fifty minutes to Barbados. There we will land, then take off again. I'll get through it, Kṛṣṇa willing. I might have to speak even today at the temple. I will be grateful for the reception. I hope they are all following their vows. Śrī Kṛṣṇa says if they worship and serve Him, they will go to the spiritual world.

3:05 P.M.

Twenty minutes until landing. I have taken two Esgics for the right-eye pain. Told M. about an improviser's dedication and search for innovation, but otherwise we spoke little. The feature film preached nonviolence toward whales. Gave me hope. I'll mention it in my arrival talk. Similar mood expressed in the inflight magazine: "You Don't Have to Kill Them"—an article about the new sport of fishing for giant marlins, then letting them go. Talk of Śrīla Prabhupāda.

I have decided that in the mornings I will speak on groups of *Bhagavad-gītā* verses and how they apply to our lives. We can appreciate the drama of the exchange between Kṛṣṇa and Arjuna, but we should also take Kṛṣṇa's words seriously. Kṛṣṇa is speaking to *us* as much as He is speaking to Arjuna. Thus scripture should be read alone, or at least with one's heart attentive. Kevin is carrying my typewriter. I plan to use it.

December 9

3:35 A.M.

At Viśvarūpa's house. The arrival went all right. Devānanda was waiting for me with a new white car. He said it belonged to a Trinidadian *paṇḍita*, who lent it because the devotees had told him the car would be blessed by my riding in it.

I spoke on the *Save the Whale* film and how the airlines could show that but serve chicken for lunch. Still, the devotees should remain hopeful as they try to preach Kṛṣṇa consciousness. Spoke later with a devotee who poured out his feelings, mostly positive, about how things are going in Trinidad. He said he wrote me three letters but received no replies. He hasn't been practicing *sādhana*, but says he no longer feels guilty about it. I didn't know what I could say to that. But I felt relaxed in the tropical climate, even though it took me two Esgics to get through the pain. I wanted to be up for an arrival talk, not to be carted off to bed the moment I arrived.

After my talk I gave everyone a prune stuffed with peanut butter. Arriving at Viśvarūpa's house, they served me a fruit plate—papayas, bananas, and an apple. During the night I didn't use earplugs and heard either a bird or a frog going off over and over like the first note of a burglar alarm. When I awoke at 12:30, I was afraid to put on the light because it would attract mosquitoes. The windows have open slats and no screens. I walked back and forth in the big room in the dark and chanted thirteen inattentive rounds.

The plan is to go to the temple for *maṅgala-ārati*, sing, come back here for a while, then return to the temple at 7 A.M. for Deity greeting. During class I'll speak on the first three verses of the *Bhagavad-gītā's* second chapter. I want to demonstrate that Kṛṣṇa is demanding and is not pleased when we don't act according to the standard expected of a *kṣatriya* (or whatever *we* are).

I don't know . . . I thought about a talk I could give on Vyāsa-pūjā day. I could tell them about things that are important to me—honesty and art. But then I would probably have to explain what I mean by "art". Do I mean these diary reports? Doesn't literary art mean writing a novel? No.

Śrī kṛṣṇa caitanya prabhu. I have the typewriter Kevin carried down here. I'll use it in Trinidad but send it back with him when we go to Guyana. Kevin also brought colored markers. I hope to find the time to use them.

On the plane I looked through the *Caribbean Beat* magazine. It featured an artist whose work was similar in some ways to mine—primitive forms, and especially the use of key emotional words or sentences with the illustration. I liked it. Hare Kṛṣṇa, Hare Kṛṣṇa. Never any loss if it's done for Kṛṣṇa.

A little boy dove over the side of the whaler and went under to play with the whale. Incredible story. He didn't like his daddy killing whales and he tried to prevent it. In the end his father was converted to nonviolence when the whale saved his life. Prahlāda and his father.

All right, fellow. Be a good guru persona, give out fruit and relax and speak about the *śāstra.* Come and go. These devotees have been here almost twenty years, some of them, so it's no joke. I have been coming and going all that time. Śrī Kṛṣṇa Caitanya. Tell the men to get up early and chant their rounds. Tell them not to quarrel so much. That sort of thing. Same old. It's true there's no joy in Mudville, but we are not supposed to leave our hearts in Mudville. We have to find a way to allow Kṛṣṇa to uplift us. I mean, we have to respond to His will. If a whale can uplift a bad man, then all-kind Kṛṣṇa can uplift a struggling devotee. And the spiritual master has the right to speak strongly and call you all impudent fools, non-Aryans, whatever it takes to break through. After all, the guru's our friend.

And Kṛṣṇa spoke like that to Arjuna. That's the basis of my whole presentation on how to read the scriptures personally. It's meant for each of us alone, just this one person, ourselves. Get down to it. If you see it as merely objective, what use is it?

Śrī Kṛṣṇa Caitanya. There is a Prabhupāda lecture tape on the table here labeled "No More Pains." I'll have to listen to *that* one. Long-range and short-range—we're all equipped to surrender, even though we lack so many qualities.

I told the story of Beech's liniment and how the inventor died happy when he heard he had one customer. A preacher should be that enthusiastic to help others, yet not attached to the results, which are in Kṛṣṇa's hands. Hare Kṛṣṇa. That's what I said.

Honesty and art and what else? Good example. Die without shame.

4:25 A.M., IN THE TEMPLE ROOM

Dark temple—small, black Gopīnātha Deity. Flies. Hard floors. Wild dancing in the old days. People pressed to join. Now slower.

9:02 A.M.

The class lasted at least an hour. Jaya Lalitā asked about performing Kṛṣṇa consciousness out of social pressure. As she spoke I listened to hear if a Trinidadian accent had mixed in with her native British. I answered her as well as I could. Then I thought how much I operate under such social pressure. M. and I agreed that all I will do today is to give one class, but I'm already worried that that's not enough. I need to make my own decisions and stick to them. I can't live worrying what others will think. If I open myself to public opinion, the public would have me performing and parading all day long, eating at someone's house, meeting with troublemakers somewhere else, and yeah, lay *off* that stuff. Tomorrow is the Big Day, so better I keep cool. I had to take two pills yesterday, so today I had better rest and get ready for the possibility that I will need more medication tomorrow, my birthday.

Someone else wanted to know what happened to the focus we had when we were young devotees. I told him it wasn't so important. What *is* important is that we go forward from the moment we are living. Maybe we were better then, or maybe we were just more naive. We were certainly idealistic, and perhaps now we have realized how much work lies before us before we can attain our ideals. What to do but continue with our quota of rounds, reading Prabhupāda's books, and looking in our hearts for more and more sincerity? We all need reform, real reform. No point living in the past, which has been made greener by our minds.

Bright green leaves on trees and grass—more yellow-infused green than in Ireland. In Ireland the green is rich and deep because they get so much rain. Here it's sunlight brilliant—mango trees, blue sky, and so warm you can't even wear a T-shirt. My *kurtā* was stained purple by this morning's garland.

Hey, if the guru calls you a fool, does he still allow you to have potential? Someone asked me that. Sure, why not? He's not like those people who paralyze you when they call you a fool. He doesn't curse his disciple.

Then should we avoid those who call us fools and who mean it to be demeaning? Yes, we don't like to be around such people. We want to be criticized constructively, be encouraged. I don't know if I fell into some local controversy by answering the way I did. I told them I have selected special *Bhagavad-gītā* verses, ones in which Kṛṣṇa speaks directly to us. No one had questions on that.

Temple room full of men, women, and children—our Hare Kṛṣṇa movement in Trinidad. Some of the young devotees have a tanned complexion that I find pleasing. It reminds me of the impulse to select a tan crayon out of the box. But I also looked away from it. I am not meant to enjoy the hue of people's skin.

Delicious fruits for breakfast again, and nice sweets with them. Hare Kṛṣṇa, Hare Kṛṣṇa—this day is mine to putter around and to get past the all-pervasive rock beat. Get away from it. Be here and chant Hare Kṛṣṇa.

I want to free-write in the free way we entered through Trinidad immigration yesterday: allowed to enter with no questions asked. Not even a hello or a "Welcome to Trinidad." When *I* said hello, she ignored me. Just stamped me in, bored as hell. Made me feel a little left out. Of course, the immigration people here are not really representative of this country's general mood. They just don't like us Hare Kṛṣṇa gringos. They have no interest in anything but staying out of trouble. Nothing more human than that.

Free-writer hot iron sweet, gave out fruits after a lecture. Eccentric person talked to me while I was trying to pay attention to each person coming up to exchange. He spoke about the "inner life of a preacher." Might have had something valuable to say, but I couldn't understand his accent well enough to focus on his words through the crowd. I nodded as if I understood, and that seemed good enough for him. An ex-cop looked at me and I felt apologetic that I won't be visiting his temple. Will they ever understand?

10:40 A.M.

Dreamt the other night of yearning to produce a literary creation. In waking life, I simply write this.

Then write deeply, individually.

I kept stumbling onto the word "deeply" in my lecture. I wanted them to know that we each go before Kṛṣṇa as individuals when we perform our service. Also, it's hard to be absolutely alone with the word of God. I spoke with conviction.

We receive our place in life and can't escape. That's karma. A woman, for example. A heavy designation. Most want to get married and have a child. How can you *not* act according to social pressure, Jaya Lalitā?

I said, "Imagine wanting to go to Kṛṣṇaloka just so you could say, 'If the devotees in my temple could see that I made it to Kṛṣṇaloka, that would show them! They always thought I was a fool.'"

How can we act with courage? It may not always be possible; it may *never* be possible. Therefore we shouldn't be proud.

She wrote, "I don't live at Rādhā-kuṇḍa." She wrote a letter purporting to be in the mood of *rādhā-dāsya* and said, "Why not? Do you object?" I object not to *rādhā-dāsya* but to her (or anyone) talking with me as if we're both servants of Rādhā just ready to head out to the *kuñja* with our brooms and jewelry or whatever. I don't want to be included so easily in that trip, not at least until it's real.

I say that, so they think I must be in Vaikuṇṭha *bhāva.* Geez. Listen to these birds chirp. If I had enough energy I'd take a walk. Plenty of hot sunshine beating on this tin roof to wear a body down. Only a strong body can work in de jute field. Dumb old place.

FREE

𝄞 Up and down the scales, merry boys
just to free up the adrenaline.

Happy or not? Free
        he sez and we
say
they're laughing at me.
White-haired,
        me in field
        no shirt
        old flames burning
and him with the key.

Pastiche pasta—
I saw into your kitchen
your noodles
hard and buttony, but
Prabhupāda said,
"Mind your own business."
I saw a scar-faced
doodle-haired woman
Trinidad-talkin' to the captain of the ship
got a good view of Long Island.

Oh, freedom no
freedom
from God but
limitations
toy trumpets for
toy devotees and
a pet cat.

On my birthday give me
honors, towels, a
straw ring,
a couch I can't carry
        a wooden recorder
the right to preach to
rest atop a bed with

a fan and an
extra blanket
and I won't be sad.
        Better to be wise to
minimize.

So I ate a big lunch
of boiled-in-*ghee* gobbers
and dipped-in-wax honey
ferms of local radish
and hoarsened chestnuts
then grinned
and was sorry
wanted to run home in safety
to my Father
        O Kṛṣṇa O Prabhupāda
you know me better
than this. ‖

2:43 P.M., NOTES FOR LECTURE ON MY VYĀSA-PŪJĀ DAY

Reading the Fourth Canto purport stating that if a nonliberated person follows the liberated, he can become a spiritual master. He will have nothing to say on his own. Nothing except that it's hot here in Trinidad.

I want to be honest. I'll say that for myself. I'm no longer "Gurupāda," but I'm still their Guru Mahārāja. Thus I receive their honor, this comfy rocker.

I met His Divine Grace and gave him my money. That's what I did. He wrote it into his diary and that proves my story true. He named me and then called me "Satsvasvarūpa dāsa" in his diary. It gives me a right to share him with others.

Things I always say on this day: The guru is the servant. He has been ordered to take disciples just as a post-peon is ordered to carry the mail. The guru must set a good example. He must leave his footprints in the mud or on the marshy path so others can follow. He must bring his subordinates over the head of Death and back to Godhead. To do that, he may have to first deliver himself.

Too exhausted to discuss the rest.

Does he have to take part in the campaign to save the whales? How many Ratha-yātrās does he have to attend before we have to listen to him? How many books distributed, how many read, how many carried from room to room? How many does he have to understand? How many roads must a man walk down before you call him a man?

Are your doubts assuaged? Whew.

3:28 P.M.

Everything I do right now is meant to help me conserve energy to get through the heat of the day. It will cool down later, when it's time for bed. Kevin went to stay at a devotee's home because he couldn't find quiet in the temple and could not write his Vyāsa-pūjā offering. As for me, I already told you. I'm just a castor-tree guru. No question of quitting now. I plan to prove my points with *śāstra.* I plan to speak from the philosophy, but also from the heart. I plan to show some prowess and not speak of myself as a disciple but as a master.

And so he stood up, favoring his bad left ankle, and danced a bugaloo by the light of the moon. They could hardly believe it. They now thought he had shown them the authorized stuff. He strummed his geetar and smiled and proved that he was indeed the genuine article. After that he relaxed his joints and they began to read their homages: "Dear Guru Mahārāja," etc. He tried not to judge them, but listened instead to their Caribbean accents and said, "By the light of the moon indeed."

4:47 P.M.

Thinking of what to say in public is not so deep, is it? What do I *actually* think of being a spiritual master? To be honest, I'd rather be left alone more. However, I'm grateful that my writing career is supported by disciples. My whole life is supported by them—medically—and room and board, an audience, and so on. I can't conceive of living without them. It's almost a moot point to raise the question, "Would you do better without this?" Or, "How could you do without them?" For better or worse, we have each other, and the real question is how to live with them in a way that we all come out Kṛṣṇa conscious. All my children. I could never leave them. Better to die honorably.

But it's good for me to take into account how much this role molds my life and thinking. It forces me to become a better disciple of Śrīla Prabhupāda, a better devotee of Kṛṣṇa, and a more honest person—all of which automatically contribute to the kind of spiritual master I can become for those who have chosen to follow me. They say they want to take shelter of me, but what does that mean? We don't always know—them or me—what it means to give such shelter.

Sometimes I wonder how I can possibly function as spiritual master for *anyone*. I see such hesitancy as similar to when I have some doubt about the scriptures. I may have a temporary doubt that Kṛṣṇa is God, and I may also doubt that it's best for me to mold my life according to my spiritual master's teachings. Similarly, I may doubt whether I should function as spiritual master to others. These are all articles of faith. As I fight for each one, I fight for them all simultaneously. It's possible to be both a disciple of Prabhupāda and not be a guru for others, but it's too late for me to back out now. Still, my disciples should know what I actually am, and if they still want to follow me after that, then fine. But their following shouldn't compromise me.

The worst heat of the day is over. I just took my third shower. They ran out of water, but it's back on. Spoke with M. about tomorrow's schedule. Lying on the bed is pleasant at this point in the day. I hear the pleasing sound of the Trinidadian countryside and drift to that place that Kṛṣṇa allows us, the place of energy-replenishing sleep.

I try to find quality time in Kṛṣṇa consciousness, but also seem to want an easy-going life. I can't take on hard work—or I don't want to. Seek God in quiet ways. Hare Kṛṣṇa. Bursts of energy we use. When they come, write something down to penetrate the coverings of superficiality. See something genuine. Ask Kṛṣṇa for acceptance and help. May He reveal Himself to me as He pleases. I pray to Him to inspire me and empower me to perform the difficult, to accept the austerity. I just have to reach out and accept His love. It arrives by carrying out the spiritual master's order. O Kṛṣṇa, I want to take an honest look. May I become more single-minded.

BRIGHT TRINIDAD

(Sunset. Cooler. Tanager and sparrow. Dog barking. Can you be true to your own? To whom do you belong?)

𝄞 This way, please, workers
comin' home
        to chicken but not in
this house—we're
        nonviolent.
But that same bebop music
exists even here
so
this way
pleeze.

Bright Trinidad
        bright sun
Kṛṣṇa in the cloud—His
mercy—just coming from
behind that jute field
while I sit here alone
in my villa, a book
at hand

etching a prayer
a
paean
to the Lord
and guru
my Prabhupāda.

Sorry, I already danced, he said.
No reruns. Now listen
to the tanager—his own
beat. ‖

My man is out there straightening it out with the temple president so that we follow my plan on my birthday, not his. I'll give the lecture as early as possible. Other than that, we always emphasize the bright side in
bright T'dad.
Death-bound all
and aspiring for Kṛṣṇaloka
through solid *bhakti.*

December 10

3:56 A.M.

"Happy birthday, although it's a performance . . . " The cock crows and the mosquitoes bite through my socks. Another day. Cat howling outdoors while I chant *japa* in the dark room. At least all these sounds are keeping me awake with the holy name as my companion. Lord knows, no one was watching me while I was chanting. That was His compassion upon me: to give me that space not to be a performer.

I can and must agonize over whether I am qualified to be a spiritual master. Aside from that, there's a job to be done. A necessary job, ordered by Lord Caitanya, and I won't comment on whether or not it was ordered by my spiritual master. I'd rather not get into that. But people need a link to one of Kṛṣṇa's living representatives.

Looking forward to time at Gītā-nāgarī. It might even snow. Then Baltimore for an intense four-day gig, then the flight back to Ireland, that haven for retired sailors. I know that no place is really home in this world, and Kṛṣṇa reminds me of that from time to time.

I wanted to think of India, of Vṛndāvana, while chanting *japa*. Vṛndāvana has many *sādhus* and just as many loudspeakers. None of those here. And of course, Vṛndāvana has the secret, unmanifest presence of Kṛṣṇa's pastimes. The *līlās* still take place at *rāsa-līlā* sites (Yoga-pīṭha, Rāsa-sthalī), they say. There is no place on earth like Rādhā-kuṇḍa. Those who live there usually have enough faith to know.

Fortunately, if we are unable to live in Vṛndāvana, we can contact Vraja-kiśora wherever we are in the world by chanting, hearing, and remembering His beautiful Vṛndāvana form. That's another manifestation of faith in the power of Vṛndāvana.

That it's my birthday doesn't touch me much. I just want to get through this day.

I had a dream last night that seems to sum up my mood this morning. In the dream, a man was living in an expensive Manhattan apartment. He was a great drummer, and other people liked to play drums with him. One character came (who later turned out to be me) but left the drumming circle. As I left I realized I had nothing; I was out on the street with no money. When I awoke I realized I am being maintained in exchange for playing the role of spiritual master. I had to conclude that it's all right that I'm maintained as long as I am giving Kṛṣṇa consciousness.

4:52 A.M.

Well, friends, you may not know me, but I am Trinidad Joe. I work in the house next to the devotees. I heard there's a big shindig today. I'm going over there to see what's going on. Heard it's for their guru.

Their loud voices—strangers in that house—echoing above the rooster and chickens. When I say something that draws a laugh from my audience, which usually begins with Ananta-śeṣa dāsa, I chant in my mind, "Kṛṣṇa, Kṛṣṇa." The scriptures say we need a guru. Here's a guru. He's not shiny new, but perhaps that's better. Old men have already gone through most of what they will go through. They're safer. He's not untarnished. I mean, he was one of those original eleven, and although that was once seen as the greatest honor conceivable in ISKCON, it gradually became a source of shame and infamy. Such is the nature of fame and fortune in this world. Best not to be attached to it. A tisket a tasket, a green and yellow basket. "Roll over," he said to his dog.

Saw a dog passing stool on the street. Prabhupāda walked in a Toronto park one morning and saw the sign intended for dog owners: "Stoop and scoop."

Friends, I tell you, the scriptures say we need a guru. And what are our expectations of the guru? We place him on a seat, ask if he'd like to be fanned. We wave a *cāmara* with artistic motions. We inquire as to how else we may serve him. Of course, many things are forbidden to him, and he's not supposed to even want them. No sex love, no cigarettes, no alcohol, no meat. When we ask him, "Guru Mahārāja, is there anything you want?" we don't really expect him to come up with much. We *hope* he'll say something memorable like, "I don't want anything. I have no material desires." Or more appropriately, "I would like *kṛṣṇa-prema*. Can you give *that* to me?" And he smiles in a brilliant-foolish way.

O Gurujī, how about apple pie?

No, you fool, it's Ekādaśī.

Don't worry, he's got his Esgic and a sparrow on his sleeve. He wrote early this morning.

Guru, is there anything you want?

No, don't ask me, or I may want things you can't deliver. But I appreciate your asking. You know, you have provided many of the comforts to which I have become attached. Therefore, I want a new pillow, a fresher bed, running water that doesn't cut out on me, some soap and toothpaste, paper that I can write on, and . . . should I go on?

But Guru, can you give us an enlightening talk?

Yes, but first, listen to the mockingbird. If winter comes, can spring be far behind? Please accept Kṛṣṇa as the supreme savior of your life. Chant His holy name. Worship His Deity form. Be serious about devotional service. Be kind to others. Now I will read from a book and make a few comments on it.

The birds whistle; the chickens go on crying despite their doom. Nobody knows for sure when the ax will fall on their own neck. Hope it doesn't happen to the guru in public. Otherwise, both he and his followers will be embarrassed. Better he leave from Vṛndāvana so that later they can be solaced that he died there, surrounded by the chanting of the holy name as he passed away through the tight straits on his way to Goloka.

HIS FOOTSTEPS IN SAND OF JUHU

𝄞 Please don't interrupt or say this
isn't allowed/ don't ring
my bell.
Beard and hat—don't cross out
anything it's
all allowed
we remember (bite on, mosquitoes)
our guru walking on
the sands of Juhu.

We were there with him growing tired
not of his but our own
proclamations. I prefer to remember now
how he saved me.

Any little ditty I accept
these days. Did you know a toad
with horny eyebrows
crawled up my
wall?

Yes, students, we are gathered here
today to honor SDG's
        belly-button birthday. He's
well known for his funny
dissonant words and for
dropping extra steps in the dark.

But Prabhupāda I am here
to honor you,
honest, smart, and
true.
Take me by the hand
        my master/ take me
by the hand/ let me walk
in your footsteps
on the Juhu's sand
        my words
following yours.

12:08 P.M.

I'm on the borderline of pain after three hours of sitting in the temple room. I spoke for about twenty minutes, then allowed the disciples to speak one at a time. *Kīrtana* followed, then a song sung by the *gurukula*. The *puṣpāñjali* grew tiresome, and they stacked the garlands higher and higher, photographing and videotaping all. I tolerated all that, felt no particular emotion. The best was when that *gurukula* girl led the singing and played the harmonium. I felt tears come to my eyes and roll down my cheeks with perhaps a little self-pity mixed in with the emotion. But more, I thought of all of us and our small efforts at devotional service. I also thought of Baladeva and his wife, whose child died a few years ago. The tears comforted me.

Now awaiting lunch. At 3 P.M. I'm due back at the temple to read from the diary Śrīla Prabhupāda kept in New York City in 1966. So far, no pill. M. thanked me in his homage for being "vunerable" (sic).

2:25 P.M.

Blame it on the heat, but my energy here is quite low. Kālachandjī dāsa ended his homage, "For time is sure slipping away." Don't *wish* it away. Anyway, even if you wish it to stay, it won't. My friend, my dear teary friend, the violet flowers and their creeper look lovely in the day, but . . .

Distant drumbeat. The new, summer-weight *dhotī* and *kurtā* stained purple from the flowers—the second new set ruined in two days. I'll go into the temple room and read that diary. I'll tell them that this is "my" day, so I can use it to worship Prabhupāda. After all, I am made of his mercy. He told me he was my real father. He gave me my real birth when he gave me initiation. He was already seventy, but he was closer to me than my own dad.

5:12 P.M.

Read from *The Beginning*, how he often bought just one banana a day, spent very little, sold a few books. Snow came and he couldn't go out to bathe or cook at Dr. Mishra's apartment. Patita asked about austerity. Someone asked me to tell more about how I gave money. I said I got a solid start in Kṛṣṇa consciousness by giving money to Śrīla Prabhupāda. It's certainly nice to talk of those days and to remember Swamiji.

"Do you still have the three *Bhāgavatam* volumes you bought?"

No, I lost them.

"Please tell us about how you bought them."

I told a few stories and spoke for an hour. Nice way to end the day's activities.

Then I dictated replies to letters, mostly standard things: "Thank you, everyone. I can't seem to say much more."

The details of Prabhupāda's wonderful activities are not fully known to me. Kṛṣṇa sent Prabhupāda here. India would not help him. He did everything single-handedly. Who can understand? I read from the diary how he tried to start a temple, how he did this, how he did that. Our dear Swami. The cleaning man came to his room and Śrīla Prabhupāda gave him a cold drink—of water, I guess. He said the man was glad to receive it. Śrīla Prabhupāda hosting a cleaning man. Hare Kṛṣṇa, this is very nice to hear, our spiritual master alone in NYC, depending on Kṛṣṇa.

I can hear those birds out there amid the greenery. Hare Kṛṣṇa. Day has ended. I can't squeeze more out of it. Don't forget Kṛṣṇa.

December 11

3:40 A.M.

Sleep when noise distances you, thoughts too, motives. I don't want to forget to strive for Kṛṣṇa consciousness, but sometimes you just have to let yourself be. Float to Kṛṣṇa and rest in the tropics. The body seems to want extra rest in the tropics.

Finally I had to get up. When I turned on the bathroom light, I saw a frog hanging on the wall with his suction feet. Cool water—no need of hot. A long day ahead—*Bhagavad-gītā* lecture, etc. I want to make my talks pertinent, because that's all I can give them directly. Yesterday's homages have passed. "You are glorifiable . . . "—I am a stand-in for God, so they praised me, each sincere. We are each sincere, although usually our sincerity is mixed with selfish motivation. Those motivations are material because we think we need matter to cope with our lives, and because we are covered by illusion. A magnanimous person doesn't become angry when he sees selfish, mundane people; rather, he understands they are victims. He sees the larger perspective, how they are functioning by karma. More than anything, he sees how much of this is true of himself. When he is mistreated by fools, he understands that he is suffering due to his own past deeds. When he mistreats others, he feels sorry that he is forced to suffer by causing others to suffer.

In Bg. 2.38, Lord Kṛṣṇa tells Arjuna to fight for the sake of fighting, "because [Kṛṣṇa] desires the battle." Śrīla Prabhupāda underlines the point: Arjuna should fight simply because Kṛṣṇa wants him to. I have added that verse to my personal prayer collection. Do your duty because Kṛṣṇa wants you to.

Of course, devotees instantly ask how we can know if a specific task is the one Kṛṣṇa desires of us. Therefore, the first task is to know the nature of duty and the nature of the self, and to find a bona fide spiritual master.

When we act for Kṛṣṇa, we get no karma. When we act for ourselves, we suffer the reaction. The materialists usually don't even believe in karma, although they are faced with reactions at every moment of their lives.

Kṛṣṇa gives a stern order: Act because I want you to and for no other reason. Do not be concerned about happiness or distress, victory or defeat. Free yourself of duality. Try at least to think you are acting for Me. Only this will free you from *saṁsāra's* web. No other scheme will work.

Work for Kṛṣṇa. How? Tag on the motto, "This is for Him"? Give up—how? I don't seem to be able to grasp it in my life. Something rubs me the wrong way about it—is it false ego? It says, "Why do I have to become Kṛṣṇa's slave? Why do we translate that into working for the temple under authorities who don't always care for us? And what's wrong with acting according to our own inclination, anyway? Can I give to God from my own self rather than by always being told by others what to do?"

So you see, I'm not grasping it.

Flies and chickens and cats and M. making bathroom sounds. My *Bhagavad-gītā* study in preparation for class is not sustained. Three verses—I'll do what I can with them. I can't get it all perfect and ultimate. These devotees know the philosophy as well as I do anyway, yet all of us are equally unable to love and surrender to Kṛṣṇa. Or we don't even recognize our failure because we're too distracted by other issues. Oh, the external life.

Act for Him and there is no sin. Even a little *bhakti* can save us at death. Usually we relate better to acting to save ourselves at death than to the idea of simply pleasing someone just by our acts. Regardless, it's appealing to think of nonkarmic action because everything we do is subject to destruction except this one thing.

We often have to admit we like one verse better than another; one proposal sounds more appealing. Still, we have to consider the difficult ones and see how to get closer to them, to accept them. Admit we don't even get some of them—how they can be possible. Be "honest to God."

Ideals, absolutes. The devotees act only for Kṛṣṇa and are resolute in purpose. (Bg. 2.41)

I talk and talk, trying to consider the audience, but know that ultimately they are like me, sincere but lacking. They are somewhat aware of Kṛṣṇa consciousness, yet confused too. They don't really know how to improve, how to get beyond their present state, or how to attain the reality of Kṛṣṇa consciousness. We try to help each other. The three verses I have chosen seem to move from one topic to another: "Fight for Me," "Devotional service doesn't diminish," and "The devotees are resolute in purpose." The first advertises devotional service, the second defines devotional service, and the third describes the devotees. Because Kṛṣṇa is directly speaking these verses, we should try to understand them. In our lives, how can we fight for Kṛṣṇa, have faith in the process, and be responsible? We have to hear constantly if we want to learn the answer to that question. The spiritual master will help. Dear Kṛṣṇa, I'm at the beginning again in my hearing of *Bhagavad-gītā*. Please reveal to me what You mean and how we may follow.

5:40 A.M.

I'll speak on *Bhāg*. 10.53, the chapter about Kṛṣṇa kidnapping Rukmiṇī. She's waiting for Him and thinks He may have found something contemptible in her. We may also think like that as we wait for Kṛṣṇa to reveal Himself, but we can also understand that Kṛṣṇa is *bhava-grāhī-janārdana*, He accepts the good essence. That is His nature.

We saw several large fat frogs as we walked from this house to the temple for *maṅgala-ārati*. M. led the singing. Kṛṣṇa's wig didn't seem to fit right, and His white dress and crown were a little strange too. Humble people in attendance.

LONESOME ROAD

(Hurry. You went to *maṅgala-ārati* and *tulasī-pūjā* so you're entitled to this . . .)

𝄞 The lonesome road is long
and besot with
fat frogs,
"Excuse me, sir," but he would not
budge and I would not
step over him.

We are entitled to freedom—it's
no whimsy the ISKCON
preacher said and told of Lord Kṛṣṇa's *līlās*
structured and complex
but full of spontaneity.

Below the wind the breezes
clacking bamboos, please
tell us how Kṛṣṇa

kidnapped Rukmiṇī
how She walked
that lonesome road.

Each has to trod
she said, that self-same road but
isn't association (a big word)
needed and
is it the same
as social pressure?

I made good sense of that one.
But know that road
is filled with potholes
of doubt, and
dogs and chickens squawk
on all sides.
The mayor and policemen
and the drunken machete-men
will also carp.

We have nothing to our advantage
but an attempt at speed
and to look at our words
before breakfast.
        It seems the same.

There's only one way
he said
to ride that hometown
road—to be in good company
good cheer. Know, though, that the last
mile or so will be hard,
        even the Pāṇḍavas got tired
and fell one by one
a dog left

to accompany Yudhiṣṭhira
all having to see hell, then
going back to Godhead
or hoping for that
trying our best
and it's up to Kṛṣṇa to
raise us if He chooses.
That road we walk
life after life
while begging the Lord
to give us the blessing
of His pure service.

8:52 A.M.

It was fun speaking on the kidnapping of Śrīmatī Rukmiṇī to the devotees in the temple room. They laughed a little too much, and as a result, perhaps I tried harder to make them laugh more. These are beautiful pastimes, and they contain lessons for us on how to be helpless while waiting for Kṛṣṇa to rescue us. He comes in His own sweet time, but somehow He is never late.

I spoke of the *bhāva* of expecting Kṛṣṇa to appear at any moment and the *bhāva* of feeling unworthy enough that Kṛṣṇa might reject us. But what do I know of such things?

I also invited us to be good listeners. Again, something I know little of. As the *Bhāgavatam* speaker, however, I had no choice but to rise to the occasion and speak the truth, even if I have not fully realized it. I cannot simply make confession after confession while I'm on the *vyāsāsana*, speaking personally rather than directly from *śāstra* the whole time. I have to get on with the narration and tell how the demons who wanted Rukmiṇī to marry Śiśupāla fell over backwards off their horses and elephants when they saw Her returning from the temple. I can say we all enjoyed the pastimes, even though we are not liberated souls.

Now it's over and I have no other duties for the day. Madhu has gone off to play music with Patita-uddhāraṇa. What shall I do after writing this page? Where shall I go? Stay in the house. I could sleep or I could answer more letters. Or even better, I could chant and think of Govinda.

Kṛṣṇa, the Supreme Personality of Godhead, stole Rukmiṇī. He exited slowly, unafraid. The demons condemned themselves as they watched Kṛṣṇa act like a jackal stealing the booty they thought was intended for the lion. In the next chapter we'll hear how Kṛṣṇa and Balarāma smashed them all, and how Rukmī was punished.

They gave me lovely garlands made from local flowers—silky yellows and whites, pink roses and bright orange marigolds. Let the morning slink by in Kṛṣṇa, Kṛṣṇa, Kṛṣṇa.

LATE-MORNING T'DAD MIND

𝄞 Georgia on my mind some musician sang
but now's the day the wind is playing
in Trinidad. I was lying on my bed
but said instead

there's no way but this
day is goin' by fast.

An accordion sounds out
the slat windows of the
sun-beating-down temple
and I see a white egret
yellow-orange bill
suddenly walkin'
in the grass—
temple backyard.

Is the egret looking for a tune?
Seems to be in a trance state or bored
no music and
the only one.

I have no headache and it's hot,
but I'm answering mail.
First we all sang despite the poorly
dressed Deities and someone said,
"Guru, sir, it was
only twenty-five percent my fault that
that woman and I broke up. I
ask your blessings . . . . "

Another wrote: "I stopped
writing you letters 'cause
your replies were
indirect and impersonal."
    Well, here's another and
no offense.

No fence
broken down or standing
and I'm glad I live elsewhere (the heat!)
but glad for the excellent homegrown
bananas and melons.

I *could* remember the old days
the tension between us
but why bother?
Remember something nice and
forget the rest—
    we're going home.

11:10 A.M.

As I write this, M. is pumping away on the melodeon upstairs in the *brahmacārī āśrama*, and Patita is pounding away on a drum. They are not a tailored-made match, but they keep at it. I'll ask him when he returns what he thought of it, and whether people gathered as they played.

Heat. No engagement. I read the chapter, most of it, so far, of Kṛṣṇa marrying Rukmiṇī. Balarāma's speech was philosophical and I got bogged down. It's important to read something like that while you're in peak condition. How can I handle the whole chapter in a *Bhāgavatam* class? One verse is enough. It's good to tell much of the story. I'll have to prepare more, and then I can decide. That is my assignment for today, to prepare for tomorrow's class. Today's went well, but I don't know about tomorrow.

Patita asked about Rādhā's hand of blessing. I replied that She assures us we can serve Her. We are not begging for material things, right? Yes. I don't know a damn thing.

Take a shower. People gather and want to hear about Kṛṣṇa. I told them if we just listen, that's pious, and it will help us even if we are ignorant of the purport. Bala-Kṛṣṇa asked how neophytes can enter Kṛṣṇa's pastimes. There are three kinds of persons, and each are interested to hear. All right? He said he was thinking more about *sahajiyās*.

Oh. We cannot pretend to enter the pastimes, or try to enter them in a material way. I hope they were all listening. Some of them write to tell me what I said that inspires them. I told how a lady disciple of mine is mentally ill and no longer chants her rounds. Still, I honor that she's trying to reclaim her *japa*, and she's now up to eight rounds. She's open with me about it, and that has become the basis of our exchange. She said she was inspired to hear me say that. They want to know that mercy is available, but sometimes they credit a person like me with more power than I have. Then it becomes awkward. I have agreed to be worshiped and to hear their material troubles. I have agreed to try and help according to my capacity.

The man who can't write made a tape of him speaking. That was his letter to me. Again and again he says, "You know, you know." I listened to his confession, his struggle.

As the hours pass, the sun gets hotter, M. keeps playing that melodeon out in that one-room shanty I can see from here. No one seems to live there, although there is an electric wire connecting it to the main line. No one in Trinidad uses screens to keep out the mosquitoes. They just don't do it. At night if you're inclined, you can use a net and burn a coil. Why don't they just use screens? But they don't. If I lived here all the time, I would melt. I would also give more lectures. No hermit life for me here.

O Govinda, You will appear in Your own time. I feel the anxiety of expecting You, but I have to wait upon Your sweet will. I explained that to the devotees, but then Rājarṣi asked, "Please distinguish for us between believing that Kṛṣṇa will act in His own time and the need for us to take responsibility." He wanted me to make a policy statement against slack interpretations. I don't like those kinds of questions, which seem to be intended by ISKCON authorities to check laggards. Why should we also caretake other devotees in that way? Better we ask our own questions. Don't ask on behalf of the ne'er-do-wells. Consider your own ne'er-do-well nature and ask something to help yourself. Don't set me up to be as defender of the system you have defined.

The devotees who came from America for Vyāsa-pūjā have already flown back. My birthday was a formal affair, Trinidad style. O Hare Kṛṣṇa. You are the taste of water, the light of the sun . . .

While eating my meals I'm listening to Prabhupāda speaking in Los Angeles in 1973. This series of tapes is nicely recorded. Prabhupāda said something and the audience laughed, just as they do here.

2:30 P.M.

Sudarśana dāsa warned M. of the dangers in Guyana. We will be arriving on Election Day, and in the past there has been rioting on that day. Also, there are many muggings. Tourists are a target. M. passed that information on to me, adding his own notes of alarm—how the Uitvlugt temple was recently twice the victim of armed robbery, how we stand out as targets because we are white. He suggested we take as little money with us as possible, although that doesn't reduce the threat of being mugged.

Sudarśana said that Paramātmā dāsa doesn't want us to hear about all this stuff. *He* said election day was an ideal day to enter. M. says he feels we are committed this time, but we ought to avoid going there in the future without first checking out the climate. So we are slated to go, but we'll worry. Another bubble popped—that you can just eat and sleep and lecture to submissive persons and nothing will go wrong. You can write your poems, read a little, take a pill if a headache comes, and nobody will mug you. Anyway, it's up to Kṛṣṇa. I have to die sooner or later. Better to die attempting to preach.

PUKKA PAD SHORTY: ACTIVE IMAGINATION, EPISODE 5

Imagine you get mugged by bandits in a car that follows you from the airport. They force your car to pull over. They have guns.

No, I don't like to think about that, or force the reader to think about it either. Someone said, "My life is full of disasters, most of which never happen." Don't worry yourself to death. If you are going to Guyana, then simply depend upon Kṛṣṇa and become more sober, aware that death could come at any moment. That's a fact whether I am in a country prone to mugging or I'm snug in Wicklow County. The chandelier could fall on my head; I could miss a few breaths and pass out.

Fantasy: I roll in a ditch, just as in a nightmare, then rouse myself to wake from it. But this life is real in the sense that it

Krsna devotees worship God & Guru

Jiv Jago - Wake up! Soul!
Begin

GOVINDA

KC
NITAI
GAURA

DK
tom
Be glad
you're a devotee
X

Hare
Krsna
I.S.K.C.ON
within

Hare I want to Chant With Devotion
candrika
Brings
CALM
NO guilt

Govindam
Govindam
Yes I want to be Good but die happy— I can't Control it
society
He thinks he knows

Flickering momentary enjoyment
WORSHIP GOVINDA

PURPORT
SB
ACBSP

maya
KRSNA's
energy
KRSN

Plenty
Krsna is hiding from non devotees I wish to know Him
LORD

Govinda
Bhaya hare I want to be a devotee

Kalpa
Vrksa
yasya deve para
bhaktir
Surabhi
get
the
ferry
to
Heaven
Prob dont know

SRi Baladeva Saha
Sakha
sky
Hare Krsna Hare Hare

is happening to body and mind. For example, the pain of a headache.

We can't say exactly what will happen to us when death finally wins. We know generally what Kṛṣṇa says, but I mean the details. Kṛṣṇa strongly recommends we think of Him if we wish to cross over the river of birth and death. I will try for that. Hare Kṛṣṇa, Hare Kṛṣṇa.

Here I am on a hot afternoon in relatively safe (it seems) Trinidad, chanting and writing. No mishaps. Eventually the afternoon will cool and slowly the day will darken into night. As soon as it gets dark I usually crawl under my mosquito net. That proves another day passed peacefully. That's what I wanted, isn't it?

In this room I found yet another guidebook to Vṛndāvana. Those old places. I caught myself feeling distaste, finding fault with the Vṛndāvana monkeys, not attracted. I had better check that. Vṛndāvana is the best place, even with its monkeys. Even a receptive beginner can feel Vṛndāvana's potency. It's where I hope to die.

But if I am preaching somewhere else and die along the road, that too is glorious. A *sannyāsī* may wind up in a ditch with a dacoit's knife in his side, or a few bullets in his head. Will I reach in my pocket to take a pill so it will be less painful? Will I think of Kṛṣṇa?

Does thinking of mugging make me think of Kṛṣṇa in fear? We suffer pain of death because of bodily attachment. There is no other reason. We want to live, try to prolong life, and know nothing beyond this endeavor. We don't want to let go.

But that's what we have to do. O Kṛṣṇa, that we may remember You at death will save us. We want that, although we are presently trapped in bodily consciousness. You promise that You will come to us as Death, at death. You are not only death for the demons, but for Your devotees too. "O my Lord, more powerful than fire," please let me remember You so there will be no obstruction to my progress as I leave this body.

We probably all fantasize about our own deaths. I'm fantasizing now, after hearing the news about Guyana. I don't want to die in Guyana, and will have to wait and see what happens. Best would be if I got a decent amount of notice, perhaps six months or more, so that I had time to get my Indian visa and go to Vṛndāvana.

Now what is the fantasy? That I live in Vṛndāvana to die, or that I'm pushed toward death in some place far from the holy abode? Where will my thoughts be in either place? Dear spiritual master, I wish to serve you and to live for you. You know my mind is filled with my creative projects. I hear you speak every day. I trust you to help me. I need your help.

Day by day, hour by hour. I know no more than that. This story ends with us in Viśvarūpa's house beside the temple, sweating in the December tropics and worrying, chanting, thinking about what to speak on next.

RISK FOR KṚṢṆA

𝄞 We will go anyway to that
dangerous land
we will
go with *kṛṣṇa-nāma* to the place
where they will simply be after our
money.

Facing danger is the nature of life
and when done for Kṛṣṇa and
the spiritual master—even
Prabhupāda was happy to risk his life
to preach.

What to speak of Arjuna, who
had to fight.

O Kṛṣṇa Hare Kṛṣṇa,
I am not this body and
Lord, may You protect us
all.

Melvin knows death in
jail, others chant in cells,
have cancer, AIDS, liver
disease, and accept. Dear
Lord, take me
        but it's not easy.

We who remain say he
passed away and that's it.
We have a feast on the third day
and then rid ourselves
of morbid thoughts.
We, the express
chanters.

5:47 P.M.

Dark gray clouds moving across the blue sky. This sky is not like Ireland's. It's muggy. Three-note bird calls. Now the frogs are starting and will go all night. Thought more of risk and realized that it includes taking chances to preach in writing by pouring out what wants to come, breaking molds.

I watched the clouds drift by like giant egrets and almost began to miss the clouds, as if I am going to die soon and won't see them anymore. Then I realized that they are beautiful; they are only a spark of His splendor. Kṛṣṇa, Kṛṣṇa. Hare Kṛṣṇa—my transcendental metaphor, semaphore signal to the Lord—I'm here and want to be with You. Mosquito warning in my ear.

December 12

3:45 A.M.

Could it be that Paramātmā dāsa and the others want me to come to Guyana so much that they would withhold information from me about the actual hazards? If so, what would that say about their love for me? It means only that they want my body among them for awhile and don't care so much about who I am or how I can best survive. And what is my love for them—or for any of my disciples? Which among them would I live and die for? In one sense, I am already living for all of them, and I will die for them too. But is that my true life, or am I not living from my closest self? I don't want to answer those questions here right now.

O Kṛṣṇa, why don't I love You enough to sacrifice my life for *You*? What are my *real* concerns? I chant Hare Kṛṣṇa by the full moon at midnight, but still I don't call out in earnest to my dearmost friend, my protector, my beloved.

Concerns: That I don't get bitten by mosquitoes; that I avoid headaches (or when they come, that I can endure them without added suffering); that I can eat and sleep; that I can avoid confrontations, meetings; that I not be seen as a deviant. I went to two *maṅgala-āratis* here, but today I won't go. What will they think? Will my disciples dare to criticize me for it? How much are my disciples and I living for our mutual interests? And how much do we understand what those interests are? My disciples obey, but of course, only to a limited degree. It takes time to figure out how to follow the spiritual master's order within the details of a life. Some of them don't even chant their rounds, though. Most of them here quarrel. Almost all do as they see fit. I do the same, although I'm supposed to be the best example.

So what exactly is this love between us? And what is my love for Kṛṣṇa? And for myself? The *śāstra* says we love our bodies first. We love our body because the life force, the *ātmā*, is within it. That *ātmā* is actually part and parcel of the Supreme Soul, Kṛṣṇa. Ultimately, whether we know it or not, we love Kṛṣṇa because He is the soul of all souls.

Whatever love we have, we must try to preserve it. Going to Guyana, that frumpy place, to a community that may love me according to their sense gratification, and me going with mixed motives, partly out of obligation—all this is nevertheless right. It is enough reason to sacrifice my life. What else do I have? Go and make the best of it. Make it a good bargain.

I'm planning to lecture on Bg. 2.40. There are hard sayings and easy ones. This is an easy one, similar to *su-sukhaṁ kartum avyayam*, that devotional service is joyfully performed. 2.40 is encouraging: even a little devotional service is never lost. Another easy proposal is this one: "Just chant Hare Kṛṣṇa and your life will be sublime."

Of course, these are *sūtra* statements, because when we apply them we realize the sacrifice that will be required to chant Hare Kṛṣṇa. In Bg. 2.38–39, Kṛṣṇa asks Arjuna to fight without attachment to fruitive results, simply because He wants him to. We are meant to give up personal desire and sense gratification, and to act according to the Lord's wishes. That's a difficult task, but *that's* the quality of work that never diminishes. "And a little advancement on this path can protect one from the most dangerous type of fear." (Bg. 2.40)

Yes, it's easy, I'll tell them, and "If such a little selfless devotion is so powerful, why not do a lot of it?"

But to whom do we surrender? In Trinidad it quickly boils down to that question and there is inevitable disagreement. The temple president may claim that he is representing the *paramparā;* someone else thinks he's not fit to lead. And so it goes. Even when we agree on an authority such as Śrīla Prabhupāda or Lord Kṛṣṇa, we realize that the higher the authority, the more difficult and demanding the surrender. Prabhupāda and Kṛṣṇa have the power to ask for complete surrender, but we don't always have the strength or the intelligence to deliver. Kṛṣṇa knows this, so He tries to be encouraging. Just take a little surrender at a time. Even a small amount will be useful. And remember the purport to Bg. 3.31, that if we follow the Lord's injunctions without envy and without resentment, Kṛṣṇa will help us to improve. A faithful devotee works "without consideration of defeat and hopelessness." Such a devotee "will surely be promoted to the stage of pure Kṛṣṇa consciousness."

Chickens and roosters crowing. *Maṅgala-ārati* is about to begin. I hear humble Ananta-śeṣa blowing the conch. The Deities here look somewhat bedraggled and are usually surrounded by flies, but still the devotees attempt to worship Them with love.

I didn't go this morning, but they have to maintain the temple worship out of their own desires, even if I am not there, and even when I come.

PUKKA PAD SHORTY, ACTIVE IMAGINATION, EPISODE 6: MIXED FANTASY

PART 1

A rubber-band guru enters the room in the afternoon. It's still hot, just beginning to cool. The room is filled with devotees, the curtains blue.

"My dear disciples," he says, "I am lord and master of nothing much. Still, I want to tell you that Śrīla Prabhupāda said we should get along with one another. We should chant Hare Kṛṣṇa. We should live until we die. We should be individuals who live in a devotional community, and we shouldn't listen too closely to the nondevotees. We are not Hindus, but neither are we pure devotees. We are simply striving."

On and on he talks, and old ghosts enter, but no dacoits with machetes, no blues singers in ensemble or parades or Derek Walcotts or schools with their respective flags. No money showers down, so no honey on cake handed out sticky into each waiting palm.

He says, "I will tell the truth." But they have already heard enough, especially as ten thousand mosquitoes, flying in the dim light afforded by the fluorescent bulb, head in and begin to circulate. The fields are dark, the moon behind a cloud.

They dress Rādhā-Gopīnātha and receive credit. Nothing will be lost. Those in the funky kitchen also get credit—and the rubber-band guru, and even you, dear reader, get credit. Sing Hare Kṛṣṇa first and everything else will follow.

"Any questions?"

"Is it true you are going to Guyana to face real danger?"

"There is no danger in this world. Everywhere is my home in Kṛṣṇa's shelter. Śrīla Prabhupāda was told not to go to the Bowery, but he saw no danger. Kṛṣṇa protected him."

"Wow! Are you really that fearless?"

"Timid me? I don't want to be thrown into a ditch like a bloody bag, or even mistreated or delayed. I don't even want to *talk* about it. Any other questions?"

"What about us in Trinidad? Why don't you do something to help us? Many householders feel unwelcome at the temple. The temple is not a place of love or even cleanliness and order."

"Wait a minute," a temple inmate objects. "You householders are no help at all. Therefore, you have no right to find fault. We are the *paramparā* and you are an outsider."

"Wait," the rubber-band guru says, sticking his hand into the gooey cake. "Do you see this cake? This is like the devotee community. The gooey covering is cooperation. When we cooperate, the guru will be satisfied. When the guru is satisfied, Kṛṣṇa will be satisfied. Get it?"

"Is it true there are crocodiles in Guyana?"

"Yes, and the world's longest waterfalls, King Edward VIII Falls, deep in the jungle."

The curtains rustle. It is mosquito time. The disciples' meeting is played out. The guru says they ought to read his books, and they say they will, but they can't get anyone to carry them from North America.

Then the rubber-band guru reaches back into the cake. He says, "You see this cake? This is my books and the gooey stuff is the structure of my teachings. Do you see this cake?"

No, they don't. They don't see any cake. They have already eaten it. Then someone stands and asks, "What's that ItM?" The guru doesn't want to talk about it.

"Why didn't you look at the Bharata-natyam dance that woman performed on your birthday?"

"The truth is flying in the window." And so it is, just at this moment.

PART 2

It is pretty obvious that the meeting is about to end. He puts on his slippers, grasps his cane, and begins to knead his red hat. They laugh as he juggles the wool, and when he says he will be back next spring, they don't quite believe him. "We think we have met your goodness just to become the captain of the ship to cross over the ocean of Kali, which is so filled with vices."

He says, "It's about time someone gave us a waft of śāstric breeze. Thank you."

"You see this cake?"

The end.

Two disobedient disciples showed up at the meeting. They looked ragged and called me Gurupāda. One has become a professional boxer. The other did not become a rock star.

Finally I left the meeting and the devotees wandered off. I heard a few cars pull out—those householders, probably.

I went back to the house and soaked my dentures, put in my earplugs, and prayed, "Whatever comes, Lord, I want to go to You. Please accept me." I really do wish only to serve the *saṅkīrtana* movement, and I wish the holy name would utter from my lips and carry my love to Kṛṣṇa so He will be pleased.

10:17 A.M.

The morning class went all right. The theme was "Easy and Hard Instructions." M. and I considered holding an initiation tomorrow, but the candidates didn't receive their recommendations. Instead I will speak this afternoon and again tomorrow. The devotees usually have questions. I just have to get the talk off the ground with a speech lasting about twenty minutes, a speech that leaves questions in the air.

Like? Like what it means to be a disciple of SDG—how to please me. Make it personal: how to maintain a relationship with me. These are standard things, but I could personalize the discussion by explaining the limits of my nature and health. Make it a real disciples' meeting rather than emphasizing more general philosophy.

For tomorrow's class I'll look at *Bhagavad-gītā*. Maybe the next verse, the one that states that we have to be resolute in purpose. It reminds me of the *Bhāgavatam* verse in the Second Canto, *śrotavyādīni rājendra.* Those interested in many things are not interested in *ātmā-tattva*.

There are two ways I could address this point. One is to simplify more, and the other is to convert as much of what we do into genuine Kṛṣṇa consciousness by dovetailing it.

BREEZE ON A HOT DAY

𝄞 Going with mind and wind
I'll be okay

a twinge begins, so
a pill while
M. plays his melodeon
like the wind.

We eat and sleep
look at old faces
reflected in the glass.
I'm the only one I
know who runs like this—
let's go
let's go
to the open way
open and
clear
looking for Him
but this
way.

Am I splayed? Smile, man, you're
too
Kṛṣṇa serious.

Japa
in this
kuṭīr.

In this room
the breeze opens the door
sannyāsa top-piece hanging over it
lifting in the
breeze.
A man writes, "He's independent" so
won't give
the recommendation. Wants him to return
as congregation.

Searching my mind for themes.

11:47 A.M.

Hasty *gāyatrī.* Shower. Still don't know what I'll speak on in tomorrow's *Śrīmad-Bhāgavatam* class. I saw a letter-report on ISKCON Guyana. Buddhi-yoga dāsa (whom I initiated) goes on TV, talks against Hindus and Christians, then introduces his father, Ṛṣabha (whom I also initiated) as a self-styled guru, ready to take disciples. ISKCON says they get negative response from Buddhi-yoga's talks because he uses Śrīla Prabhupāda's books. The GBC advises they make a public disclaimer.

Other good news? No rodents in the kitchen, as far as I can see.

O Stephen, do your parents allow you to act like that at home?

No, ma'am.

Then why?

Red-faced apology. You should know that I cut up because I want to be approved by the mob. I want to get through without being singled out as a fruit or sissy or brown-noser. Actually, I am somewhat anti-establishment at heart. After all, we're teenagers.

Back to Kṛṣṇa, but no splayed intelligence. I can't tell you how I free-write.

I always feel a little crazy here in the tropics—as *they* are crazy. For me it shows in my writing. I start to live a fantasy. For example, I choose mugging scenarios (as if I had a preference).

12:17 P.M.

If for some reason I was forced to live here all the time, I could write a fantasy along with my diary reports. The fantasy would be a mad-tropics-induced float and tell-it-as-it-is story. Or so I think.

I can't pay attention to the scripture right now, so there's no use trying to come up with a theme for tomorrow's class.

I heard that the temple president here was inspired by a visiting GBC man to develop a strategy to engage the devotees who live outside in temple service. Unfortunately, that strategy doesn't seem to work "because of so much independence and skepticism." I can sympathize with the independent skeptics, but I can also see the other side. I don't think any of the devotees are bad, and I doubt they are deeply skeptical or independent. The *gṛhasthas* are probably just normal *gṛhasthas* who are not being accepted for what they are. Temples often call them "negatively independent and skeptical" because they appear to be skeptical about surrendering themselves to the temple president's assignment of "do the needful." Who wouldn't be skeptical of that, especially when temple managers cannot afford to define "the needful" in a way that doesn't bring direct results to the temple?

But I also empathize with the saintly temple president here who has taken on all the management and who somehow thinks he has to represent Prabhupāda to the world, who does his best at it, serving the lotus feet of the temple Deities, holding ISKCON together in this place.

4:45 P.M.

Took Esgic an hour ago. It didn't remove the right-eye pain, so I canceled the disciples' meeting. "It's enough just to survive in the afternoons." I have chosen a verse for the morning lecture: Bg. 4.40. I assume I will be up for it. Tired of lying in bed, restless. Can't write or read. Just be. Hare Kṛṣṇa. Wait for the dark to come and then expect ease as I lay under the mosquito net. Hope to be clear for my 12:30 A.M. writing. The devotees can see by my cancellation that I am chronically in pain. M. said, "If you stayed here for a few weeks, they'd stop coming to your classes." Push on with this tour—be here for it, yet I look forward to returning to Ireland and Rādhā-Govinda.

Paramātmā dāsa spoke with M. about our trip to Guyana. He said it will be nice on election day because the roads will be empty when we arrive early in the morning. M. didn't prod him for the actual situation or for a more cogent description of the political unrest. He said it was no use; Paramātmā would have said, simply, that it's all right. We will just have to go and see. I won't disappoint them by not coming. Kṛṣṇa will protect us one way or another. I especially request He allow me to think of Him now and at the hour of my death. Amen.

December 13

MIDNIGHT

I had a dream I was threatened by a lion. I had a gun, but it didn't work. A man suggested that the ocean was nearby; I could escape by swimming across it. *Somebody* might even pick me up on the way. It seemed like my only chance, although it was extremely dangerous and beyond my powers. He thought I could alternately float and swim. I dove in, but was soon picked up and brought to the other shore, relieved. Later, I met a devotee and was able to get away from the scene altogether.

The dream reminds me that sometimes we have to take impossible risks to save ourselves, but the real relief is in meeting a devotee.

2:20 A.M.

Sixteen rounds. Hear, hear the kernel. Easy to do, at least the easy part. Little steps in the right direction. Looking up. Aware of failure, but not admitting defeat or hopelessness, not resenting Kṛṣṇa's injunctions, a man of faith.

O Kṛṣṇa, Hare Kṛṣṇa, Śrī Kṛṣṇa. I am rolling along.

M. was up before me, at midnight. Said he couldn't sleep because of the full moon. Now he is resting. I went to the sink and found a large frog in it. Then a second, smaller frog joined him. Maybe they can appear as characters in an Active Imagination story.

Someone clearing his throat. A car beeps its horn insistently, and all the dogs in the neighborhood bark. You hear dogs in Vṛndāvana too. That man in Guyana with the Dobermans keeps them shut up in a dark doghouse all day, where they whine away, but lets them out at night to prowl around his compound.

3:42 A.M.

Got Bg. 4.40 lined up for my talk. They may wonder why Kṛṣṇa speaks on faith. They also wonder how to cooperate, how to organize the preaching, how to solve the conflict between those who maintain the temples and those who live outside. If only they could see that those two parties are not really in conflict. They say the outsiders are not willing or able to participate much, and don't place themselves under the leaders' authority. From the temple's point of view, the problem is "skepticism and independence."

A large frog jumped off my clothes when I pulled them from the hanger. I heard it plop onto the wall and hang there, fat and saggy. What an ugly mess he is. And that brown insect I saw yesterday, the walking stick—I could barely believe it was a living creature. It sat camouflaged as a brown straw, but when I accidentally touched it, it bent its legs.

We can actually acquire such a body. It would take such a long time to come up again.

Śraddhāvān attends *paraṁ śāntim*. The *aśraddadhānāḥ* falls down into *saṁsāra* and is happy neither in this life nor in the next.

PUKKA PAD SHORTY, ACTIVE IMAGINATION, EPISODE 7, THE FROG STORY

My throat felt chilly—I left my scarf behind in New York City. I put my hand up to my throat and found a fat frog hanging there. "Ugh!" I cried aloud, and tried to push it away, revulsion coursing in my blood.

The frog (like Nimāi's mouse) spoke. He said, "You hate me, but I could be a prince or a demigod in disguise. If you treat me nicely, even kiss me, I might transform into something wonderful, the curse broken, and you might please Kṛṣṇa."

"You can talk!" I was surprised. "But give me proof that you are my well-wisher or a prince or demigod in disguise."

"That I can talk should be enough," the frog said. "You may have to love something you despise to get spiritual enlightenment. St. Francis kissed lepers and gained enlightenment. He was empowered by God to give mercy to others."

I began to trust the frog and I reached out to pick him up. But no, how could I?

"Not a sufficient effort," the frog jeered. "You didn't even touch me without shivering. Your revulsion still shows." And he hopped away into the darkness. Three other ugly frogs appeared at his side. I could see it all because the moon was full.

Perhaps I'll get another chance to conquer.

Then I returned to my own world, the one in which there is no way out. I turned to the *śāstra* and saw that without faith in the scripture, I will fall down. I will find no happiness in this life or in the next. Decided to go over and give class. The sun was rising and the frogs were gone, and I felt more determined to live as I am, aware that I will have to take the opportunity to love even the creatures that revolt me. I am not such a beautiful creature myself, and I like *myself.* The frogs were just a fantasy, but the point was one of truth.

Frogs are ugly lumps. Such a lump might swell up on my own body—I might get elephantiasis or some other dreadful disease. Then *I* would be an ugly frog. I'm already ugly—my cheeks sinking, my teeth false. Ugliness and disease is sin manifest in the body. I brace myself for the appearance of such ugliness, but I don't want to be afraid of it. The swellings of inevitable time and reaction are something we must learn to endure, and the expectancy of the unwanted is different than going forward to love what you initially despised. Living with such expectancy can help us love with detachment.

As for the devotees down here, they are not ugly frogs. I try to see only the good in them, whoever they are. I don't want to enter their political world or take part in their quarrels. I would prefer to see the good in each, the sincere effort to love Kṛṣṇa, and nothing more. I wish they could see it in each other. After all, we are all spirit soul beneath our coverings, all servants of Kṛṣṇa.

EQUINOX AT MAṄGALA-ĀRATI

1

𝄞 *Maṅgala-ārati*—temple sounds
a man singing to God. He says
I was born on the equinox.
I'm sad but worshiping,
trying my best.

2

They sing to Rādhā-Gopīnātha,
pious, pressured—
they are who they are—
in a group or as single souls,
shuffling feet.

O Gopīnātha, just outside these walls
dark the moon.

3

A towel wrapped around
my neck, my sweatshirt
hood up under
the cinquefoil, the
fluorescent tube,
under the weather.
Was weak yesterday,
Lord.

It's equal my being here or
there where Gaura-Nitāi
upraise Their arms.

What adventures will You put
me through, my Lord? Please allow my
love to grow.

10:08 A.M.

I strained my back while exercising this morning. Then I gave the class on faith and combating doubts. Afterwards, as I distributed sweets to each devotee, I felt the warmth of our affectionate relationship. They were awake for class and asked good questions. The nice side of preaching in the Caribbean is the easy and simple nature of the devotees' approach to the guru-disciple relationship.

Now I will have to see if I can make it without a headache until I am due to speak again at 3:30. If I do get pain, I should not allow myself another pill; I have already had three this week. Hare Kṛṣṇa.

NOTES FOR LECTURING ON "TAC CHṚṆU"

1

𝄞 Moving down a
humid soggy page in the tropics
someone—the breeze—is
banging the door
    to interrupt my solitude.

Ups and downs we want the man
to give his best in real feeling
and I am bound to respond to that.

2

"Are you lecturing on 7.1?"
How did you know?
(Read my mind?)
"Saw it at
the top of a page."
My notes—Kṛṣṇa speaks to
us. He is the *best* speaker
and every scriggle in a musician's
heart of creative energy comes
from Him.

Musician Madhu touching
people who hear.
Good. I am on
the corner too, blowing
an inspired hymn
with paper and pen, no
idle moment
of sadness.

3

Yeah, I'm lecturing on 7.1,
probably straight,
that reading books
is required,
hope to get them to feel it
as if
as if *I* read a lot.

4

Can't tell of my
secret love because I
have none.

Just the experiment, the
scratching, the knowing there is
better than this, the
expression of self as honest—
is this love?
At least it's my offering. ‖

3:05 P.M.

I am on for the disciples' meeting at Indira's house. Tell them my disciples should develop themselves, etc. I need to be sincere and care about what I say. That's more important than the exact words or arguments I use. Convince them, touch them—I know it's another temporary attempt.

They shouldn't think I can come every year. My health and the cost won't allow it. More than that, the travel places too much strain on me. It's better I stay in one place to write and worship Rādhā-Govinda and Śrīla Prabhupāda.

I'll come when I can, but the separation and *vāṇī* is a fact. My books.

Speak on devotees living inside and outside the temples.

5:10 P.M.

The disciples' meeting went well. Indira's house is a beautiful little place. She had white walls and very clean white tiles on the floor, and it reminded me a little of a *kuṭīr*. At the end of the meeting I told her she doesn't have to go to Vṛndāvana, she can live in Vṛndāvana here. As I said it I glanced out the window and saw the green jungly surroundings, which also resemble certain seasons in Vṛndāvana. Of course, I didn't mean that she should never go to Vṛndāvana, but the fact is, few of us can actually live there full-time. And she is older. Best that she turn her present home into Vṛndāvana.

At the meeting I felt inspired by the devotees' presence. Although I tend to think of the Trinidadian devotees as "simple," I was able to speak pretty much to the heart of the topics about the guru-disciple relationship. I told them that there are general instructions about how to relate to one another and personal ones having to do with our particular natures. I don't have to repeat it all here. We have been through a lot together already, many of us, for almost twenty years. I hinted to them that I might not come so often.

One devotee asked what I thought of the fact that he couldn't approach my books other than the ones about straight philosophy. Another devotee asked me to speak about the inner life of a preacher. I told him about the plot of *Choṭa's Way*. Another asked me to speak about how devotees can get along with one another.

After the meeting I returned to Viśvarūpa's house. It seemed like a different world. I think it's because I played up the role of guru. I became their spiritual father.

December 14

MIDNIGHT

Loud music, reggae or whatever. I will chant anyway. Intend to go to *maṅgala-ārati*. Always some noise.

3:21 A.M.

Head slightly stuffed on top, but I decided to show up at *maṅgala-ārati*. Now let's see.

Last night at the meeting I boasted on a few occasions. I said I am breaking new ground in Vaiṣṇava literature. Also, I indirectly implied that while other ISKCON gurus have fallen, I will not. Pride and boasting. Please forgive me, Lord. I say things sometimes I don't mean or wish I hadn't said. I should proceed with fear and trembling. I don't know if my offering is even acceptable.

Swami, you're not fearless so
when did you get that name?
In L.A. in '72 when I asked
for it. Prabhupāda said only,
"Preach, preach, and don't regret."

Will you carry paper to Guyana? Got a gun? They pick on the weak, and the white stand out. I am not physically strong, so don't take my passport and don't leave me with broken limbs. I am on a mission for God, Kṛṣṇa.

Although we know we're not supposed to, I think many of us have a heartfelt prayer for protection, not just of our *bhakti* but of our bodies and resources. Yet we know Kṛṣṇa is not our servant. We are meant to please Him. He is *svarāṭ*, and ultimately we will bow to His will. Surely the Lord has our interest in mind. He doesn't give us only general care; He wants to help us enter the internal energy. He will arrange how best to do that—what experiences we must have. If sudden or violent death is one of them, then we shouldn't waste time criticizing devotees. Learn to appreciate the sacrifice of others.

Manmohan says he can't appreciate books like *Wild Garden* or *Journal and Poems*. He prefers the *Nīti-śāstras*. Well, I write something for everyone. We intend to provide education about my books, the way scholars teach us how to appreciate an author. It's easy to understand what I am writing, but first you have to remove preconceptions you may have about what constitutes Vaiṣṇava literature.

Some may not be willing to do that. They may feel their preconceptions are standard and that they cannot venture into a new field with me.

Honesty, I say, is important. Can't imagine this Hindu-cultured Manmohan entering *Songs of a Hare Kṛṣṇa Man* or an ItM poem. But *I* have to go there, to where the energy rises in me, and capture it for Kṛṣṇa. The *cognizetti* will like it, and a new generation will find it accessible.

5:30 A.M.

Someone is playing one of my lecture tapes at full volume. Sent M. to tell them to stop it. Still stuffy in head, but if it doesn't get worse, I will give the *Bhāgavatam* class.

Cocks crowing. I didn't make it to *maṅgala-ārati*. Slept in due to pain. M. too. The nature of the tropics—how they work on the body.

What else? Don't exalt me or demean me. Let me go off to my corner of the world to read and write.

In today's class I will speak on the need to read Śrīla Prabhupāda's books. I will probably read from my own book, *Obstacles on the Path of Devotional Service.* Subheadings ask, "What's wrong?" "Where is the nectar?" And I say, "Be willing to change," "What's the best way to read?"

What's wrong is that we don't worship Kṛṣṇa. That's not a slight oversight, either. We don't taste nectar because we are jaundiced. If we read, the sweetness will come. Manage your time better, those of you who say you don't have time to read.

I like to read in small amounts during peak times in the day. I like to mix writing with reading. I like to read in an unmotivated way, not preparing for a class.

11:20 A.M.

Things on my mind: I took an Esgic twenty minutes ago and am still waiting for it to take effect. Pain in the right eye. At least I have a fan here. I can hear Madhu playing the melodeon on the second floor of the temple; Patita-uddhāraṇa is on cardboard box drums.

We will be going south, and have definitely fallen into the Caribbean mode in terms of stripping ourselves of unnecessary supplies. It's not easy to replenish what we use up as we travel. We're short of batteries, and my small travel container of shaving cream cracked. Although I taped it together, I don't know how long it will hold up. Madhu borrowed the batteries from my dictaphone to copy EJW tapes. I can't do much work here without them.

Bhakta Kevin, who is here with us, will leave for New York City tomorrow. We are loading him up with things we aren't bringing to Guyana. We'll pick them all up later at Rasarāja's. We also decided to give him most of our traveling money so it won't be stolen from us in Guyana.

After my lecture this morning the temple president made an announcement, thanking me for coming to Trinidad. Then they made me stand by Prabhupāda's *vyāsāsana* while they took photos. Some devotees trailed with me out of the room, and I heard girls squealing, hoping I would throw them a garland. I gave it to a man standing near me. As we entered our host's house, I said to Madhu, "It's time for us to leave."

Madhu's musicianship is irrepressible. I see him like a teenage son with whom I share a life. Our tastes are different, but I appreciate his enthusiasm.

2:50 P.M.

Devotees gather by the car for the send-off. They pelt me with hard-cored flowers, which feel like rice hitting my skin. The flowers rattle against the car. Smiles, nods, waves good-bye—they don't know I have a headache. Patita (Madhu's new friend) hands me a tiny marigold and says something humorous, then "Bon voyage!" Writing this on an extremely bumpy "Prabhupāda Road" just as heavy rain begins to fall.

At lunch Śrīla Prabhupāda was speaking on *Bhāg.* 2.1.1, *varīyān eṣa te praśnaḥ*. He said we may die at any moment, so we should be like Mahārāja Parīkṣit and prepare seriously for that moment. Big worldly men think they are secure, but Mahārāja Parīkṣit, although world emperor, wanted to know his duty now that he was about to die. He accepted the curse and utilized his last seven days for perfecting his spiritual life. A devotee is never afraid.

December 15

2:10 A.M.

We are at Baladeva's house, five minutes from Piarco airport, Port of Spain, Trinidad.

We are planning to leave the house at 2:45 A.M. I have been up since midnight and have chanted twelve rounds. My night was peaceful, thanks to the electric fan that drowned out any other noise. The mosquito net and the pain go down together. M. spent a "terrible" night with no net, and was bitten despite the coil. He took a few showers and applied baking powder to the bites.

Here we go. The airport queue will already be long by the time we get there. I'll try to meditate on the *Gītā* verses that I might share when I get to Guyana.

M. said as we drive off from the airport in Guyana I can lie down in the back "so they (muggers) will only see one white head." Do they block the roads or pull up beside you and shoot you, as crooks did to the German tourist leaving the Miami airport?

"We're doing all we can to avoid being robbed," M. said. We sent most of our belongings and money up north with Kevin. What else can we do outside of hiring armed guards? Post a *chaukīdār* at our house in Guyana? No, that's ridiculous. I'm sure I will think about this all the way there until I see the situation for myself, but let me chant and read.

A young Mormon—white shirt and tie—looking at us and us at him. He was clever enough to go up to the empty agent's desk and get himself an immigration form. We followed suit. I think the Mormons have a two-year compulsory preaching tour. My tour is still on after thirty-one years. It's better this way.

"Is ISKCON becoming an ethnic church?" the sociologist asked. He hoped not. He said when the anticult movement hit hard in the late 1970s, ISKCON turned to support from Hindus. Yes. But we shouldn't abandon our thrust to reach Americans, Europeans, or people of any other nationality. He also said ISKCON purists have a right to be concerned about the fact that many devotees no longer live in temples. These are outer, important issues about ISKCON's future. He said ISKCON will survive, but we don't know in what form.

Travel anxiety. I looked at Bg. 7.3. That seemed a good one for a lecture. I don't have the purport here. Thank you, Śrīla Prabhupāda, who created our good fortune. I cannot assume to be *kṛṣṇa-tattva-vit*, but I am trying for that. Maybe one day, one lifetime.

Writing this under the sick fluorescent light in the airport. A radio announcement said that passengers to New York and Guyana should arrive three hours before flight time because of the Christmas rush. We are here, but there no agents to attend us.

4:17 A.M.

TV on in the distance. I can hear the tone of the voices and the canned laughter, but can't make out the words, except a few: "I dream all right." "Talk to me in dreams . . . " "Oh, what's the difference?" "Dream or no dream . . . "

Baladeva chanting insistent *japa* beside me. He is wearing a black T-shirt with bright purple letters—"Matchless Gifts"—on the chest. In the entire departure lounge (the shops are closed), there are only the three of us and the young Mormon. At this rate, I doubt we will be leaving by 5 A.M.

4:45 A.M.

"I just want to sleep I am so tired," says M. The TV perks and boings and laughs in the distance. Cheap Christmas displays hang on the wall—low budget. A plane offloading. Probably ours. Still sitting around.

The devotees will be glad to see me. So as not to disappoint them, I have to play the role. The one thing I can do in earnest is to give lectures from scripture. Then we ascend to transcendental subject matter. That's my act of faith.

Always unafraid the great
bhāgavatas (that's not me)
know the spiritual world
know eternality
are not afraid of the body
or what may happen to it
are simply
not fearful.

5:05 A.M.

Our sitting places on plane were trashed by previous passengers. Dinner plates and food strewn on floor and seats, and smashed into the upholstery. M. put the garbage in the aisle. The stewardess asked, "What's this?"

M. told her, "It was on the floor."

"Oh, all right," she said, as if she expected us to live with it. We insisted she take it away.

We are stray whites in a black nation. Poland Spring water from Maine. Reality is always different than what we imagine it will be. I feel solace from that fact, and always thank Kṛṣṇa and pray to Him to help me.

One way for me to be Kṛṣṇa conscious is to reach out to devotees. I am here for them, and to act as spiritual master doesn't mean only to receive honors, an elevated seat, a garland, and to give a lecture; it also means expressing my real concerns.

6:10 A.M.

Descent into Guyana. The river. Mist. Dawn. Soft tropic vision. Prepared for the formal, unfriendly immigration confrontation, but they never seem to stop us. A quick stop at customs, a few snide remarks from the taxi drivers and hangers- around, and then we enter the affectionate reception of the "Hindu" Haribols, who are oblivious to snide remarks as they garland me with flowers. They see only their guru. And that's who I'll have to be, only their guru. Flying low over the forked, muddy river, over the jungle, to Timeheri Airport. I have been here many times. Whatever happens, I chalk it up to providence. I used to think in the 1980s, "If they refuse me entry, I'll just go back to America," but they never have. It was in these thick jungles that Jim Jones and his followers committed mass suicide.

11:35 A.M.

I am at Paramātmā's house, or rather a house he built for me. It's a small white "mansion" (by Guyanese standards), built with devotion. I told him I was relieved to have finally come here; they're probably relieved too. "Relieved" is probably not the right word, but "glad" stuck in my throat. I read to them from *Kṛṣṇa* book, the same section I was reading in Trinidad about the kidnapping of Rukmiṇī. In today's installment, we heard how Kṛṣṇa received the *brāhmaṇa* messenger. I spoke about how we honor *brāhmaṇas* by washing their feet, and that they reciprocate by giving instructions.

After the lecture, a headache developed. I took an Esgic, the second in two days, then took rest.

Nice facilities here.

1:00 P.M.

We're way out in the country where people live in shanties instead of houses. People keep goats and cows in their yards, and of course, chickens. Egrets roam among the cows, picking off the flies. A ribbon of road runs straight through the center of this scene, frequented by speeding cars. It's not quiet. Our house is right near the road.

Today is election day. I saw flags all along the road, and signs for only one candidate, the black man, Hoyte. We asked Paramātmā if there was rioting in the cities. He said, "Oh, that was long ago."

Parked in the yard across the street is a truck with a hand-lettered sign: "The Lord Reigneth". Of course, the owners' yard is also full of chickens, which they slaughter. A boy there lazily throws a stone at a cow to chase her from their front yard. Their dog also harasses the cow, who swings her head with her long horns toward the cur. The stone doesn't chase her far, and she stops to eat grass from the roadside. On our way here from the airport, we saw a dead cow lying near the road. Also saw a caged bird. Was it for sale?

MEMORIES OF YOU

𝄞 That girl was so
young, just a child really,
hair drawn back tight, rings on
her fingers, she sniffled as if she had
a little cold,
yet she was the Government of Guyana
        and let me into her country.

I've been here before—same
slats on the windows, same
fears, same teachings to deliver
from Prabhupāda from
me
from the GBC.

Can't hope to capture it—the big
river of events. Do I think when I return
to New York, I'll be the
homecoming hero?

Memories of Kṛṣṇa consciousness—
ethics, *līlā*—of
temple receptions, lunches
at airports.

But Prabhupāda, your memories
flow in a river through my mind
sometimes muddy, forested
a wonderful tide. ‖

KṚṢṆA PROTECTS HIS DEVOTEES

𝄞 I'm from NYC.
What's all
this race stuff? Aren't we all
souls and the music free?

God, people of Guyana
are religious.
"The Lord reigneth."

The clown,
the shepherd's crown,
poor goats and birds—

"meat bird for sale"—
me not doing much to
save them.
O Kṛṣṇa, please protect Your devotees.

3:35 P.M.

Happiness is when a headache goes away, or when you eat lunch and it disappears somewhere into your body, digested, during the post-lunch nap.

A nice thing about a preaching tour of the Caribbean is that they don't expect you to do much more than give a lecture each day. Since your energies are stolen by the tropical heat, you are satisfied to spend the afternoon selecting verses and preparing outlines. Thus the day becomes a simple round of lecturing and preparing to lecture.

An outline for a lecture on Bg. 7.3:

How fortunate we are to be among the rare group of devotees. We can't claim we climbed through karma, *jñāna*, and yoga perfection before arriving at the *bhakti* process, but 18.54 states that *bhakti* comes after liberation. The quality of a person experiencing *brahma-bhūta* is that he neither laments nor hankers. Rather, he is equal to all. Practice and aspire for such joy.

What mercy—*brahmānda brahmite kona bhāgyavān jīva*—water the seed.

Bhakti, they say, is easy to perform, but real *bhakti* according to rules and regulations is not so easy if we attempt it in unauthorized ways.

We can't claim we are *kṛṣṇa-tattva-vit* or that we act as if we believed "Vāsudeva is everything" in life, but Śrīla Prabhupāda has pointed us to the goal. We *are* better situated even than an advanced *yogī* or *jñānī*.

4:00 P.M.

Moments: When we came through customs and the devotees approached, Paramātmā came right up to me and bowed at my feet. He didn't even hit the ground before I gave him a strong tug upwards. No bowing in public!

It was a good, no-nonsense exit from the airport. Aside from that one *daṇḍavat*, everyone was subdued and efficient. They directed Madhu and me immediately to the waiting car. Paramātmā was driving. Although he is tall, he seemed slouched low in the seat. But he knew what he was doing as he maneuvered the car to this house.

In the parking lot, there were quite a few maxi-taxis. They were parked within yards of one another, each booming rock music with the bass amplified and creating a wall of sound. It's a way for these drivers to show off their opulence. Some of the cars were painted and waxed. Even though we moved quickly, the taxi drivers had time to take a good, long look at us. I wondered if we looked like good targets. They could follow us down the road and pick us off. Whatever they thought, Paramātmā soon outdistanced them and brought us safely onto the strange roads that make up travel into Guyana. The roads here are long and narrow, banked not with sidewalks but with dirt, and with plenty of people hanging around outside like they do in India (with nothing to do). They stare vacantly as the car zooms by. Although it's the blacks who are supposed to be rioting, I saw only a Hindu man, young and bare-chested, striding along and swinging his machete the way an American would brandish a baseball bat.

5:28 P.M.

Try to get comfortable. Cow grunting. They tied a small log to the male goat's foot so he can't wander off. I've seen them do the same in Vṛndāvana, in that field by the Oriental Institute.

I don't know who is winning the presidential election here today, and I don't know what it will mean to this country. I saw a large man riding a small bicycle with purple-covered wheels. He didn't seem to care about the election, except perhaps that it provided him a holiday from work.

Small ants crawling all over me. I ignore them until I suddenly feel their bite. You can't blow them off—they hang on for dear life.

The list of disciples I initiated in Guyana stops at thirty-seven. Some are gone. One (Bir Kṛṣṇa dāsa) died in a car accident.

A *brāhmaṇa* shouldn't be disturbed; he should be peaceful. Kṛṣṇa said that to Rukmiṇī's messenger. I agree, of course. He shouldn't get stirred up by controversy or debate. If that happens, he will lose his ability to be equipoised, and then won't be able to deliver the pure nectar. I told them that today. Wash his feet, then let him speak. Listen to the depth of meaning that comes despite any surface botheration.

If I sleep peacefully tonight, it will be Kṛṣṇa's mercy. He takes care of me. *Śrī kṛṣṇa caitanya*. Dark already.

6:10 P.M.

Paramātmā dāsa often wrote me that he was building me a house. I got the impression he had his own house, and next to it was this "guru's house." Just now I put my foot in my mouth when I asked him, "Where is *your* house?" He told me that *this* is his house, and the other house, his rented house, he no longer keeps. In other words, there is no separate guru's house, I am staying in *his* house. Even when I arrived I somehow had this misunderstanding and thanked him for the house. I have no desire to own a house in Guyana, but I was going along with the impression he gave me—an impression he *wanted* to give me—a euphemism.

But what he has built is very, very nice, and I have full facility here. So there is no problem; it was just a surprise. The only drawback is that all the disciples and their children must also stay here—there's nowhere else available—and it's noisy.

December 16

12:10 A.M.

Frequent creative dreams. The last one was filled with anecdotes of funny things people do. Several books had just been published on it and it was a fad to collect them.

It was noisy in the house when I took rest at 6 P.M. The earplugs helped. Now I have another chance to hear the holy name.

Dreamt that Madhu challenged Mādhava to a fight. Mādhava didn't want to fight, and he said he had a headache. Madhu beat him up anyway. Then Mādhava made an announcement on his behalf: "I had a headache. I didn't think Madhu would insist on fighting with me. If he tries it again in the future, I will give him a solid blow on his nose."

I came in and asked Madhu, "If you insist on fighting, what will happen to you?" As I spoke, Mādhava smiled because he knew street fighting. Just wait until he was ready to fight back! Then I addressed them both. "All right, then both of you, both my sons, will be damaged. *Māyā* couldn't have done a better job herself."

PUKKA PAD SHORTY, ACTIVE IMAGINATION, EPISODE 8, TALKS AT THE DINING TABLE AND ELSEWHERE

I was sitting at a dining table with long, tall D. Prabhu and B. Rasa. I didn't have my dentures in—I had forgotten them!—and my mother was in the background.

"Thomas Merton asserted that a monastery shouldn't have more than ten or eleven people in it."

B. Rasa was impressed. Then I realized I was toothless! In public! I excused myself and went to get my dentures.

Yes, I said to myself, to see Kṛṣṇa in all things is not easy. We will talk about this important subject later.

Then I met M. "The danger of being mugged in Guyana or the possibility of the country rioting after the elections—they all seem unlikely now. I have a new worry. Will our flight from Guyana to Trinidad get there on time to connect with the flight to New York?"

I speculate on contingencies: will the BWIA early flight from Trinidad to Guyana be late and cause our flight to Trinidad to be late? How easy it is for them to be forty-five minutes late. Then what? I didn't want to spend the day hanging around the Trinidad airport!

Yeah, M. heard me out, and what he said back was reasonable and solacing.

Then the fantasy moved to new heights as dirigibles flew between the window slats—or so I thought. I then realized they were large flying insects.

You poor fellow.

My sister told me things. Then a girl-woman named . . . I won't name her here. Anyway, she said, "If someone wanted to serve you hand and foot, you would accept it. I can see that about you." She was right, and that opened my eyes. Perhaps that same false-ego willingness to be served as kings was what allowed us eleven to become zonal gurus. We reigned after Śrīla Prabhupāda.

Gee whiz.

This is too hard to sort out. The vicious ISKCON attackers act as if they're the only ones trying to doing it.

Yes, Oona, you are right. I seem like a quiet guy, humble and all, but if a disciple comes forward and does a little thing for me, I'll accept it all and more and more and never say "Enough."

I think I deserve it.

I heard that Vaiṣṇavas in Bengal won't even let you open a door for them. They are too humble to allow anyone to serve them.

Then what happened?

It's a secret. But at the dining table I hinted at smaller monasteries and didn't encourage preachers to move more people into them. Anyway, it was just talk.

Told the guy last night that I needed a pill to quell the pain: "I can't tolerate it."

"I feel for you."

Listening to my inner voices, which tell me that despite the anxieties and inconveniences here, I should stick it out. To preach in the Caribbean is a responsibility, and I owe something to these devotees. I can show compassion for their struggles by speaking the message of *śāstra*.

"Oh, that's another thing I wanted to say," I said to the subpersons who looked at me earnestly yet casually, under the mosquito net where we rested almost bodiless, considering how we share this one form. "I see myself as a person with various interests. I want to preach, but I also want to write poems. I'm also interested in Vedic philosophy, and I like to read Śrīla Prabhupāda's books. How to integrate into an entire person when

I am put into a situation where I can only act on one of these interests?"

"I don't think having varied interests makes me less of a devotee, but I have to be honest about that. When I lecture and tend to disciples, it is, we might say, my religion. But there is more to me than that."

Raining hard and heavy. Doors and windows shut. I'm calm.

5:30 A.M.

"Single bells, single bells"—he was singing it to amuse me. I kept him in rein, though, as a servant should be kept.

Then Karandhara popped into my life, telling his subordinates that he and I were working together. Where did *he* come from?

I CAN'T SEE HIM EVERYWHERE BLUES

1

𝄞 Don't know. No one knows
the old strains, the
conversation I had
with a friend.

Then we were kicking back.
I said I can't, can't
work more than this.

"Go into old Kṛṣṇa conscious memories
then." Tell us.
Kṛṣṇa ate the melon what
Kṛṣṇa did in *Kṛṣṇa* book.
Paint a picture in guru's
āśrama.

2

Kṛṣṇa was king of Dvārakā
and anyone doing anything is a
part of Him—this
philosophy I don't
grasp. Does it mean
if a gruff and lovable
trombone is playing
some human blues
off the levee
        it'd be Kṛṣṇa conscious?

Yes, he said. Smiled too.
But I don't want a tacked-on
Kṛṣṇa
but something real, Him
coming.

3

Śāstra-cakṣus means put on blinkers
like black shades
and say I dig the world
in Absolute Truth colors now
three modes
        four miseries and
Kṛṣṇa at top in Goloka.

And *Bhagavad-gītā*
says whatever he sees
        he sees Kṛṣṇa
and God likes him
and he is never lost.

Young Kṛṣṇa carries a
calf and
I love Him
        His aura
        Himself. ‖

10:04 A.M.

Tired. Hope to survive the day's activity, preferably without getting a headache. So far I haven't prepared the lecture on the disappearance of Bhaktisiddhānta Sarasvatī. I want to remind the devotees that we understand him through our Śrīla Prabhupāda. I also want to tell of the exchanges between them, especially the last ones. They have no *Caitanya-caritāmṛta* volumes here, so I can't read Prabhupāda's "Concluding Words." At least I know what he said there and can try to paraphrase it. I think the most important material for my lecture is the letter Bhaktisiddhānta Sarasvatī Ṭhākura wrote to him.

It's a struggle to be a devotee, said Haridāsa dāsa. I didn't quite agree with him. I said a devotee doesn't struggle with the four rules and sixteen rounds; he follows his vows. If not, he is not a high-class devotee, as Śrīla Prabhupāda writes in his purport to the *api cet su-durācāro* verse.

I'm always afraid that I don't care enough about what I say in my lectures, and that it doesn't mean enough to them or to me. Do I say anything practical? What was the best thing I said this morning? I can't remember exactly, but something about the importance of admitting that we are fortunate to have come to Kṛṣṇa consciousness. Kṛṣṇa consciousness is the best process, even if we are not great at applying it.

I *could* have praised Prabhupāda more, said his name more often to make it clearer. We're here by *his* mercy. *He* created our fortune.

They didn't have many questions. Silent fronts. Is it because they already know what I am saying?

This may not be so important. It reminds me of the Benson & Hedges Gold cigarette billboard ads: "The government advises that cigarette smoking can be hazardous to your health." I considered those words and their careful choice of "can be hazardous." Why not say simply, "Smoking is hazardous"? Because for some it's not? That possibility is carefully allowed.

Similarly, in my talks I have to allow that I may not really care enough about what I am saying. I may not even know what I am talking about. Also, what I write in EJW may actually be more important than what I say in a lecture. It may be the best I can offer.

Śrīla Prabhupāda wrote his letter and received a reply just a few weeks before Śrīla Bhaktisiddhānta Sarasvatī's disappearance. That's the point. Then he followed the *vāṇī*, and that's why he is so great, why he received so much of his guru's blessing. Bhaktisiddhānta Sarasvatī Ṭhākura, the missionary, the great devotee—my words may be bloated ("can be dangerous"), forced rhetoric for the audience. I am a lecturer, but a bit reluctant.

10:56 A.M.

I did the outline for tomorrow morning's talk. You can get by with a simple presentation here. They know the philosophy, although perhaps they don't read much. They receive my words quietly whenever I speak. I am not sure—I can't read their minds—what they think and feel, but it seems they are satisfied.

MESSAGE TO DEAR ONES

1

𝄞 Don't forbid me, don't watch me
I am in Guyana and the breeze
moves the sheer curtains.

The men outside dig holes.
I am weak—pain in head—
        but not sorry.

Day before another lecture
I made my outline
on soggy paper.

2

What can I do for these people who
hear me simply?
Blankly?
They live their duty—small houses
countrified, almost backward,
Hindus and blacks and tension and
tamas—although we are trained
to rise above it.

3

Saw one man bathing his naked four-year-
old son, one bucket and another smaller
pouring water over his little brown body, a
cloth to dry offered, a few
instructions.
I watched from above.

No, I didn't tell these people to
make a charge of the Light Brigade
on World Enlightenment Day.
I tell them to do
as they are able.

Crawling along, these ants
on my flesh, mottled and head
weak, a whitey.
Don't follow *me*
        but read my books
what Prabhupāda said
serve devotees
        preach Lord Caitanya's message
as much as you can.

Dear ones, dear words,
expressions, can you
find something strong and live by it?
Silent
    keep struggling,
    as I do. ‖

3:30 P.M.

Chanting Hare Kṛṣṇa, pacing the wooden floor to the strains of the accordion wafting up to me. Hey, it's Joey grinding out those polkas.

Here comes a maxivan down the road, carrying news that Hoyte won the election. No bad news for us because we are Kṛṣṇa's devotees.

We are preparing for an initiation. I already selected names. I'll reuse Ekeśvara, since the first person I gave it to isn't living up to it.

Microphone encased in cement. Man across the street building a house. Goats with artistic patterns, black on sides and tan on top. They all freeze alert whenever a dog approaches. The cur's a bitch and looks pregnant and harried. Her teeth are bared, but she walks past the goats and they (defenseless) go back to eating grass.

4:08 P.M.

M. has been playing for forty minutes and is still going strong. I wish he would stop. My head has no control. Where am I going? Fog coming in. Just lie down and let time go along as I do when I have to wait for a plane. Waiting in pain. Gives me time to consider the nature of time's passage and how my whole life is passing away. I once thought I had forever at my disposal. Now I know better. M. will eventually call it quits and I'll be able to ask him to help me put up the mosquito net on my bed. Another day played out.

Lord Govinda promises eternal play, variety, no boredom or fear or death, when we go to His abode.

6:18 P.M.

Taking rest early, although the house is noisy with devotees. A *loud*, one-note birdsong right outside my window. Maybe it's a frog, but whatever kind of animal it is, it has a queer whistle. That creature is not self-conscious. That's what makes it beautiful, that the creature will go on with its one note, unabashed, all night. Never bored.

December 17

2:10 A.M.

Fourteen rounds done. M. said that when I get to America I should give my attention to the Press workers, because they are the ones who are working hard to produce my books. But we are already in close contact through our mutual service; our thoughts come together over that. What more can I give by being physically present?

Art—the purpose is to break through for better Kṛṣṇa conscious expressions. The unconscious, the creative drive—ultimately, Kṛṣṇa is the source. If I can't write as a pure devotee, I can only admit struggle. Breakthrough then means confession, truthfulness, and prayer—seeing who I am, what I want, and expressing it to Kṛṣṇa from my own personal heart. And through that, to help others.

Art . . . music. Straightforward presentation scheduled for 7:30 A.M., when I'll discuss what Bhaktisiddhānta Sarasvatī Ṭhākura means to us. He is the grandfather of ISKCON. He wanted us to preach, to be truthful and genuine, and to cooperate with others. Fulfill Lord Caitanya's instructions to the *brāhmaṇa, yāre dekha, tāre kaha 'kṛṣṇa'-upadeśa*. Let us encourage one another.

VERY EARLY MORNING JOG
ALTERNATIVE: PREDAWN JOG IN ISKCON HOUSE

𝄞 Now this light forsooth
is art on stage.
Please pray for me.

Danced, mimed
for folks
audience—Please
listen this man
prays feeling.

There's a special
wail; a little boy
presents.

Lime juice for sale
two cents each on stand
in front of father's
house.

Then we met our guru.
Remember? Same thing.
Look at slats in ceiling
and die then, in some
room
somewhere.

Has the cloud of grief passed?
Yes, much better. They decided their
son wasn't meant to live
here long. Astrologer said
he didn't mind dying, but
it was pain for *you*.

A pineapple
smashed into jam and put
into three-sided triangular
baked
    samosā.

Dance lessons and music so
when she grows up and
leaves ISKCON she
won't say she was ripped
off by her parents' religion.

Don't ask me. I am giving
all I can. Got a ticket, got
room in my passport
for a few more stamps.

Run out of ideas?
No, never. We gave
no veto on imagination.
The train
    that said
"I think I can, I think I can."

Kṛṣṇa muscled in
on me as Time and
pain and bugs
until the gig is over
and I go back

alone
or with others
to dream and dance
forever. ‖

4:17 A.M.

I reason that I play the role of guru and that's why I have to speak Vedic *paramparā* lectures. I want to do them right, even though I am not a pure devotee. I don't have to spend time describing my unworthiness. Just give the teachings.

Here, it's different.

Today I will not ride on a pony or go out and feed the semi-wild (at least not penned in) ducks of black and red. I won't flirt with the black girl across the street, and I won't pinch pennies or loaves of sugar. *Neti, neti.* Won't dig with a shovel. Will write with pen and ink and stain my fingers. Hope to be well enough to speak on Bhaktisiddhānta Sarasvatī's contribution, and on his relationship with our Śrīla Prabhupāda. Same as I've done for thirty years.

5:05 A.M.

I plan to give initiation to a man named Vishram Narine. He came here last night with my disciple, Nityānanda dāsa, who has been training him. Vishram presented the collection of letters I have written to him since 1993, in which I said I was reluctant to initiate him. But I will do it. I am, after all, the soft white guru. I am the one who sits up high on the *vyāsāsana*.

I asked them to submit questions for a disciple's meeting. So far, only one has been turned in. This is it: "Suggest discussions about our relationship with you as disciples and each other as Godbrothers and sisters, and how to improve them."

That question again. It's a little dull. I guess I can't expect their questions to come with a new twist. They are still in the "Gurupāda" mood. Well, if they can't come up with new questions, then I needn't come up with new answers.

Wonder how that Mormon is making out in Guyana. Is he getting his white shirt laundered? Preaching to the natives as I am? We have the *Vedas*, *Upaniṣads*, the *Gītā*, and the *Śrīmad-Bhāgavatam*, all as old as time.

6:47 A.M.

Do you want to be a pure devotee, or is that too "Indian" for you? Do you want to be an artist who expresses himself in the Kṛṣṇa conscious milieu but whose main aim (and satisfaction) is honesty and self-expression, or do you want to live an idealized Kṛṣṇa consciousness? Whew. What questions. No one else can answer them for me.

I dreamt I was going on a journey and wanted to take a big dog. The dog was friendly, but old. It didn't seem like he was going to be much of a protector.

The dream lingered even after I awoke. Is that dog a symbol for something?

My dear Lord Kṛṣṇa, I am foolish, timid, and crouched in this body, identifying solidly with it. Being in Guyana makes me more aware that I am attached to my psycho-physical persona. I am aware that the persona is played up as ISKCON guru, especially in a place like Guyana, where all the disciples are of Hindu-Indian descent. A sociologist wanted to know if we had become an ethnic church. If he saw the movement in Guyana, it might look true.

But then who am I and what am I doing in this movement? Am I the *brāhmaṇa* guru leading the ethnic church forward in this country? I say that is not me, but I don't know where else to turn. Am I an American ISKCON devotee who belongs with other American devotees? Do I belong with the disciples of Prabhupāda? If I want more association, I could always get onto e-mail. That's not really what I want. I definitely belong to the insular ISKCON world where I go from temple to temple and don't really visit any countries. What I see of Guyana is what I see from these windows. When I go to America it's pretty much the same. I'll stay for one day in Jackson Heights with disciples, and I won't venture out onto the streets. Later, I'll go to Gītā-nāgarī.

All this would be all right if I could use my aloofness from the real world as a form of freedom and then turn my attention to the *Bhāgavatam* and my *japa*. Supposedly the great benefit of living in the holy *dhāma* is that the environment is as spiritual as we want our practice to be. That doesn't work for me—I can't live there. I will continue living in Ireland in my inner world.

Anyway, I have few choices. I titled a volume of EJW *Accepting My Limits*. I have come to accept my boundaries.

9:15 A.M.

Lectured before a packed house. Devotees came from various places, and not just my disciples, but Godbrother Bhūtādi Prabhu too. I felt relaxed, no head pain, and I spoke with enthusiasm.

Afterwards, there were two different agitating questions about the fact that one of my disciples is initiating his own disciples in Guyana. I was clear that his activities weren't authorized, but the temple president wanted "blood." I stopped there.

Later Bhūtādi Prabhu and I spoke in my room. Our exchange was pleasant, but at the end, he told me more about the nation's problems. He told me that things were more open now, and that it would be safe to have *kīrtana* at the airport when I left. Would I mind? I guess I would. I have heard too many stories about Hindus and whites being attacked.

Bhūtādi Prabhu also said that there was certainly racial tension in Guyana right now. He said there was rioting during the last election too. Just yesterday he and some devotees went by car to Georgetown, but they were stopped by some blacks on the road. The blacks told them, "You are wearing *dhotīs* and *sārīs*? It's just a matter of time before we get around to beating you up." Bhūtādi and his party immediately turned around and left. He said that sort of thing would happen in Georgetown because most people there are black, but there's not much threat out here where we're staying.

Of course, this news didn't cheer me up. My mind went immediately on the alert. I asked him who won the election. He said it would be announced today or tomorrow, and if the Indian party wins, then there is a greater likelihood that the fighting and rioting will increase. He said the real motive is not even racial; the blacks here have a tendency to loot and rob those of other races who are above them economically. The election will provide them with an excuse.

We hope to get through safely by leaving at 3:00 Monday morning for the airport. Bhūtādi broke through my illusion that everything I had heard was exaggeration.

9:23 A.M.

Mistuh, pull over. We gonna rob ya.

Tension. Riots. Who won the election? Paramātmā dāsa didn't tell us the truth. He kept it covered so it would seem peaceful and I wouldn't cancel my visit.

So, Mistuh white scum, we gonna beat on yo face and body now.

No, please. Nṛsiṁhadeva! (In a slightly raised voice.) Don't worry. It won't happen like that. And if it does . . . at least you've got some of EJW 17 sent up north. The world won't be deprived of your ramblin'.

Jayanti dāsī writes me that because her husband feels this is the best place for him to preach and live, they have moved back to Guyana. "It is a challenge being here. It seems like each day brings a new test to pass. Therefore we have to depend fully on Kṛṣṇa . . . I am mostly engaged in Deity worship and cooking at the temple. I feel happy and blissful in my new service despite the difficulties. My realization is that if I just assist my husband in any way, my position is safe. It is so dangerous here that I am praying to you to give me strength and courage to continue. It takes all of your saintly qualities to make it, especially humility and tolerance."

10:58 A.M.

Initiation tomorrow. I don't want to emphasize the guru in my lecture. Better to speak on Kṛṣṇa or the holy name. Initiation means the disciple will promise to follow the Lord's instructions, give up sinful life, and always chant Hare Kṛṣṇa. How about *yeṣāṁ tv anta-gataṁ pāpam* (Bg. 7.28)? It's a good verse, and the purport refers to the need to follow the regulative principles of religion. "Only those who have passed their lives . . . and who have conquered sinful reactions . . . " Regulated principles of freedom. If we can't think spontaneously of Kṛṣṇa, follow *viddhi* (12.9). Speak on initiation in terms of following *viddhi.* That will lead to love of God. Especially mention the holy name in that context. Chant and have faith.

I noticed in one purport how a devotee is not troubled by reverses. That's a deep quality. I probably have dormant reserves of it, but on the surface I am nervous and attentive to hear even rumors of rioting and trouble.

12:02 P.M.

Madhu is setting me up well and giving me support on how to respond to the controversies among the devotees here. I make my statements, but don't get dragged into it unnecessarily. He also reassured me that our passage from here to the airport, and our time at the airport itself, will probably be straightforward. My anxieties have faded. Getting all the way to New York in one day would be great.

Bhaktisiddhānta Sarasvatī Ṭhākura both braved opposition and used things in Kṛṣṇa's service. I have to do my little bit sometimes. The world is not a safe place.

Hare Kṛṣṇa. I can hear something boiling.

2:41 P.M.

Got a title for this volume yet? *The Lord Reigneth.* Because it's painted on the side of the neighbor's truck.

Is there a deeper meaning?

God is in control, even here, even when the chicken-killers proclaim Him, even though none of us are aware of His full and mysterious reign. Some say the Lord is the God of Christianity or Islam, but the Lord reigneth despite our petty designations.

Actually, I liked that sign on the neighbor's truck. It reminded me every time I saw it that I can remember Kṛṣṇa, and I can take Him personally into my life. I trust Him to protect me in whatever way He sees fit—protect my remembrance of Him—while I'm in Guyana. I'm no fearless preacher, so I took solace from that sign.

That the Lord reigneth means that even if some mishap occurs here or elsewhere, Kṛṣṇa is in control, and I can worship Him through the mishap: *tat te 'nukampām.* A devotee finds Kṛṣṇa even in material reverses, and because he continues his submissive worship, accepting the token karma he receives, he earns the right to go back to Godhead.

It seems to be a large family who own and operate that truck. They definitely use the truck for their livelihood. Just now another large truck, painted army brown, has pulled in alongside the "Lord Reigneth" truck. They are loading up white bags, which seem filled with seed or sand or something, from the family truck onto this other truck. At least half a dozen men and a few women are helping. I'm not sure what their business is. They have a big yard around their ramshackle house, and it appears to have pens in it, and I have seen chickens. Maybe they live by selling whatever it is that goes into those white bags. All the family members are strongly built and full of confidence.

Anyway, as far as I am concerned, regardless of what politicians or crazy people do, God's will is in control of every situation, and He has promised to protect His devotees. Ordinary humans think their president or the modes of nature rule, but the Lord reigneth over all, and His justice prevails, both in this world and the next. And blessed are the devotees who suffer persecution for the Lord's sake.

3:15 P.M.

You wanted the news, so you got it. The *Starbroek News* states that the PPP presidential candidate, Janet Jagan, is leading the election by five percent over the PNC candidate, Mr. Hoyte. The U.S. observers said that the elections were fair; there had been no cheating. But there is considerable concern about the long delay in reaching a final count. The PNC is particularly unhappy about this, and has started rumors that there may be foul play involved.

The newspaper said that the voting fell almost entirely along ethnic lines. Blacks voted for the black candidate and Indians for the Indian. A lot of candidates fell away with few votes. In other words, there was no platform except race. I somehow thought it would be safer for us if Hoyte won, because it's the blacks who are liable to riot if they lose.

Even in this backyard, one cow with horns pushes around the cows with no horns, and a truck passes, packed with live cows standing side by side in a row.

It's not Guyana, but the whole crazy world. Chant Hare Kṛṣṇa. The Lord reigneth.

4:55 P.M.

The disciples' meeting went well. At least I didn't get a headache. We talked a lot about using intelligence in approaching the relationship between us. Don't read my books and use them to push your own cause. Don't make me a collection of quotes. If you read widely and catch the *siddhānta*, you will learn intelligence. Intelligence is a spiritual quality—at least the kind we want. Such intelligence should lead to humility and cooperation, not aggression and quarreling.

While lecturing I forgot my fear of the inevitable post-election riots, the airport delays, and so on. I sailed over it all and spoke in *paramparā*. After I distributed *prasādam*, I returned to this tight little room to face the same issues, looking out the same window, looking at the same canal with the same cracked clay on the same banks. And I can still see that truck: "The Lord Reigneth." It's odd how much environment shapes our consciousness.

5:18 P.M.

Lots of goats and kids running along the canal bank. They come to the macadam road and hesitate. A car rushes by and the goats freeze, some falling back. As soon as the car passes, however, they dart across the road and continue along the canal bank. A boy thinks the goats are too near his yard, so he throws stones at them. They bleat and keep moving. Another boy runs down the road to retrieve an escaping cow.

Initiation is next. What name to give to someone whose name since birth is Manmohan Persaud? *Man-manā bhava mad-bhakto. Mad bhakta. Mam. Mamata. Mamaivāṁśo*. Can't be Madana-mohana because I have already given that name. I've also given Mahā-mantra, Maha-yajña, Maha-prasāda, Mahā-puruṣa.

NIGHT COMING ON IN GUYANA

𝄞 This way pleeze/ night action
not NYC this is
guy-anna
this mud-baked canal bank
this sweated body
the melodeon player next door
and the kazoo player too
my head
        careens to
His lotus feet.

Now this way go down the same
aisle walked by Guru Mahārāja
they laugh and
laugh—see?
He's on the high seat this
do-goody
    writer of many
homespun books.

Forgetting his self he meeks
and the meeks shall inherit
what? Hear that bang-bang stick
against the tree?

The night imprints
the ink imprints on
previous page and the man said
even if he wasn't a Negro he'd
make music. He tried hard to hate
white men but then one
good one would come along
and ruin everything. ❚

December 18

MIDNIGHT

Dear Lord Kṛṣṇa, You are always with me and with all souls. I ask you to bring me close to You through prayer and revelation. You know how I am afraid of material suffering, especially when it is meted out by cruel demons. Does this mean that I am not willing to pay the price for *kṛṣṇa-prema*?

Please, please, I petition You like an unworthy, sentimental disciple begging his guru for mercy.

You are kind and I am slow. Please grant me the power to improve. Let us all improve. And please let me chant.

In a dream I was challenged with the reality of Kṛṣṇa's pastimes. Somebody left us. I shouted to Lalitāmṛta and my sister, "Look, now we're left alone with Kṛṣṇa's pastimes. Do you think Kṛṣṇa is going to come walking in the door the way His *līlā* describes? How can we believe this? Now all we're left with is this, our lack of faith." I was hoping that by saying that, someone would come to help us understand the transcendental reality.

4:24 A.M.

Most of my disciples here live outside the temples, so I encourage them to practice Kṛṣṇa consciousness at home yet maintain a connection with the organized ISKCON preaching. Yesterday we discussed how my books can instruct them, but they have to be read and acted upon with discretion and intelligence. Paramātmā dāsa asked how to find such intelligence. It's not material but spiritual. If they read a lot, they will grasp the *siddhānta*. They can also learn from experience, both mistakes and successes.

Counting the days until we leave. Four days left. Seems like we scheduled too long a stay. The election aftermath and racial tension still make me nervous. I'll be relieved to get out. Why can't I just live here for a few more days in the ever-present moment? There's no difference between Guyana and America except in externals. I will have a heart there as well as I have one here, and my mind will accompany me through both places. I will experience the same challenges, the same faith, the same taste, read the same books. I will also do the same writing. Take advantage of wherever you are to remember Kṛṣṇa. May Kṛṣṇa protect me from calamities.

BODY AND SOUL

1

𝄞 Body and soul this man
I like.
He wants me to be happy and
from his suffering comes
a light that fears no
darkness.

The saintly person must
suffer—just between him
and God.
        His way isn't ours
But we've got to
find one—
a way, I mean.

2

Warm weather and cold
nice people and not nice
the indifferent money-
makers.
        Engines, inane TV
the art soul
        and body
he's trying . . .

our burden of God consciousness
        topmost
heavy.

Smile with me, brothers,
sisters, daughters, sons
as I make light
asides
        in Kṛṣṇa conscious
        books
        Kṛṣṇa conscious
        looks.

I'm no angel
but I'm telling it
through the rhythms I was am born with
born of Swamiji
learning to love

at all costs
and it
costs.

3

Dawn not far away will
turn to tropic heat, to more trucks
and angry shouts and goats
and ducks
the baked riverbank
the plethora
beyond my grasp/ I
eat and rest
and hope

and sing my hymn to God
beyond all hearing to
Kṛṣṇa in all things
Kṛṣṇa in the heat.

Build a fire for *yajña*
give spiritual names
your soul's in heart
they say
and body you know
is here, your sweet
and burdensome
flesh and body
and blood
given by God
'cause you wanted it.

4

My Lord I bow to
You. You are my
body and soul.

You are my preferred
sweet slow chariot
may You see me at death
and me see You in Your holy name,
holy name, holy name
what else
can I do even
at best? ǁ

PUKKA PAD SHORTY, ACTIVE IMAGINATION, EPISODE 9, PRE-YAJÑA FANTASIA.

The *śāstra*-man said, "We hereby give out these spiritual names: Gopīnātha dāsa, etc."

"Wait," interjected another from the fireside. "What right have you to do this? Do you care enough? Can you give them freedom from death? I know what's on your mind—it's petty material stuff, fears and desires."

"Oh, no," said the man of *śāstra*. "You don't know how Kṛṣṇa sees and accepts me. I intuit the same, have faith, although I am a man of part-time *śāstra* only." He was not actually fully absorbed in *śāstra*, but anyway, he sat on a pillow and gave them enduring names, an assignment for life.

Filled the *yajña*
made the peace pipe
and joined the mantras one to another.

Got his *śrī viṣṇu* prayer? Got *gāyatrīs*? Will his eye hold out? Will he take a pill if he needs to so he doesn't have to cancel this event?

The head asked these questions, and good questions they were. The doctor went to church but not to temple and the cocks crowed endlessly outside. The *yajña* hour drew nearer.

Before the *yajña* he lay down in peace and his neck and head and entire body relaxed. There was a chance he'd make it through.

Rurus and ghosts
can't stop him, he is
working for the Lord
even if he expires or
cancels he'll get
through somehow on behalf
of Swami our
master.

Please, disciples
in my charge—Lord knows
these people try and have
a natural pious tendency.
But please, disciples,
four rules, sixteen rounds—
I order you from
the mast of this
ship, the forecastle.
I give the command:
    no mutiny
    watch out for P-boats
    our ship is Safe Wake
worship the Lord of sacrifice,
and Goloka is yours.

10:35 A.M.

The Lord reigneth. I did the initiation *yajña* with many photo-takers in attendance and at least two video cameras. It went all right, but by the time it was over, the pain in my right eye had flared up. I took an Esgic about forty-five minutes ago, but the pain is still going strong. I'm trying to recover so that I can give the two *brāhmaṇas* their *gāyatrīs* and meet with the three initiates.

Really playing up the role of guru. Spoke about the four rules and sixteen rounds. It's good for me to do that, but it's heavy. I'm looking forward to being free of it and relaxing with more intimate friends. Madhu is a real right- and left-hand man in the way he helps me get through these days. The songbook I used to read the *maṅgalācaraṇa* prayers was literally falling apart, and Madhu held the pieces while I read the words. Then we all went for the "*Svāha*!"

I just asked for a second pillow to prop me up. Next thing to plan is for tomorrow morning when they want to have a *guru-pūjā*. Maybe I could sing *bhajanas* and explain their meanings. A guru should speak *kṛṣṇa-līlā, kṛṣṇa-kathā.*

I find I have a healthy sense of duty. I don't always like everything I am expected to do, partly because I doubt much of what I do carries as much weight as people make out, but I do have a strong sense of duty. I don't want to neglect anything that might help.

1:00 P.M.

Martin Carter is Guyana's greatest poet, they say. He died last week at age seventy. We told the cooks here to stop serving me deep-fried preparations. My headache took a few hours to go down. I suppose I should try to see the *brāhmaṇas* this afternoon.

I am privileged, having been born in the richest nation, but I am not rich. I'm a guru for a poor ethnic church. I'm a pestiferous usurper, some say. Or a slouch, an invalid now, a semi. I'm also a quiet madman and a recluse. Alas.

I chose three *bhajanas* to sing and explain tomorrow morning: *Parama koruṇa* because they have such lovely Gaura-Nitāi Deities here, *Śrī Tulasī-praṇāma* so we can talk of the eternal residents of Vṛndāvana, and '*Gaurāṅga*' *bolite habe*.

Overeat? Hot stuff in gut. Too many spices. I'll need to rest if I am to see the *brāhmaṇas* this afternoon.

3:30 P.M.

Just met with the three new initiates, Viśvambhara dāsa, Gopīnātha dāsa, and Ekeśvara dāsa. All three are sweet men.

Viśvambhara told me how he heard that I wasn't initiating, but he had decided to accept me and follow through on his determination. Ekeśvara told a similar story. He has been keeping my picture for seven or eight years. He heard I wasn't initiating, but his wife and mother, who are both my disciples, told him to remain sincere. I told them that Kṛṣṇa had answered their prayers and overcome my resistance. In their presence I am forced to speak the *paramparā* in a straightforward way. I don't know what I am going to say, but things come out and they sound right.

Viśvambhara also told me how years ago, he saw pictures of me in an album one of my disciples owned and stole one. He asked if it was all right to steal like that. I told the story of how a devotee stole Prabhupāda's *mahā* sweet ball from Tamāl Krishna Mahārāja's plate and how Prabhupāda had laughingly approved.

The initiates are all householders and all have outside jobs, so I encouraged them to think of Kṛṣṇa at work and to give the fruits of their work to Kṛṣṇa.

When Ekeśvara spoke, I had difficulty understanding his Guyanese accent. He kept saying "me" instead of speaking of himself as "I". Once I got used to it, I understood him better.

Now I have to meet with the *brāhmaṇas*. They forgot to have the *brāhmaṇa* threads ready for the ceremony, so they have just made them. They only have enough string for one thread to have three strands and the other to have six. I can laugh, but I'm equally unprepared spiritually. I chanted on their threads regardless, but I told Rādhā-kānta, who received the three-strand string, that he would have to replace his thread with a proper one.

Rādhā-kānta said he couldn't do that immediately because there is rioting in the town.

"In Georgetown or the local town?" I asked

"Georgetown. Maybe it will quiet down tomorrow or the next day."

He also said that this thread is rare in Guyana and is only available in one store, which is now closed. I told him not to worry about it.

4:02 P.M.

Calm out here. Breezes. Pretty canal, a duck floating in it. Madhu on the porch playing melodeon. The rioting seems far away, but it's on my mind. They still haven't announced the election results. M. assures me that we'll bypass all the trouble Monday because we will be leaving so early. "They'll have returned home with whatever they've looted." We'll go with Kṛṣṇa and pray for no roadblocks or flat tires.

These days passing slowly. I keep functioning with my lectures, resting in between to overcome the eye ache. It doesn't seem good for meditation, this schedule down here, but it will soon be done. I speak of duty, *viddhi*. Hare Kṛṣṇa.

Newspapers of the last two days have expressed a kind of fingers-crossed hope that calm will prevail, but both sides have claimed victory and that has only aggravated the problem. Give us peace.

Swami spoke on subjects basic
I wanted to hear better but
at least I heard the *śāstric* truth
methinks me better run the booth
instead of post-election fears,
be sense-controlled
be fearless (duty-bound).

STAYING CALM

𝄞 There's calm, he says, and I don't
know if his nervous talk
refers to reality.

I mean, if this man can
keep the worst elements
calm

he's a peacemaker but
others are not.

So I sit it out and hear him
and think of profound and soft
moods of God conscious
poets.

Will he run out of patience—
hear the siren plow down
this road. It's an ambulance!

Could be a man lost a limb
but we keep on praying
there's a way
to get to Kṛṣṇa

and it doesn't seem
to be through peace
in *this* world, Peace,
paraṁ śāntim, is with
the soul and his God and God
and His beloveds.
Please Lord
Let us remember You.

O Kṛṣṇa, my soul can't die
and You will protect what's important
my remembrance
of You.
        You reigneth over me,
a tiny
part
of You.

Hare Kṛṣṇa Hare Kṛṣṇa.
Hare Kṛṣṇa.
    Soft tones of the
strong one do well
each moment
of breath
    until end.

4:46 P.M.

A very dark brown cow and her young calf walked by. There's a knee-high barbed wire fence, and at first she couldn't get past it and was bellowing. She spent some time eating greenery, then tried again to step over the wire. This time she succeeded. Her calf walked under it. Then another cow came. This one seemed more experienced, and she ducked smoothly under the wire with surprising agility.

Maxi-taxis roar by, dropping people off at local stops. Are they coming from town? I wonder what's going on there.

Two ducks loiter on the hard banks of the canal. One folds its wings and nestles into a crevice in the sun-baked mud. In this house it sounds as if someone is playing the radio. I hear a newscaster. Oh, it's my lecture tape.

5:53 P.M.

I get under the net around 6:00 P.M. each night. There seems to be nothing else to do. I like to settle down early so I can get up at midnight. While under the net, I pray to Kṛṣṇa to reveal to me how to act in Kṛṣṇa consciousness. I read in Śrīla Prabhupāda's 1966 New York journal and highlighted sections earlier today, and I plan to read some of them tomorrow afternoon. Each day I come out of this room, bow down to the devotees and the Deities, take a seat, and lecture. Then I return. I haven't left the house since I've been here. Neither has M. There is nowhere to go. Today devotees tried shopping in Georgetown but were forced to return without being allowed entrance. Don't exaggerate. There is rioting and the shops are closed.

Read that Śrīla Prabhupāda's room was broken into. Then he got a letter from Bon Mahārāja stating that there was a precarious situation in Bengal with the loss of property and life. Śrīla Prabhupāda took an offer to move into a Bowery loft, even though he was warned by a friend. It's dangerous everywhere.

Śrīla Prabhupāda, please accept my activities as service to you. They are obviously flawed. My desire to preach is not strong, and I have lost conviction for a certain kind of preaching. I want to reach people through my writing and to care for those who have come to me for that.

Prabhupāda, you see what a worrywart I am, so self-absorbed, distracted, and physically afflicted. Still, I beg you to accept me. I have no other hope. Please give me the inspiration to cross over the inevitable troubles life hands me and to finally step on the head of Death—and mount—if not the chariot back to Godhead, at least a rung up on the devotional ladder.

December 19

1:05 A.M.

Nine rounds done so far. That's not bad for me, since I'm under more pressure here to lecture and I've had some pain. As I read past volumes of EJW, I see the undeniable boredom that occasionally creeps into my quiet routine. That's another challenge I face—to live in the quietness and to go within. Of course, as we read Prabhupāda's books, we see continual references to the preachers and how they take risks. I think of my Godbrothers crossing dangerous borders or meeting with so many obstacles in their preaching. Now it's the Prabhupāda marathon, and devotees in the U.S. cities or wherever are going out, sometimes being arrested or beaten, but are accepting the voluntary austerity of distributing Prabhupāda's books.

Thus it's probably good for me to be down here with this pressure and even anxiety. I too have taken a risk to come here to preach to my disciples.

Also, I have been regularly making fun of the fact that I am offered an elevated seat, and it's true that especially in places like this, such honors can tend to get exaggerated. But sitting on that seat is also my duty, as well as giving the kind of classes I have been giving. I shouldn't think of my service here as useless just because every time I come, the devotees are experiencing the exact same problems. I don't seem to be advancing very quickly either. But that is no reason to become hopeless.

Whenever I'm in the tropics, I think of my innards as melting. Instead of thinking of the guru as being a puffed-up false persona, I melt until I feel like a functionary preacher. Let me function as guru if that's what this body is for. Choose the text on which to lecture, and deliver it with all the rhetoric and earnestness you have.

3:30 A.M.

Fear. I'm trying to examine it. Excessive attachment for material things puts one into bewilderment: " . . . such fearfulness and loss of mental equilibrium take place in persons who are too affected by material conditions." (*Bhāg*. 11.2.37, quoted in Bg. 1.30, purport)

We can't be fearless unless we are completely Kṛṣṇa conscious. "A conditioned soul is fearful due to his perverted memory, his forgetfulness of his eternal relationship with Kṛṣṇa." (Bg. 6.13–14, purport)

"Fear is due to worrying about the future. A person in Kṛṣṇa consciousness has no fear because by his activities he is sure to go . . . back to Godhead." (Bg. 10.4–5, purport)

Others are in constant anxiety about the next life. Be free of fear in Kṛṣṇa consciousness.

Sounds simple. Fear is due to material absorption. A Kṛṣṇa conscious person knows he cannot be killed, and in his next life he will be with Kṛṣṇa.

How to be free of fear: "One who takes shelter of the Supreme Lord has nothing to fear, even in the midst of the greatest calamity." (Bg. 1.19, purport)

"There is no fear in transcendental realization," because even loss of life is only a material consideration. (Bg. 1.29, purport)

"This is the secret of Kṛṣṇa consciousness—realization that there is no existence besides Kṛṣṇa is the platform of peace and fearlessness." (Bg. 5.12, purport)

A devotee knows that even danger is part of Kṛṣṇa, and He is our protector. Śrīla Prabhupāda was not afraid when Calcutta was being bombed. He knew that if Kṛṣṇa wanted to come in the form of a bomb or rioter to kill him, he would accept such a death. Whomever Kṛṣṇa wants to kill, no one can protect, and whomever Kṛṣṇa wants to protect, no one can kill (*māre kṛṣṇa rākhe ke, rākhe kṛṣṇa māre ke*). Bhaktivinoda Ṭhākura prays, "Slay me or protect me as You wish, for You are the master of Your eternal servant (*Mārobi rākhobi jata car, kṛṣṇa dāsa prata tua adhikara*)."

BODY AND SOUL (TAKE TWO)

1

𝄞 We are with Kṛṣṇa and have
music to accompany us—
no drum and bugle for war

'cept war on fear
of being a body that must
die.
    Sweet love attachment
to day and night and
    heat within but
    let it go.

Soul is real person
learn *Gītā* lessons
from masters
and see Kṛṣṇa in sacred in
everything.

No sentimental slush
I improvise and speak
of the sweetest thing and
I want to be with
You, dear Lord Kṛṣṇa.

2

Let go even this
charming melody 'cause body
and soul got to part
again and again until
the spiritual body enters
Vṛndāvana, Goloka.

Be safe with Kṛṣṇa.
Group your *abhaya*
mottos
        like *japa*
Be with
us, Lord.

Sharp intake of breath
adrenaline fear
flee or fight,
anger and hate
        all bunched up
you can't know
pure peace.

O Prabhupāda, you came
in light
to this unworthy son.
Told me, "Do something practical." Yes,
I will. ‖

PUKKA PAD SHORTY, ACTIVE IMAGINATION, EPISODE 10, WORST-CASE SCENARIOS

Suppose as the cock crows and we're on our way to the airport, we get stopped and beat on the back of the head and we die. Maybe I die thinking, "Hey, I'm an American. This isn't supposed to happen to me." Or, "I didn't get a chance to send the last dictation tapes of my writing up north." Then I might have to come back to live again as an American or as a writer in ISKCON.

That might not be so pleasant. I could be born in a family of Hare Kṛṣṇa devotees who might be in good standing, but who might not be expert parents. Or perhaps my parents will be great, but I might grow up in a bad or nonexistent *gurukula* system. Or the *gurukula* system is first-class, but I don't like it, and when I turn sixteen I run away from home and join the circus or the Mormons.

Yeah, maybe I'd meet that strong-shouldered, strong-necked Mormon with the white shirt we saw on the plane. He'd convince me to follow his path and I would have to live in Salt Lake City, Utah. While out there, I might meet some descendants of Cāru Prabhu, and they might reconvert me to Kṛṣṇa consciousness. I might become a happy manager on their open farm, take care of the llamas and collect a lot of money. I might really like reading Śrīla Prabhupāda's books, and I might start to preach what they say. It would all be so natural to me that when I read the *Bhagavad-gītā* statement that I must have been a *yoga-bhrasta* in my past life, I would know it to be true.

Well, the problem with this scenario is that it's all speculation, fantasy, fiction, and I want to hear of a successful ending, how I lived happily ever after.

All right. I graduate from taking care of llamas and go to work in Salt Lake City's Govinda's. While there, I read more seriously in Prabhupāda's books. I decide I want to move to Vṛndāvana, and when I arrive, I fall in love with the *dhāma*. I decide to live near the temple, which is still operating as Prabhupāda's ISKCON. I then begin to preach by emphasizing chanting and hearing. I die in the holy *dhāma* when I'm about fifty-nine and go back to Godhead. Right?

And *then*?

No, that I can't reveal until you're liberated. If I told you now, you would become a *sahajiyā*.

Do you mean our hero gave up every last attachment to this world? You mean to say that he was no longer in love with the beautiful Guyanese sunrises or the Irish sky dramas? You mean he stopped looking forward to breakfast to please his stomach and started honoring *prasādam*? You mean he gave up feasting his eyes on tones of green and brown in the canal and enjoying the reflections of palm trees in the water?

Well, no, it's not that you have to be blind and deaf to be a pure devotee. I mean, when our hero saw such things, they drew his mind to Kṛṣṇa. Yes, that's what I mean. Did you know that the sun-god has some connection to Rādhārāṇī? So what do you think he was thinking about when he saw those sunrises? And doesn't that canal just remind you of the Yamunā?

The one thing our hero would have done is survive those Guyanese riots way back in 1997, back in a previous life.

6:15 A.M.

Yesterday I gave the *gāyatrī-mantras* to two devotees simultaneously. I did it because I had pain. I asked Prabhupāda to forgive me.

After I pronounced the words for them and presented them with the translation, Rādhā-kānta dāsa asked, "What is the purpose of this?"

"What?" His question caught me off guard. "The purpose? It's to . . . say prayers. These are prayers. You might as well ask what is the purpose of the Hare Kṛṣṇa mantra, or what is the purpose of *śāstra*. It's to help us think of Kṛṣṇa. The Muslims pray five times a day, and we stop at three of the day's junctures to remember Kṛṣṇa."

I fielded the question all right, I guess, but somehow it remains in my mind with its almost dumb innocence. It's actually a profound question, and one to live with rather than to answer glibly.

In the Sixth Canto, Chapter 17, where Mother Parvatī curses Citraketu, there are interesting instructions about a devotee's suffering. King Citraketu accepted Parvatī's curse without complaint. Even if he is offenseless, a devotee accepts whatever happens as ordained. "A devotee is naturally so humble and meek that he accepts any condition of life as a blessing from the Lord. *Tat te 'nukampāṁ susamīkṣamāṇaḥ* (*Bhāg.* 10.14.8). A devotee always accepts punishment from anyone as the mercy of the Lord." (*Bhāg.* 6.17.17, purport)

"A devotee is always eager to return home, back to Godhead, and remain there as the Lord's associate. This ambition becomes increasingly fervent in his heart, and therefore he does not care about material changes in life . . . The Lord wanted Citraketu to return to Godhead as soon as possible, and therefore He terminated all the reactions of his past deeds."

If I get a dose of suffering, it can be Kṛṣṇa's mercy finishing up my last material attachments or reactions. It would purify me and make me more attracted to Kṛṣṇa. I may be praying not to be disturbed in the material world, not to have a rough ride, but a rough ride might be more for my ultimate good. I am not brave enough to pray for calamities.

10:32 A.M.

The morning *bhajana* and commentary with the devotees went well. Then I sat and endured a *guru-pūjā*. Back in this room, trying to keep cool so that I can do a 3:30 P.M. lecture.

Right now I am looking out the window. I see some brown goats butting heads with some white ones. Neither have horns, and they are a little hesitant to bang their heads from such a distance, but they are definitely unfriendly with one another.

Today's newspaper has pictures and a story on mob action in downtown Georgetown. The perpetrators were mostly thugs and supporters of the PNC. Together they formed a crowd of 1,500. The police were able to repulse them with their Black Beret forces. The final results of the election have still not been announced. They keep reaffirming the votes, whatever that means. The delay is causing more and more agitation, and nerves are getting more and more frayed as the days go by. The opposition calls the whole procedure irregular.

11:31 A.M.

Speculations. Worries. Sitting it out. Pressure to give lectures. But don't complain. Newspaper, one per day. Pills, how many? None today. I have a head vise. If I don't feel free of it by 3:30, I'll cancel my talk.

12:05 P.M.

I just spoke with Madhumaṅgala about the position of my disciples here. Some of the senior ones don't want to be involved in ISKCON management. I think they have a right to live the way they want, but I have to be careful how I advise them. As we spoke, I said we have stayed here too long. I have been getting too many headaches, and they are becoming difficult to endure. When headaches come, it's not only the pain that disturbs me but the fact that if I have to cancel, people get disappointed. When I'm alone, there's no role to play. Here it's different. A group of devotees are living here just to hear my classes.

At first M. and I thought about possibly changing our departure, but I think we have solid bookings for Monday, and I don't want to play around with that given the political situation here. I'll wait it out.

The immediate result of our talk was that I decided to cancel all my classes except the one tomorrow morning. That means today I can try to ease up, and on Sunday I will have no engagement at all. That will give me a day to rest before we leave.

STICK IT OUT

𝄞 Janet Jagan is Hindu—she won—
and blacks in town are *angry*.

Don't foment on me, guy-Anna.
Let me out, me and M. and our
hand luggage and our plan for up north in
the prosperous good karma.
        We want to see that ten-week-
old baby Rasa, the snow the
        lay back
        the the the
what?

Freedom illusion, new books
records I can't enjoy and don't want
anyway
        the big meals I can't eat
but at least I can look.

This free mix of lines, M. pumping away
on that melodeon his
good cheer near
Christmas. Guyana, don't blow up or
burn down the Election Hall or even
the Freedom House
        guard them, that
        "vicious bunch"
while this semi-invalid
flies out with his blues-filled
toes. ‖

4:17 P.M.

Ladies lounging in spacious yard under the palm trees. Maxis and cars zoom by, beeping horns to clear the road of children, chickens, goats, and cows.

The guru canceled his remaining afternoon engagements. I don't know if they understand why. He expects to be escorted out of the country by a guardian angel. This isn't Vietnam, the roof of the embassy at Saigon. This is civilized Guyana. You can expect . . .

I got through the wars and the Cuban blockade. Our ship was in dry dock, or I was too young or too old. I caught the last ferry home the night the lights went out. But sometimes I got it too—attacks, glass, bad deals, etc. It was a bad deal, for example, to put eleven gurus on top.

Just now another pen has run out. I have enough left, Captain Scott, to last me awhile longer. And a song. He decided he's a poet. Can't sustain.

Two more days. Just relax and don't look out the window much. Boy hacking with machete. Young woman in shorts. Truck passing, crowded with live cows. Waiting for my daily copy of *Starbroek News* so I can see what happened in the incredibly, unforgivably delayed election.

The Lord Reigneth truck is parked for the night, and it looks quiet over there. Letters come in and I reply: "Do as you think best. Serve voluntarily. I respect you."

As the sky darkens, I expect to hear that frog's one-note "Wheet wheet!" I'll be grateful to rest.

This is eternity. Or a day in eternity. I will not be sorry later that I lived here and didn't run away. Gave me a chance to look within. Hare Kṛṣṇa.

5:12 P.M.

Buster, you calmed down. De roughest people is also spirit soul, and so is de goat and de lizard and de horse. But dose animals cannot receive Kṛṣṇa consciousness. De humans can, although some are like two-legged *paśus*.

I'm not much better myself, pretentious fellow with a pen and a B.A. degree. Do I have a *bhakti-śāstri* degree? Am I listed in the Book Distributors Hall of Fame? Am I a GBC member or did I quit? Am I Kṛṣṇa-centered or self-centered?

Read about the Lord in His many incarnations. Understand they all come from the original Kṛṣṇa in Vṛndāvana. Even from Guyana you can tune in on Him via the spiritual television in the heart. You can receive the sound vibration of *nāma-saṅkīrtana* coming straight from Kṛṣṇaloka. You can, despite the humid climate and fears and distractions.

Oh, Hare Kṛṣṇa. As this day cools down, I pray to chant with attention.

Trucks and tractors, bare-chested boys, everyone a shade of brown. The houses on stilts, lightly built. O Kṛṣṇa, I see a little.

I will like to read of Citraketu's tolerance and Lord Śiva's praise for him as *nārāyaṇa-parāḥ*. Maybe it will give me a drop of tolerance and fearlessness. *Abhaya caraṇāravindu re*. Prabhupāda was also fearless.

All glories to the Supreme Lord. Two more days. Read to devotees. Tell them Śrīla Prabhupāda was a great and humble soul. Savor his life story. Remember his days in NYC before the movement began? He was looking for an audience, some followers, help to spread Lord Caitanya's cause, but never certain what would develop. He depended on Kṛṣṇa, and the Lord sent money and men. Śrīla Prabhupāda had to wait patiently for awhile with very little. No one seemed interested. In his room in Mishra's yoga studio, he followed up on leads, but little happened. He thought of returning to India, but went to the Bowery instead where he began to meet interested young people.

December 20

1:47 A.M.

Last night I took rest at about 6:15. I woke at 7:30 feeling closed in. I was inside the mosquito net, and it was too hot. As I lay awake, I began to feel the anxiety of being in Guyana at a time of political unrest. Just before taking rest, I had received a letter from a devotee here who has been searching for thread to make himself a better *brāhmaṇa* thread. His note said that all the stores in town were closed. When I woke up, I again felt the uncertainty and threat. This country could boil over into revolution at any moment. No one has been able to assure me that that's not a possibility. That would mean Madhu and I wouldn't be able to get out.

As I sweated under the mosquito net and listened to the sounds of passing cars and beeping horns and an occasional voice, I imagined that every sound was connected to the political and ethnic tension. Then I remembered Madhu's last words before I took rest. He was saying that we're uncomfortably hot down here, but when we get to New York, we will probably be uncomfortably cold. He added, "We have no idea what to expect in New York." Trying to use my intelligence, I thought how New York could be full of another kind of anxiety. I can't count on New York being an improvement in security. I knew the anxiety was emotional, so I tried to take a hold of myself by using my intelligence. Intelligence not only means seeing through the eyes of *śāstra;* it also means not allowing yourself to expect anything other than the mercy of Kṛṣṇa. It seems to be a prerequisite for thinking of Kṛṣṇa to acknowledge that we have no safety in this material world. Kṛṣṇa is our only protector. This is one of the symptoms of *śaraṇāgati*, and we have to make it real for ourselves.

2:50 A.M.

"Mistuh Kurtz, he dead." A bullet in his head. Mr. Smith he alive, a bee bite in a hive. Mrs. Jagan, she won, a person with a mom. John T., he recalled, an artist in a fog. Bobby Jones, a name, a golfer of past fame. The lists were weighted, the flight was nervous-rated, and he climbed the skies. Was Stevie onboard? Does it matter in the end, in the front, in the words?

Get down and pray no matter what they say. Your rounds are your ticket to Kṛṣṇa meditation. Kṛṣṇa is in your life as well as in His *līlā*. The *līlā* and *upadeśa* are in the *śāstra* and in the spiritual energy—for those who qualify. I am a student of the same.

O Govinda, You are the Kṛṣṇa in my life. I know I often start with impure prayer, but please help me to actually reach You. I worry about my safety. Then go on, as Gajendra did, to pray for pure Kṛṣṇa consciousness.

BYE YA

𝄞 Merry men squeak
we want home, We
want our pres!
Recount!
Not now, I'm from New
Yawk
        Yeah bye Ya
to this place.

I can say bye at any time
'cause I'm a sold-out
servant to my master.
        The sound of mantras leaking
through police barricades
while pellets shoot
man's eye lost
save it and
        his sight.

Mr. Philadelphia Q
and Bob Rains and
Reebey Good is
all in Georgetown hospital but not me
        I'm for Kyber Pass
no rifle among
        my goods.

These riffs fit me and I'll
make peace with
rioters in my heart
from a more distant place.

"This material world resembles the waves of a constantly flowing river. Therefore, what is a curse and what is a favor? What are the heavenly planets and what are the hellish planets? What is actually happiness, and what is actually distress?

Because the waves flow constantly, none of them has an eternal effect." (*Bhāg.* 6.17.20)

So prayed Citraketu to goddess Parvatī after she had cursed him. In his purport Śrīla Prabhupāda quotes Bhaktivinoda Ṭhākura: "If the living entity tries to understand that he is an eternal servant of Kṛṣṇa, there will no longer be misery for him." If we surrender to Kṛṣṇa, we're no longer under the category of sufferers (or enjoyers) of cause and effect in the material world.

I am therefore making too great a distinction these days between the unrest I feel in this country and the supposedly better condition I'll find in another country. I should be more like a true devotee who preaches in one place or another, who doesn't see the material situation as a cause of misery. "The so-called temporary happiness of the world is also misery, but in ignorance we cannot understand this." I cannot imitate the higher platform, but I definitely want to attain it. Why allow my heart to burn with attachment for a better material situation? Don't be afraid here, and don't try to rest anywhere. Every place is simply a pit stop on the road of service.

nārāyaṇa-parāḥ sarve
na kataścana bibhyati
svargāpavarga narakeṣv
api tulyārtha-darśinaḥ

> Devotees solely engaged in the devotional service of the Supreme Personality of Godhead, Nārāyaṇa, never fear any condition of life. For them the heavenly planets, liberation and the hellish planets are all the same, for such devotees are interested only in the service of the Lord.
>
> —*Bhāg.* 6.17.28

From Śrīla Prabhupāda's purport: "Despite the disturbing dualities of the material world, devotees are not disturbed at all. Because they fix their minds on the lotus feet of the Lord and concentrate on the holy name of the Lord, they do not feel the so-called pains and pleasures caused by the dualities of this material world." (*Bhāg.* 6.17.29, purport)

To feel such anxiety is a mistake, like when you think a flower garland is a snake. Why be in anxiety about something that is not actually real, but which is more like a dream? When we distinguish between happiness and distress in this world, considering one good and the other bad, that's illusion. "A devotee accepts the distress of this material world as happiness only due to the causeless mercy of Śrī Caitanya Mahāprabhu . . . He was never distressed but always happy and chanting the Hare Kṛṣṇa mantra. One should follow in the footsteps of Śrī Caitanya Mahāprabhu and engage constantly in chanting the Hare Kṛṣṇa *mahā-mantra* . . . Then he will never feel the distresses of the world of duality. In any condition of life one will be happy if he chants the holy name of the Lord." (*Bhāg*. 6.17.30, purport)

As if in follow-up to these thoughts, I took a nap and dreamt I was in a combined Navy-devotee office with Draviḍa and Yamarāja Prabhus. I was putting on *tilaka*. Then someone broke into a song that sounded like a Broadway musical, which was related to something we were discussing.

When I awoke, I felt a sudden anxiety that I may not be able to leave Guyana when I want to go. Because of the song in the dream, I remembered the Broadway musical "Gypsy," and the song the man sings as a duet with Gypsy's mother: "You'll never get away from me/ even if you try." It actually made me sad. Then I realized how much I have to use my intelligence and not allow myself to give in to anxiety. It appears that my Kṛṣṇa consciousness is not so much an easy or natural feeling as it is a correction of the mind by the intelligence. It's discipline, and a strained, stiff upper lip.

5:25 A.M.

I could call M. in to talk, but maybe there is nothing we really need to discuss. We know we have to wait two more days. We want to be philosophical. We—especially me—have limited energy, so no point wasting what little we have on an early-morning talk that can't change the situation. I am scheduled to speak at 7:30 this morning. I plan to speak on Citraketu tolerating Parvatī's curse and Lord Śiva's praise of devotees. Today if I can, I will read a little about Gajendra.

Don't look out the window
or look
down
look down that lonesome
road before you travel
on—

do you think you can see a supposed future?
Only imagination.
Active imagination
even
over-active, hypertension—
the milestones being birth and death then
rebirth and
not so much in between
but the Kṛṣṇa conscious tests.

O Kṛṣṇa I hope to meet You
down that road
we people of the world are
crazy, I know, and
wild, so wild the police can't
contain us all. But when I look
down the Kṛṣṇa conscious way,
I remember the matted grass walkway
near the entrance to that shed
the sweet shed where I
mix my
mix.

Although I'm often pinched with pain there, I float lightly on top of it and refuse to sink deep into the present. The light hearts of Hare Kṛṣṇa devotees even in heavy times—be transcendental.

6:50 A.M.

I speak of my anxieties in Guyana as if there's some specific danger. There are some wild people here in Georgetown. But as I read of Gajendra's crisis, I see reference to "the great serpent of time which brings death." This serpent makes people fearful, and chases everyone endlessly, ready to swallow them up. The snake is an image that allows us to understand time and the inevitability of death. Our death. I am being chased by that demon here in Guyana. Why worry about it, then? Now that I have readily admitted my fears, I should take recourse by accepting Kṛṣṇa's shelter. "If one who fears this serpent seeks shelter of the Lord, the Lord gives him protection, for even death runs away in fear of the Lord." (*Bhāg.* 8.2.33)

"We are always in danger because at any moment death can take place. It is not that only Gajendra, the King of the elephants, was afraid of death. Everyone should fear death because everyone is caught by the crocodile of eternal time and may die at any moment. The best course, therefore, is to seek shelter of Kṛṣṇa, the Supreme Personality of Godhead, and be saved from the struggle of existence in this material world, in which one repeatedly takes birth and dies. To reach this understanding is the ultimate goal of life." (*Bhāg.* 8.2.33, purport)

Prabhupāda states that a devotee also has to die, but a devotee's death is his last one; he goes back to Godhead.

11:30 P.M.

Latest news: The doctor came immediately after the lecture. I already had the beginnings of a headache, and as I spoke to the doctor, the pain began to increase. He told me to drink six glasses of water a day, and gave other naturopathic advice. He's against medicine, even Āyurvedic medicine, and I listened agreeably.

After he left, the headache sharpened and I took my fourth Esgic this week. To hell with just sitting around in pain. It's harder to endure down here under these circumstances.

Madhu brought the newspaper, and despite my pain, I read it. Janet Jagan has been inaugurated as the new president, but right up until the last minute they were still quarreling about her legitimacy. The person in charge of declaring the elections made a surprise announcement that she should be installed. They were still counting the votes! The newspaper says it's a complete farce the way the whole thing was conducted, and it would remind the reporter of a Gilbert and Sullivan comic opera if it weren't such a serious event. Anyway, my main worry was that rioting would prevent us from leaving the country. There doesn't seem to be that kind of threat now.

Lying down, hoping the Esgic will work, although I took it rather late in the pain stage. I did the opposite of what the doctor advised. He said let the headache continue, and rather than do something artificial like blocking the pain with allopathic medicine, find the root. *He* can talk like that, but I'm the one who suffers from the pain.

The doctor was about thirty-three years old. He was a likable person. After he insisted I drink so much water, I told him that Kṛṣṇa says, "I am the taste of water." He smiled and said I could associate with Kṛṣṇa all day long by drinking water. He then added that he liked the devotees very much.

But from the medical point of view, he is clearly of the "heroic" school, which insists that the body is sick because we have polluted it, and now we have to take our medicine in the form of tolerating pain while the body makes its repairs. I'm too far gone for that.

4:40 P.M.

Low point of the Caribbean tour. Sharp pain all day since 8:30 this morning. The talk with the doctor pushed it. If only I had taken the pill at the start, I might be free of the pain now. But I am always reluctant to try another pill at this late stage. It's hot, humid, noisy. Cars zoom by, beeping horns. The cow moans just outside. Why are the cars beeping so insistently? Is there some reverse in the election proceedings? A protest? I lie down awhile, then sit up again.

December 21

3:20 A.M.

Last day in hell? No, our leaving won't be so easy. Last night I couldn't take the pain, so I became restless. Took a second Esgic and finally slept.

CAMPTOWN RACES

𝄞 Good morning, we are shaking
our little crew
we are in Camptown
      going to the races
somebody bet on the
bay.

I bet Sats will make it
awright to the Bee Wee
counter. But I can't
say it will be a pain-free
as-per-in.

Then will he eat pine
jam crushed
        then will Kṛṣṇa
be in my life—it's up
to me.

Down the narrow pass
        the band swinging
in America the great. ‖

CAMPTOWN RACES (TAKE 2)

𝄞 Let's try that one again.
Same tune? Well, a little different.
        We held up a banner
took a urine bottle in
back
        Swami said take two
we took all
        Kṛṣṇa consciousness
waitin' waitin'

remembering—pains
joys, perks, the tunes and luck
my travel mate
who loves music and therefore
he's happy.

We wait. Careful slices of
papaya and mango
a lush banana and

then the sounds
begin: goats and cars just one
more time.
Abide in His name even here. ‖

4:12 A.M.

While in Trinidad I wrote a letter to Madhumatī and said something like, "I hope you have good adventures ahead." She wrote back and told me about some of the wild adventures they had upon arriving in Trinidad. She also mentioned that it was a "fun adventure" to be traveling with just one other *mātājī* without their husbands. Since then I have been thinking about the word "adventure". It seems on the one hand that I have had my fill of adventures in this lifetime, and even this past while in the Caribbean. Nowadays I prefer to be free of them. I remember reading a letter that an Englishman wrote to a friend after they had spent a day together. The friend had traveled home, then written a note back to tell his companion that his return journey had been uneventful. The word "uneventful" seemed very British to me. It was used to point out a virtue of the travel, a blessing. I empathized with it.

Yet without adventure, what could an author write about? Well, I'll tell you what. With an uneventful life, an author can write plenty. He or she could take time to find inner adventures, adventures that appear only through routine and not through hair-raising events.

Objectively speaking, I know my anxieties about being safe in Guyana and my mental difficulties in trying to leave the country are probably exaggerated. Still, I think it has been good for me to write them out and examine them. If I am more objective with myself, I can conquer such anxieties easily, but that's not who I am. My imagination flies off from whatever facts I hear. Anyway, sorry to have said it all, dear reader.

5:17 A.M.

"Every devotee should practice in order to chant some mantra perfectly so that even though he may be imperfect in spiritual consciousness in this life, in his next life he will not forget Kṛṣṇa consciousness, even if he becomes an animal . . . Therefore, we should not forget the chanting of the Hare Kṛṣṇa mantra under any circumstance. It will help us in the greatest danger, as we find in the life of Gajendra." (*Bhāg.* 8.3.1, purport)

Oṁ ajñāna-timirāndhasya. The spiritual master insists that we face the truth: "Although one may struggle for existence in this material world, to live forever is impossible." We should therefore desire liberation from the cycle of birth and death, because that's our only safety. We are meant to be safe in eternal existence. "We are making so many plans to live happily, but there cannot be any happiness in this material world, however we may try to make a permanent settlement in this life or that." (*Bhāg.* 8.3.25, purport)

Māyā covers us with the contamination of forgetting God, in which we then make our own plans to enjoy the material world. "As long as this contamination continues, the conditioned soul will be unable to understand his real identity and will perpetually continue under illusion, life after life." (*Bhāg.* 8.3.29, purport)

"Gajendra had been forcefully captured by the crocodile in the water and was feeling acute pain, but when he saw that Nārāyaṇa, wielding His disc, was coming in the sky on the back of Garuḍa, he immediately took a lotus flower in his trunk, and with great difficulty due to his painful condition, he uttered the following words: 'O my Lord, Nārāyaṇa, master of the universe, O Supreme Personality of Godhead, I offer my respectful obeisances unto You.'" (*Bhāg.* 8.3.32)

Śrīla Prabhupāda writes that a devotee does not see danger as dangerous, because in that position he can fervently pray to the Lord in great ecstasy. "He does not accuse the Supreme

Personality of Godhead for having let His devotee fall into such a dangerous condition." There is a thin line between Gajendra's praying for release from the crocodile and repeated birth and death, and his approaching pure submission to the will of God and to worshiping the Lord. Prabhupāda admits in an earlier purport, "Sometimes, when there is no alternative, a pure devotee, being fully dependent on the mercy of the Supreme Lord, prays for some benediction. But in such a prayer there is also a regret." (*Bhāg.* 8.3.20–21, purport)

It is important to remember that Kṛṣṇa is always trying to deliver us. "He is within our hearts and is not at all inattentive. His only aim is to deliver us from material life. It is not that He becomes attentive to us only when we offer prayers to Him . . . He is never negligent in regard to our deliverance."

From the Collins College dictionary:

Adventure: (1) noun. risky undertaking, the ending of which is uncertain; (2) exciting or unexpected events. An *adventurer* is a person who seeks *adventure*.

Eventful: adj. full of exciting or important incidents.

Uneventful: adj. ordinary, routine, or quiet.

PRAYER FOR SAFE PASSAGE

1

𝄞 A country's got to be free
and the black man the
white man the Hindu—they
gotta stand up for what's right
and all that.

I'm just one soul
with a small circle of friends.

Śrīla Prabhupāda put us in this circle
of devotees and
doesn't encourage us
to go the nondevotees
except to
preach.

We live alone, insular, a time table
the days spent ranting
out to Kṛṣṇa
the sweat pouring down our sides.

2

Oh, you gremlins, I will continue
  to pray for those
vitamins to be released,
  and the endorphins
into my bloodstream.

I pray for safe passage
to airport over potholes and
  oceans—Carib, Atlantic
    the River Styx
  and the Plutonion
  regions.
Please take me back to Godhead
although I don't deserve it.
One man's rant
and he leaves a trail
for others to find the way
  back.

3

We will go/ we will go
a smart ride
a passport (good)

right look on face
pills for back-up
money, phone card
appropriate friends,
the Supreme Lord to
        lift us up.

But if Death jangles them bones
a skeleton dance and we can't
save our lives—the ticket's up
        Cheddi went
        Forbes went
        Janet too
Abe Lincoln, everyone
had to die or will
        as Hemingway agreed—

then we devotees will know
        the paradise
        of self in Lord—no more
        war against madness
        no more search for peace no
        righteousness
that rough ride held us up.

O Kṛṣṇa, to be Your soldier-monk-
poet with no disgrace
        to pray those Hare Kṛṣṇa mantras
to bubble out our love
                O Prabhupāda. ‖

9:50 A.M.

M. playing melodeon on the porch. He brings me another cup of coconut juice. I promised the local doctor I'd drink six cups of water and some dobs every day. M. says he plans to join the

Wicklow branch of the Irish Music Society so he can enter competitions. He is excited that his playing is getting better. "This is a good place to practice," he says, meaning the front porch. While he was playing, I was lying down. I haven't been able to recall dreams. Things are fuzzy. Last day. At least no headaches right now.

Janet Jagan was born in the United States, but she renounced her citizenship in 1947 in order to live as a citizen of Guyana with her late husband, Cheddi Jagan, after whom the national airport is named.

Paramātmā's daughters are named Revatī and Gaura-priyā. I gave Gaura-priyā a ballpoint pen. Revatī already has a pen.

Paramātmā said it would be great if I came here for a writing retreat. I mentioned the country's political unrest. He said out here where he lives, it's always peaceful. The black neighbors are good Christians and would rather protect him than give him trouble as some other blacks might. Who knows, maybe I'll renounce my citizenship and come down here. The atmosphere in Guyana is healthy, and the fruit is good. Did they think I was seriously considering it? One talks like that.

I admitted to Paramātmā that down here I am cut off from ISKCON communication. No one can reach me until I get back. Then they hit me with their latest demands and news. There are benefits to living here. P. said the ocean breeze comes straight from the Atlantic and is "very pure." Pure water, fresh air, coconuts, papayas, and no snow or ice on the roads. And as I said earlier, no e-mail, no faxes, and no phones.

So folks, it has quieted down to normal in Georgetown, or so we hear. We'll be getting out on time with reliable-unreliable BWIA. Looks good. The last I heard, the U.S. dollar was tolerably strong, and the cold war was over with Russia. The fanatics? Well, you never know. Better chant an extra round.

LAST DAY FRAGMENTS:

(1) Goat on rope tethered, bleating.

(2) Shooting and racial tension in Georgetown. When?

(3) Madhu, while reading *My Search Through Books*, liked the definition of "free-thinker." We discussed it for forty minutes, starting with how to develop art and expression and how to steer to Kṛṣṇa. "Friendly" as preaching, etc.

(4) Rādhā-kānta dāsa asked Madhu, "Why are you doing this (playing the melodeon)?" M. replied, "I'm going to make a record." Said he did not want to, and could not, relate to the question.

(5) M. chanted a round after lunch thanking Kṛṣṇa for the nice meal His devotees had prepared for us.

(6) Chickens clucking . . . clothes, mostly white—looks like diapers—on neighbor's backyard clothesline. Billowing in breeze.

(7) No chimneys here.

(8) M. suggested I take rest by 6 so I can be ready to leave at 3:00 A.M. We are getting down to that. The ever-present moment—the present—until the end.

(9) See Kṛṣṇa in all things? See what you see. Steer to Him.

(10) Read *śāstra* as free-thinkers *within* Kṛṣṇa consciousness; get deeper appreciation in your own mood.

NOW'S THE TIME

𝄞 (Last day?)

Now is the time sweatin'
for fathers
we hope you enjoy it and
thanks.

We heard in '66 and they
say he's a genius
the bird of many notes,

playing that way those
riffs—O Kṛṣṇa
I don't want no interference.

Madhu sees me looking down through bifocals.
Now's the time—he brings the dob juice early.
Well, I'm not dizzy
not like this—
not in Guyana. Janet promised
the government would be inclusive.

In the meantime, Kṛṣṇa consciousness
revolves.
We want to be with our
master now not
later—sweatin' no jive just
eternal service.

In the old days
when *devas* visited here—one
flag under Yudhiṣṭhira—
Kṛṣṇa consciousness flourished.

I can't condemn or judge
the state of it now, but as our master said,
I try to "encourage them more and more."

When I play Madhu picks up his own horn
and the cow bellows most unhappy.

Kṛṣṇa, Kṛṣṇa in trance of dull
routine sweating sticky bare
feet on wooden floor.
Prabhupāda was preaching back
in 1944.

3:27 P.M.

Whiling away the hours on our last day here. The wind is up, and it knocked over the vase of artificial daisies. I pace my *japa* around the main room before Gaura-Nitāi. A delicate *tulasī* sways on her stem. Trucks go by and I imagine things. The goats won't leave here by tomorrow. Paramātmā's wife is making us travel snacks. Madhu says we will eat a fruit breakfast at the airport—you know the scene as you wait for the plane's arrival from Trinidad. It's usually late, and we need to make the connection from Trinidad to New York City. I will be trying to solace myself that getting to Trinidad will be itself enough to accomplish in a day. If we go all the way, great. There is no rush for me to be at Gītā-nāgarī by Christmas. I can arrive whenever I arrive. The main thing is to keep my stress levels down and to keep on living.

The *main* thing is *śravaṇaṁ kīrtanam* followed by *kṛṣṇa-smaraṇam*. For that I can be in Trinidad, New York, Pennsylvania, or even Guyana. Anyway, just let me make a quiet, efficient, safe exit, and move on.

It gets dark here by 6 P.M. I'm simultaneously relaxed and tense, on hold. As if I'm not really living while here. But I am. It is time spent, devotional life, and these are sweet, pious people.

4:56 P.M.

Satyavrata prayed to Matsya-avatāra, addressing Him as the supreme spiritual master. God is the original spiritual master, and the guru is His representative. Yes, He is the original spiritual master of my heart.

Goats cry like sad humans. The kid follows its mother at every step; it won't let her go anywhere without following her shadow. That's a stage of life. I'll see something similar in that little baby tomorrow in New York City. His mother told me he's colicky and suffers. He's helpless, his mother said. She sees the suffering of a newborn and says she is in no illusion about it, although she loves her child. Father goes to work to earn for them.

Through all that, this guru comes flying in from the tropics with tales of his adventures. Then he'll want to be left alone in a room to sort out his mail.

I already have six or so pieces of mail, but I don't want to read them now. I am tired of advising people, pumping out rhetoric. I'll do it when I get to the next place.

M. talking with the little girls here. They are becoming less shy. Madhu is a daddy too. They like hearing him play his melodeon.

Swami, you wear a turban?
Will you sit on nails?
Ah, he's not that kind of Swami.
"My master told me preach
in Kṛṣṇa consciousness."

December 22

1:40 A.M.

Dog barking constantly for the past hour. I wonder if the barking woke others. I've been up since 12. I have already chanted fifteen rounds. Before that, I thought clearly that I should aspire for writing more "formidable" or structured literature. Then I decided against that. Whatever I write will never be equal to Kṛṣṇa Himself. I am aiming only to please Him, and to do that I have to write honestly.

Bringing people to Kṛṣṇa consciousness is the best thing we can do, yet a person comes of his or her own accord. Maybe I can help maintain people. Maintain myself.

Thinking of lectures I'll give from January 8–11. The guru in his more sophisticated, more demanding performance in America. First get through the upcoming travel.

2:52 A.M.

May there be no brigands on the road. May—but how much should I pray for? May I learn my lessons. May I chant inner, vital Hare Kṛṣṇa mantras. May such mantras become a non-stop prayer. May I endure pain without so much distraction from the center. May I pray in faith that the self-soul does not perish. May he go to Kṛṣṇa and Prabhupāda when he leaves this body.

Remember Gajendra, Prabhupāda, the *gopīs*—at least their names—in love and while seeking protection. Like Gajendra, I start by seeking physical safety from the only One who can protect us, and my prayer goes all the way to hopes for devotional service.

4:38 A.M.

The ride was okay. Now on airport queue. I was alone in back of car, eyes closed or looking up at sky. Calm. Restless. A long drive. Now nervous amid people passionate even though it's *brahma-muhūrta*. In the car I thought of my Rādhā-Govinda. I hear someone say "canceled" and I get nervous. Let them say "crash" and I'll say Hare Kṛṣṇa, my all-encompassing prayer. We're on flight 484. There is a shorter queue, so people get into line for other BWIA flights thinking to convince the agent to take them. Sign mentions limited size for cabin luggage. Some people "merge" toward the front of line. Don't exaggerate, and don't hypertense or flip out.

New image airport. Oh! There is that Mormon we met in Trinidad. He is with three other Mormons, each wearing a white shirt and tie, each a beefy guy. He looks happier in the company of others of his kind. I heard men talking behind me, saying the election was a rip-off—or why did they swear her in in secrecy? Waiting for breakfast. I said some nonsense to M. about Mormons. I should shut up unless I can speak properly.

O Kṛṣṇa. So far so good. We now have our boarding passes. The BWIA agent, a young black man, kept furrowing his brow at us. BWIA makes its agents wear tasteless, tropical-print neckties. Our saffron is definitely a more pleasant color. But that doesn't make me a *sādhu* just because I wear it! Remember that.

Can't write absolute, ecstatic revelations. Can't pay that price. As I said, I was thinking of my Rādhā-Kṛṣṇa *mūrtis* and knew I wanted to live with Them. Can't see myself running around a lot, giving lectures and seeing people in various places, not at this point in my life. Time runs out on guys like me. So where's breakfast?

I didn't like how the Hindu-looking guy inspected my passport to see if it were bona fide. This was *after* immigration. He looked at it, pressed it, turned it around. Anyway, it's real.

When devotees came into the hall, I thought, "Oh, boy." Was I ashamed of them with their *dhotīs* and big shoes, the ladies in "old-fashioned" Indian *sārīs*? I was seeing them from the worldly stand point. And what about me? What do *I* look like from that point of view? Then I realized that these are my people. I went and spoke some last words with them. Paramātmā told me that the country is becoming better developed (but he always says that). Kṛṣṇacandra wanted to take a photo, and I agreed. They liked that. We ate fruit, and I left a lot behind. I said to one devotee, "Be a good devotee," and to another, "Be a good example." Someone asked when I was coming back. I have no plans right now. Then we walked outside, a light rain sprinkling, into another building where the terminal is. The devotees couldn't come with us. I turned and waved farewell. I shouldn't be so uptight in public, but I'm usually not so ostentatious with good-bye scenes.

Now M. and I are dumped off into the departure lounge. The check-in area is new and air-conditioned, but this place hasn't changed in all the years that I have been coming here. Fans overhead. The man behind us is speaking with a loud Guyanese accent, making his pronouncements about politics,

Indians, racism, and other topics. First light in the sky, although the sky is filled with dark clouds. They are talking of Janet Jagan—don't like her.

The guy behind me is bragging. He seems to be the kind of person who talks not only to his companion but loud enough that others can hear and appreciate him. He says he knows some ambassador and that he got a contract to write a book on African-American trade unions or something. Now he's talking about the mismanaged election. Śrīla Prabhupāda told us we shouldn't be interested.

6:20 A.M.

The plane is here and appears it will leave on time. The sun is up. A captain went out to a plane; maybe it's ours. Read verses in the eighth chapter of *Bhagavad-gītā*. Kṛṣṇa is clear: whatever we think of at death we attain as our next destination. I liked reading it, and I tuned out the guy behind me, although the harsh loudspeaker announcements threatened to break my absorption. Hare Kṛṣṇa. When I went into the bathroom, I thought I heard Madhu chanting *japa*. It was some other sound that I had identified as the Hare Kṛṣṇa mantra. You could say it was an auditory hallucination. I'd like more of that! In the car coming here, Paramātmā dāsa sang Hare Kṛṣṇa for a little while, and I liked that too. At the end of life, people sometimes chant for the one who is departing. At death, we may not be able to do it for ourselves.

6:40 A.M.

Here it is again, the Guyana squeeze. Waiting in the departure lounge through a delay. It's hot.

The Liat Airlines flight is now queuing up, so we won't be able to queue up until they get out. Only one line, one agent, one squeeze.

Guy behind me talking away with a man who sounds like a Hindu—friendly village talk. I wonder if I will make the New

York connection since the plane from Guyana won't leave on time.

7:03 A.M.

Sitting in the plane finally, but we still haven't left, although the departure announcements were made some time ago. What's the delay *now*? Windows covered with beads of water from the humidity. I see a guy standing outside with a paddle to wave us off. A cool Trinidadian guy sings snatches of songs from his seat. Another passenger fans herself. No air-conditioning here.

Sign: "Welcome to Guyana. We ♡ you."

Finally the man raises two red paddles, and we start to move. A good-looking and very young steward does the safety and emergency features demonstration. I'm writing out of nervous energy, alternating this notepad with a drawing pad. Hare Kṛṣṇa.

7:35 A.M.

Madhu struck up conversation with a young white man sitting across the aisle from us. He's a musician too, and he and Madhu are talking about that. A devotee is friendly. Before that, he was listening to Irish music on earphones. A little of it was leaking out, and I thought of Jimmy Duncan and what a wild, undomesticated Irishman he was.

O Kṛṣṇa, this material energy is "wonderful" and strange, but ultimately, it annihilates everyone and everything. At the end of Lord Brahmā's day, everything is wound up.

You get old. You . . . die . . .

Saw over a man's shoulder this magazine headline:

¡Frank Sinatra *ha muerto!*

81 Años

Mujeres cran su pasionsu fortuna era de million.

Back in Trinidad. One and a half hours before our scheduled flight to New York. There are birds inside, wild swallows!

Frank Sinatra—death finally got him.

The young musician Madhu met on the plane was from England, but his girlfriend lives in Guyana. He likes it there and says he may move there. It's a simple place, but I wouldn't want to live there myself. I'd prefer to go back to Ireland and to my little Rādhā-Govinda and Śrīla Prabhupāda and my solitude. In the meantime, I can serve in Northeast U.S., trying to enliven my friends and disciples in Gītā-nāgarī and Baltimore.

It's very crowded here. We found a seat, but they just announced an "assembly call" for our flight to gather at Gate One. A baby wailing. I wonder how that baby will endure the flight. Faces interesting—karmic twists of age, race, clothing, and style. It bewilders, threatens, lures, repels. First-class and others getting on the American Airlines flight. Don't take too many bags on. It's a controlled pandemonium, but I am grateful we are here, and not late out of Guyana. The Lord reigneth and allowed me to do my Caribbean *yajña*.

11:15 A.M.

On plane, five hour plus, from Trinidad to New York. Thank God everything went smoothly. "Uneventful," they say. I got a right-eye twinge and took Esgic an hour ago. But that's expected.

Movie on. Guy walks in cemetery . . . I thought again about writing fiction or my own version of Kierkegaard's spiritual books . . . but . . .

I keep coming back to EJW.

With plenty of poems.

I don't want to do something too daring. Keep close to Kṛṣṇa.

One hour and twenty minutes to go. Spoke with M. about what we will do during this next month in America. I hope it will be relatively uneventful. They just put on some movie called *Conspiracy Theory*. It's a mad, action-packed crime thriller, "too exciting" for my senses. It reminds me that if you want to give a reader a riveting experience, you have to make up a story, and when it's over, make up another. Or, like Chekov, you have to invent characters. I am not inclined to either fictive plot or fictive characters—I don't have the talent for it, or the capacity to maintain it. It takes too much energy, that kind of writing. I am more committed to giving my prime time, physical and mental, to *japa* and reading *śāstra*.

One-and-a-half-hour car drive
two-and-a-half-hour wait
fifty-minute plane ride
two-hour wait
five-and-a-half hour plane ride
waiting at the baggage claim and for M. to get through immigration
ride to Jackson Heights—
about fourteen hours of journeying.

One Esgic so far. Tomorrow I want to simply stay indoors and putter around, write a little poetry, answer a few letters, and depend on Kṛṣṇa: the Lord reigneth.

Glossary

A

Abhiṣeka—the bathing ceremony of the Deity.

Ācārya—a spiritual master who teaches by his personal behavior.

Aghāsura—a demon in the form of an eight-mile-long serpent.

Aiśvarya—majesty, opulence.

Aparādha—offense.

Apāna—the down-going air, part of the yogic process in controlling the breathing.

Ārati—a ceremony of worshiping the Lord by the offering of various auspicious articles, such as incense, flowers, water, fans, ghee lamp, etc.

Arcā-vigraha—Deity.

Arjuna—one of the five Pāṇḍavas. Kṛṣṇa spoke the *Bhagavad-gītā* to him on the Battlefield of Kurukṣetra.

Āśrama—a spiritual order: *brahmacārī* (celibate student), *gṛhastha* (householder), *vānaprastha* (retired), *sannyāsī* (renunciate); living quarters for those engaged in spiritual practices.

Ātmā—the soul or living entity.

B

Bābājī—one who devotes the major portion of his life to solitary devotional practices, especially chanting the Lord's names.

Balarāma—Kṛṣṇa's elder brother and His first plenary expansion.

BBT—The Bhaktivedanta Book Trust.

Bhagavad-gītā—lit., "song of God". The discourse between Lord Kṛṣṇa and His devotee Arjuna, expounding devotional service as both the principal means and the ultimate end of spiritual perfection.

Bhagavān—lit., "one who possesses all opulence". The Supreme Lord, who is the reservoir of all beauty, strength, fame, wealth, knowledge, and renunciation.

Bhāgavata—anything related to Bhagavān, especially the Lord's devotee and the scripture, *Śrīmad-Bhāgavatam.*

Bhāgavatam—*see: Śrīmad-Bhāgavatam.*

Bhajana—devotional activities; a devotional song.

Bhakta—a devotee of Kṛṣṇa.

Bhakti—devotional service to the Supreme Lord.

Bhaktisiddhānta Sarasvatī Ṭhākura—the spiritual master of His Divine Grace A. C. Bhaktivedanta Swami Prabhupāda; an *ācārya* in the Gauḍīya-Vaiṣṇava-sampradāya.

Bhaktivedanta—a title conferred upon Śrīla Prabhupāda by the Gaudiya Math, meaning "one who has understood that the conclusion of Vedic scripture is *bhakti* (devotional service)."

Bhaktivinoda Ṭhākura—an *ācārya* in the Gauḍīya Vaiṣṇava disciplic succession; the father of Bhaktisiddhānta Sarasvatī Ṭhākura.

Bhāva—the stage of transcendental ecstasy experienced after transcendental affection.

Bloop—an onomatopoetic word used primarily as a verb to signify an extended, serious falldown from devotional service into material sense enjoyment, similar to a pebble falling into a pond; to leave the association of devotees.

Brahmā—the first created living being and the secondary creator of the material universe.

Brahma-bhūta—the liberated or spiritual platform of consciousness.

Brahmacārī—a celibate student living under the care of a bona fide spiritual master.

Brahman—the impersonal aspect of the Absolute Truth; spirit.

Brāhmaṇa—one wise in the *Vedas* who can guide society; the first Vedic social order.

Brijbasi—(*var. sp.*,Vrajavāsī). A resident of Vṛndāvana. This spelling also generally refers to the company which produces the typical religious posters and calendar art seen everywhere in India.

Burfi—a fudge-like delicacy made from cooked down milk and sugar.

C

Cādar—a shawl.

Caitanya (Mahāprabhu)—lit., "living force". An incarnation of Kṛṣṇa who appeared in the form of a devotee to teach love of God through the *saṅkīrtana* movement.

Caitanya-caritāmṛta, Śrī—the biography and philosophy of Caitanya Mahāprabhu, written by Śrīla Kṛṣṇadāsa Kavirāja Gosvāmī.

Cakra—a wheel or disc.

Cāmara—a yak-tail whisk.

Capātī—a whole-wheat, griddle-baked flatbread.

Cātuḥ-ślokī—the four core verses of the *Śrīmad-Bhāgavatam*, spoken by Lord Kṛṣṇa to Brahmā at the beginning of creation.

Celā—disciple.

Chaukīdār—a security guard.

D

Dāl—a spiced bean soup.

Daṇḍavats—lit., "like a stick". To offer prostrated obeisances, extending one's limbs in a straight line.

Darśana—vision; audience.

Dāsa—lit., "servant" (masculine). An appellation which along with a name of Kṛṣṇa or one of His devotees is given to a devotee at the time of initiation.

Dāsānudāsa—lit., "servant of the servant of the servant".

Dāsī—feminine variation of *dāsa*.

Dāsya-rasa—the spiritual relationship in which the devotee acts as the Lord's servant.

Demigod—a celestial being, superior to humans, deputed by the Lord to manage one or more aspects of the material universe.

Dhāma—abode; the Lord's place of residence.

Dharma—the duties prescribed by one's nature and social position; ultimately, *dharma* means devotional service to the Supreme Lord.

Dhotī—a garment wrapped on the lower body of men, commonly worn in India.

Divya-jñāna—spiritual, transcendental knowledge.

E

Ekādaśī—a day on which Vaiṣṇavas fast from grains and beans and increase their remembrance of Kṛṣṇa. It falls on the eleventh day of both the waxing and waning moons.

G

Garbhodakaśāyī Viṣṇu—the expansion of the Lord who enters into each universe.

Garuḍa—Lord Viṣṇu's eternal carrier, a great devotee in a birdlike form.

Gauḍīya Vaiṣṇava—a follower of Lord Caitanya.

Gaura—a name of Lord Caitanya Mahāprabhu, meaning "golden".

Gaurakiśora dāsa Bābājī—the spiritual master of Śrīla Bhaktisiddhānta Sarasvatī Ṭhākura.

Gaura-Nitāi—Lord Caitanya (Gaura) and Lord Nityānanda (Nitāi).

Gāyatrī—a prayer chanted silently by *brāhmaṇas* at sunrise, noon, and sunset.

GBC—Governing Body Commission, ISKCON's board of directors.

Goloka—Kṛṣṇaloka, the eternal abode of Lord Kṛṣṇa.

Gopa—a cowherd boy; one of Kṛṣṇa's eternal associates.

Gopī—a cowherd girl; one of Kṛṣṇa's most confidential servitors.

Gosvāmī—one who controls his mind and senses; title of one in the renounced order of life. May refer specifically to the Six Gosvāmīs of Vṛndāvana, who are direct followers of Lord Caitanya in disciplic succession and who systematically presented His teachings.

Govardhana Hill—a hill in Vṛndāvana, the site of many of Kṛṣṇa's pastimes.

Govinda—a name of Kṛṣṇa, meaning "one who gives pleasure (*vinda*) to the cows (*go*) and senses (also *go*)"; may also refer to Lord Caitanya's personal servant.

Gṛhastha—a married person living according to the Vedic social system.

Guru-dakṣiṇā—a gift made to the spirtual master as a token payment for his teachings.

Gurudeva—one of many titles which may be used in addressing one's own spiritual master.

Gurukula—a school headed by the spiritual master.

Guru-pūjā—worship of the spiritual master.

Gurvāṣṭakam—a prayer, composed by Śrīla Viśvanātha Cakravartī Ṭhākura in praise of the spiritual master.

H

Halavā—a sweet dish made from roasted grains, butter, sugar, and water or milk.

Hare—the vocative form of Harā, another name of Rādhārāṇī; refers specifically to the internal spiritual energy of the Lord.

Hari—a name of Kṛṣṇa.

Haribol—"chant the holy name."

Hari-nāma—lit., "the name of the Lord".

Harināma—public chanting of the Hare Kṛṣṇa *mahā-mantra*.

I

Indra—the chief of the administrative demigods and king of the heavenly planets.

ISKCON—acronym for the International Society for Krishna Consciousness.

J

Jagannātha Purī—place of pilgrimage on the east coast of India where the deity of Jagannātha is worshiped.

Japa—individual chanting of the Hare Kṛṣṇa mantra while counting on beads.

Jīva—the individual, eternal soul or living entity; part of the Supreme Lord.

Jñāna—the process of approaching the Supreme by the cultivation of knowledge.

Jñānī—one who approaches the Supreme by cultivation of knowledge.

K

Kali-yuga—the present age, which is characterized by quarrel and hypocrisy.

Karatālas—hand cymbals used during *kīrtana*.

Karmī—one engaged in karma (fruitive activity); a materialist.

Karṣati—lit., "stuggling hard".

Kārttika—the Vedic month corresponding to October–November, in which Lord Dāmodara is worshiped.

Kavi—poet.

Kīrtana—chanting of the Lord's holy names.

Kṛṣṇa—the Supreme Personality of Godhead.

Kṛṣṇaloka—the eternal abode of Lord Kṛṣṇa.

Kṣatriya—administrative or warrior class; the second Vedic social order.

Kuñja—grove.

Kurtā—a tuniclike men's shirt commonly worn in India.

Kuṭīr—a hermitagelike residence for the practice of devotional activities.

L

Laulyam—greed; usually refers to intense desire to see Kṛṣṇa.

Līlā—pastimes.

M

Mādhurya—lit., "sweetness". Refers to the sweet conjugal pastimes of Kṛṣṇa and the *gopīs*.

Mahā—a Sanskrit prefix meaning "great" or "large".

Mahā-bhāgavata—a devotee in the highest stage of devotional life.

Mahā-mantra—the great chant for deliverance: Hare Kṛṣṇa, Hare Kṛṣṇa, Kṛṣṇa Kṛṣṇa, Hare Hare/ Hare Rāma, Hare Rāma, Rāma Rāma, Hare Hare.

Mahā-prasādam—the remnants of food offered to the Lord, generally understood to be the remnants taken directly from the Lord's plate.

Mahārāja—great king. Also used as a title of respect for a *sannyāsī*.

Mahat-tattva—the total material energy in its original, undifferentiated form.

Mahā-Viṣṇu—also Kāraṇodakaśāyī Viṣṇu; the expansion of the Lord from whom all material universes emanate.

Mandira—temple.

Maṅgala-ārati—the first Deity worship of the day, performed an hour and a half before sunrise.

Mātājī—mother.

Mauna—silence.

Māyā—the external, illusory energy of the Lord, comprising this material world; forgetfulness of one's relationship with Kṛṣṇa.

Māyāvādī—an impersonalist or voidist who believes that God is ultimately formless and without personality.

Mṛdaṅga—a two-headed clay drum, traditionally used in *kīrtana*.

Muni—a sage or self-realized soul.

Mūrti—a form, usually referring to a deity.

N

Naimiṣāraṇya—a sacred forest in central India, considered to be the hub of the universe.

Nāma—the holy name.

Nāma-haṭṭa—a place outside a temple where devotees gather to hear and chant about Kṛṣṇa.

Nārada Muni—a great devotee of Lord Kṛṣṇa who travels throughout the spiritual and material worlds singing the Lord's glories and preaching the path of devotional service.

Nārāyaṇa—the four-handed expansion of Lord Kṛṣṇa.

Navadvīpa—the province in West Bengal where Lord Caitanya exhibited His early pastimes.

Neti neti—lit., "not this, not that." A materialistic philosophical process by which one analyzes existence to search out the Absolute Truth.

Nirvāṇa—freedom from material existence.

Niṣṭhā—faith.

Nityānanda—the incarnation of Lord Balarāma who is a principal associate of Lord Caitanya.

Nṛsiṁha(deva)—the half-man, half-lion incarnation of Lord Kṛṣṇa who appeared to save Prahlāda Mahārāja from Hiraṇyakaśipu.

P

Pāṇḍavas—the five warrior-brothers, sons of King Pāṇḍu, and intimate friends of Lord Kṛṣṇa.

Paṇḍita—a scholar.

Paramparā—the disciplic succession of bona fide spiritual masters.

Para-tattva—the supreme Absolute Truth.

Parikrama—a walking pilgrimage.

Phalgu-baba—a false renunciant.

Prabhupāda, A. C. Bhaktivedanta Swami—founder-*ācārya* of ISKCON and foremost preacher of Kṛṣṇa consciousness in the Western world.

Pradhāna—the total material energy in its unmanifest state.

Prākṛta-sahajiyā—a class of pseudodevotees who take the conjugal pastimes of Kṛṣṇa and the *gopīs* cheaply and do not follow the proper regulations of *vaidhi-bhakti.*

Prakṛti—material nature.

Prāṇa—the life air of the body; vital energy.

Praṇāmas—an offering of respect by joining ones hands.

Prasādam—lit., "mercy". Food which has been spiritualized by offering it to Kṛṣṇa which helps purify the living entity; also referred to as *prasāda*.

Prema—love of Kṛṣṇa.

Pūjā—worship.

Puṣpāñjali—the ceremony of offering flowers to the Lord.

R

Rādhā(rāṇī)—the eternal consort and spiritual potency of Lord Kṛṣṇa.

Rādhā-dāsya—lit., "service to Śrīmatī Rādhārāṇī."

Rāma—as part of the Hare Kṛṣṇa *mahā-mantra,* refers to the highest eternal pleasure of Lord Kṛṣṇa; may also refer to Lord Balarāma or Lord Rāmacandra.

Rasa—the spiritual essence of a personal relationship with the Supreme Lord.

Rāsa-līlā—refers to Kṛṣṇa's pastime of dancing with the *gopīs.*

Ratha-yātrā—an annual chariot festival celebrating Kṛṣṇa's return to Vṛndāvana in which the Deity of Lord Jagannātha is pulled in procession on a *ratha* (chariot).

Rukmiṇī—Kṛṣṇa's principal queen in Dvārakā.

S

Śabda-brahma—transcendental sound, considered by Vedic philosophy to be self-evident proof of knowledge.

Sādhana—regulated spiritual activities meant to increase one's attachment to Kṛṣṇa.

Sādhu—saintly person.

Sahajiyā—a class of pseudodevotees who take the conjugal pastimes of Kṛṣṇa and the *gopīs* cheaply and who do not follow the proper regulations of *vaidhi-bhakti.*

Sakhī—girlfriend; refers to Śrīmatī Rādhārāṇī's intimate girlfriends, who assist Her in Her service to Kṛṣṇa.

Śakti—potency.

Samādhi—trance or absorption in the service of the Lord; also refers to the tomb of an *ācārya.*

Samosā—a savory, stuffed, deep-fried pastry.

Sampradāya—a chain of disciplic succession through which spiritual knowledge is transmitted.

Saṁsāra—cycle of repeated birth and death.

Sanātana—eternal.

Saṅga—association.

Saṅkīrtana—the congregational chanting of the holy name, fame, and pastimes of the Lord; preaching.

Sannyāsa—renounced life; the fourth order of Vedic spiritual life.

Sannyāsī—one in the renounced order of life.

Śaraṇāgati—the process of surrender; a collection of songs by Bhaktivinoda Ṭhākura; the name of an ISKCON farm in Ashcroft, British Columbia, Canada.

Sārī—woman's dress commonly worn in India.

Śāstra—revealed scripture.

Śāstra-cakṣus—one who sees through the eyes of the authorized scriptures.

Siddhānta—the perfect conclusion according to Vedic scriptures.

Śikhā—lit., "flag". A tuft of hair grown at the crown of the head of male Vaiṣṇavas.

Śikṣā-guru—an instructing spiritual master.

Śloka—a stanza of Sanskrit verse.

Smaraṇam—the devotional process of remembering the Lord.

Smṛti—scriptures further explaining the four original *Vedas* and the *Upaniṣads.*

Śraddhā—firm faith and confidence.

Śravaṇam—hearing about Kṛṣṇa.

Śrī—a prefix used as an honorific.

Śrīla—a term of respect given to a spiritual master.

Śrīmad-Bhāgavatam—the *Bhāgavata Purāṇa,* written by Śrīla Vyāsadeva, which specifically points to the path of devotional love of God.

Śrīmatī—a term of respect given to women or female Deities.

Śūdra—a laborer; one of the four Vedic social orders.

Sūtra—a Vedic aphorism.

Svarāṭ—the independent quality of the Supreme Lord.

Swami—one who controls his senses; a title of one in the renounced order of life.

Swamiji—lit., "great master". A common term of respect addressed to *sannyāsīs*.

Śyāma(-sundara)—a name of Kṛṣṇa, meaning "blackish," and "beautiful" (*sundara*).

T

Tamas—ignorance; one of the modes of material nature.

Tilaka—auspicious clay markings that sanctify a devotee's body as a temple of the Lord.

Tulasī—a great devotee in the form of a plant; her leaves are always offered to the lotus feet of the Lord.

U

Upadeśa—instruction.

Upaniṣads—108 philosophical treatises that appear within the *Vedas*.

V

Vaidhi-bhakti—the process of following the regulative principles of devotional service under the guidance of a spiritual master, in accordance with revealed scriptures.

Vaikuṇṭha—the spiritual world.

Vaiṣṇava—one who is a devotee of Viṣṇu or Kṛṣṇa.

Vāṇī—the instruction of the spiritual master.

Varṇāśrama—the Vedic social system of four social and four spiritual orders.

Vāsudeva—the son of Vasudeva, or Śrī Kṛṣṇa Himself.

Vedas—the original revealed scriptures.

Vibhūti—opulence.

Viṣṇu—a fully empowered expansion of Kṛṣṇa.

Vraja—Vṛndāvana.

Vraja-maṇḍala—the area of Vṛndāvana-dhāma.

Vṛndāvana—Kṛṣṇa's personal abode, where He fully manifests His personal qualities.

Vyāsa-pūjā—worship of the spiritual master, who represents Śrīla Vyāsadeva, on his appearance day.

Vyāsāsana—a special, elevated seat reserved for the speaker of *Śrīmad-Bhāgavatam*.

Y

Yajña—sacrifice.

Yamunā—a sacred river in India, which Lord Kṛṣṇa made famous by performing pastimes there.

Yaśodā—Kṛṣṇa's mother in Vṛndāvana.

Yogamāyā—the internal spiritual potency of the Lord.

Yogī—one who practices sense control with the aim of spiritual realization.

Yugala-kiśora—the Divine Couple, Śrī Śrī Rādhā and Kṛṣṇa.

Yukta-vairāgya—real renunciation by using everything in the service of God.

Acknowledgments

I would like to thank the following disciples and friends who helped produce and print this book:

Caraṇāravinda-devī dāsī
Guru-sevā-devī dāsī
Kaiśorī-devī dāsī
Kṛṣṇa-kṛpā dāsa
Lalitāmṛta-devī dāsī
Mādhava dāsa
Nitai dāsa
Prāṇadā-devī dāsī
Rādhā-Ramaṇa dāsa

Special thanks to the Greedy Readers Club for their kind donation to print this book. They are:

Dayāl-Nitāi dāsa
Dhīra-praśānta dāsa
Kīrtana-rasa dāsa
Lakṣmī-Nārāyaṇa dāsa
Madana-gopāla dāsa
Manu dāsa
Nitāi dāsa
Nitāi-Gaurasundara dāsa
Rādhā-Ramaṇa dāsa
Rūpa-Raghunātha dāsa
Uddhava dāsa